Peirce, Charles
Chance, love, and
logic

DATE DUE

JUN 17 '97			
JUN 09 1998			

CHANCE, LOVE, AND LOGIC

PHILOSOPHICAL ESSAYS

BY THE LATE

CHARLES S. PEIRCE

THE FOUNDER OF PRAGMATISM

EDITED WITH AN INTRODUCTION

BY

MORRIS R. COHEN

WITH A SUPPLEMENTARY ESSAY ON
THE PRAGMATISM OF PEIRCE

BY

JOHN DEWEY

BARNES & NOBLE, Inc.

NEW YORK

PUBLISHERS & BOOKSELLERS SINCE 1873

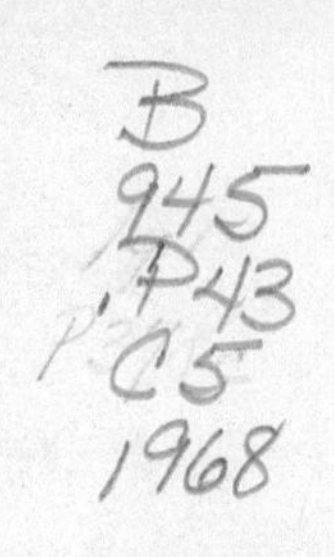

Reprinted, 1968
by special arrangement with
Harcourt, Brace and World, Inc.

L. C. Catalog Card Number: 68-23762

Printed in the United States of America

PREFACE

In the essays gathered together in this volume we have the most developed and coherent available account of the philosophy of Charles S. Peirce, whom James, Royce, Dewey, and leading thinkers in England, France, Germany and Italy have placed in the forefront of the great seminal minds of recent times. Besides their inherent value as the expression of a highly original and fruitful mind, unusually well trained and informed in the exact sciences, these essays are also important as giving us the sources of a great deal of contemporary American philosophy. Because of this historical importance no omissions or changes have been made in the text beyond the correction of some obvious slips and the recasting of a few expressions in the interest of intelligibility.

In a subject which bristles with suggestions and difficulties the temptation to add notes of explanation or dissent is almost insuperable. But as such notes might easily have doubled the size of this volume I have refrained from all comment on the text except in a few footnotes (indicated, as usual, in brackets). The introduction is intended (and I hope it will) help the reader to concatenate the various lines of thought contained in these essays. I cannot pretend to have adequately indicated their significance. Great minds like those of James and Royce have been nourished by these writings and I am persuaded that they still offer mines of fruitful suggestion. Prof. Dewey's supplementary essay indicates their value for the fundamental question of metaphysics, viz. the nature of reality.

Grateful acknowledgment is here made to Mrs. Paul Carus and to the Open Court Publishing Co. for permission to reprint the essays of Part II from the *Monist*. The late Paul Carus was one of the very few who not only gave Peirce an opportunity to publish, but publicly recognized the importance of his writings.

I must also acknowledge my obligation to Professor Dewey for kind permission to reprint his essay on the Pragmatism of Peirce from the Journal of Philosophy, and to the editors of that Journal, Professors Woodbridge and Bush, for permission to reprint some material of my own. Part V of the Bibliography was compiled by Mr. Irving Smith.

MORRIS R. COHEN

THE COLLEGE OF THE CITY OF NEW YORK.

TABLE OF CONTENTS

INTRODUCTION

Many and diverse are the minds that form the philosophic community. There are, first and foremost, the great masters, the system builders who rear their stately palaces towering to the moon. These architectonic minds are served by a varied host of followers and auxiliaries. Some provide the furnishings to make these mystic mansions of the mind more commodious, while others are engaged in making their façades more imposing. Some are busy strengthening weak places or building much-needed additions, while many more are engaged in defending these structures against the impetuous army of critics who are ever eager and ready to pounce down upon and destroy all that is new or bears the mortal mark of human imperfection. There are also the philologists, those who are in a more narrow sense scholars, who dig not only for facts or roots, but also for the stones which may serve either for building or as weapons of destruction. Remote from all these, however, are the intellectual rovers who, in their search for new fields, venture into the thick jungle that surrounds the little patch of cultivated science. They are not gregarious creatures, these lonely pioneers; and in their wanderings they often completely lose touch with those who tread the beaten paths. Those that return to the community often speak strangely of strange things; and it is not always that they arouse sufficient faith for others to follow them and change their trails into high roads.

Few nowadays question the great value of these pioneer minds; and it is often claimed that universities are established to facilitate their work, and to prevent it from being lost. But universities, like other well-managed institutions, can find place only for those who work well in harness. The restless, impatient minds, like the socially or conventionally unacceptable, are thus kept out, no matter how fruitful their originality. Charles S. Peirce was certainly one of these restless pioneer souls with the fatal gift of genuine originality. In his early papers, in the *Journal of Speculative Philosophy,* and later, in the *Monist* papers reprinted as Part II of this volume, we get glimpses of a vast philosophic system on which he was working with an unusual wealth of material and apparatus. To a rich imagination and extraordinary learning he added one of the most essential gifts of successful system builders, the power to coin an apt and striking terminology. But the admitted incompleteness of these preliminary sketches of his philosophic system is not altogether due to the inherent difficulty of the task and to external causes such as neglect and poverty. A certain inner instability or lack of self-mastery is reflected in the outer moral or conventional waywardness which, except for a few years at Johns Hopkins, caused him to be excluded from a university career, and thus deprived him of much needed stimulus to ordinary consistency and intelligibility. As the years advanced, bringing little general interest in, or recognition of, the brilliant logical studies of his early years, Peirce became more and more fragmentary, cryptic, and involved; so that James, the intellectual companion of his youth, later found his lectures on pragmatism, "flashes of brilliant light relieved against Cimmerian darkness" — a statement not to be entirely discounted by the fact that James had no interest in or aptitude for formal logical or mathematical considerations.

Despite these limitations, however, Peirce stands out as one of the great founders of modern scientific logic; and in the realm of general philosophy the development of some of his pregnant ideas has led to the pragmatism and radical empiricism of James, as well as to the mathematical idealism of Royce, and to the anti-nominalism which characterizes the philosophic movement known as Neo-Realism. At any rate, the work of James, Royce, and Russell, as well as that of logicians like Schroeder, brings us of the present generation into a better position to appreciate the significance of Peirce's work, than were his contemporaries.

I

Peirce was by antecedents, training, and occupation a scientist. He was a son of Benjamin Peirce, the great Harvard mathematician, and his early environment, together with his training in the Lawrence Scientific School, justified his favorite claim that he was brought up in a laboratory. He made important contributions not only in mathematical logic but also in photometric astronomy, geodesy, and psychophysics, as well as in philology. For many years Peirce worked on the problems of geodesy, and his contribution to the subject, his researches on the pendulum, was at once recognized by European investigators in this field. The International Geodetic Congress, to which he was the first American representative, gave unusual attention to his paper, and men like Cellerier and Plantamour acknowledged their obligations to him.[1]

This and other scientific work involving fine measurement, with the correlative investigations into the theory of probable error, seem to have been a decisive influence in the development of Peirce's philosophy of chance. Philosophers inexperienced in actual scientific measurement may naïvely accept as absolute truth such statements as "every particle of matter attracts every other particle directly as the product of their masses and inversely as the square of the distance," or "when hydrogen and oxygen combine to form water the ratio of their weights is 1:8." But to those who are actually engaged in measuring natural phenomena with instruments of precision, nature shows no such absolute constancy or simplicity. As every laboratory worker knows, no two observers, and no one observer in successive experiments, get absolutely identical results. To the men of the heroic period of science this was no difficulty. They held unquestioningly the Platonic faith that nature was created on simple geometric lines, and all the minute variations were attributable to the fault of the observer or the crudity of his instruments. This heroic faith was, and still is, a most powerful stimulus to scientific research and a protection against the incursions of supernaturalism. But few would defend it to-day in its explicit form, and there is little empirical evidence to show that while the observer and his instruments are always varying, the ob-

[1] See Plantamour's "*Recherches Experimentales sur le mouvement simultané d'un pendule et de ses supports*," Geneva, 1878, pp. 3-4.

jects which he measures never deviate in the slightest from the simple law. Doubtless, as one becomes more expert in the manipulation of physical instruments, there is a noticeable diminution of the range of the personal "error," but no amount of skill and no refinement of our instruments have ever succeeded in eliminating irregular, though small, variations. "Try to verify any law of nature and you will find that the more precise your observations, the more certain they will be to show irregular departure from the law."[2] There is certainly nothing in our empirical information to prevent us from saying that all the so-called constants of nature are merely instances of variation between limits so near each other that their differences may be neglected for certain purposes. Moreover, the approach to constancy is observed only in mass phenomena, when we are dealing with very large numbers of particles; but social statistics also approach constant ratios when the numbers are very large. Hence, without denying discrepancies due solely to errors of observation, Peirce contends that "we must suppose far more minute discrepancies to exist owing to the imperfect cogency of the law itself, to a certain swerving of the facts from any definite formula."[3]

It is usual to associate disbelief in absolute laws of nature with sentimental claims for freedom or theological miracles. It is, therefore, well to insist that Peirce's attack is entirely in the interests of exact logic and a rational account of the physical universe. As a rigorous logician familiar with the actual procedures by which our knowledge

[2] P. 190. [3] Pp. 162–163.

of the various laws of nature is obtained, he could not admit that experience could prove their claim to absoluteness. All the physical laws actually known, like Boyle's law or the law of gravitation, involve excessive simplification of the phenomenal course of events, and thus a large element of empirical inaccuracy. But a more positive objection against the traditional assumption of absolute or invariable laws of nature, is the fact that such assumption makes the regularities of the universe ultimate, and thus cuts us off from the possibility of ever explaining them or how there comes to be as much regularity in the universe as there is. But in ordinary affairs, the occurrence of any regularity is the very thing to be explained. Moreover, modern statistical mechanics and thermodynamics (theory of gases, entropy, etc.) suggest that the regularity in the universe is a matter of gradual growth; that the whole of physical nature is a growth from a chaos of diversity to a maximum of uniformity or entropy. A leading physicist of the 19th Century, Boltzmann, has suggested that the process of the whole physical universe is like that of a continuous shaking up of a hap-hazard or chance mixture of things, which thus gradually results in a progressively more uniform distribution. Since Duns Scotus, students of logic have known that every real entity has its individual character (its *haecceitas* or *thisness*) which cannot be explained or deduced from that which is uniform. Every explanation, for example, of the moon's path must take particular existences for granted. Such original or underived individuality and diversity is precisely what Peirce means by chance; and from this point of view chance is prior to law.

All that is necessary to visualize this is to suppose that there is an infinitesimal tendency in things to acquire habits, a tendency which is itself an accidental variation grown habitual. We shall then be on the road to explain the evolution and existence of the limited uniformities actually prevailing in the physical world.

A good deal of the foregoing may sound somewhat mythologic. But even if it were so it would have the merit of offering a rational alternative to the mechanical mythology according to which all the atoms in the universe are to-day precisely in the same condition in which they were on the day of creation, a mythology which is forced to regard all the empirical facts of spontaneity and novelty as illusory, or devoid of substantial truth.

The doctrine of the primacy of chance naturally suggests the primacy of mind. Just as law is a chance habit so is matter inert mind. The principal law of mind is that ideas literally spread themselves continuously and become more and more general or inclusive, so that people who form communities of any sort develop general ideas in common. When this continuous reaching-out of feeling becomes nurturing love, such, e.g., which parents have for their offspring or thinkers for their ideas, we have creative evolution.

James and Royce have called attention to the similarity between Peirce's doctrine of tychistic-agapism (chance and love) and the creative evolution of Bergson. But while both philosophies aim to restore life and growth in their account of the nature of things, Peirce's approach seems to me to have marked advantages, owing to its being in closer touch with modern physics. Bergson's procedure is largely based on the contention that mechanics cannot explain certain empirical facts, such as the supposed identity of the vertebrate eye and the eye of the scallop. But the fact here is merely one of a certain resemblance of pattern, which may well be explained by the mechanical principles of convergent evolution. Peirce's account involves no rejection of the possibility of mechanical explanations. Indeed, by carrying chance into the laws of mechanics he is enabled to elaborate a positive and highly suggestive theory of protoplasm to explain the facts of plasticity and habit.[4] Instead of postulating with Spencer and Bergson a continuous growth of diversity, Peirce allows for growth of habits both in diversity and in uniformity. The Spencerian mechanical philosophy reduces all diversity to mere spatial differences. There can be no substantial novelty; only new forms or combinations can arise in time. The creative evolution of Bergson though intended to support the claims of spontaneity is still like the Spencerian in assuming all evolution as proceeding from the simple to the complex. Peirce allows for diversity and specificity as part of the original character or endowment of things, which in the course of time may increase in some respects and diminish in others. Mind acquires the habit both of taking on, and also of laying aside, habits. Evolution may thus lead to homogeneity or uniformity as well as to greater heterogeneity.

Not only has Peirce a greater regard than even Bergson for the actual diversity and spontaneity of things, but he is in a much better position than any other modern phi-

[4] Pp. 249 ff.

losopher to explain the order and coherence of the world. This he effects by uniting the medieval regard for the reality of universals with the modern scientific use of the concept of continuity. The unfortunate war between the pioneers of modern science and the adherents of the scholastic doctrine of substantial forms, has been one of the great misfortunes of human thought, in that it made absolute atomism and nominalism the professed *creed* of physical science. Now, extreme nominalism, the insistence on the reality of the particular, leaves no room for the genuine reality of law. It leaves, as Hume had the courage to admit, nothing whereby the present can determine the future; so that anything is as likely to happen as not. From such a chaotic world, the *procedure* of modern natural and mathematical science has saved us by the persistent use of the principle of continuity; and no one has indicated this more clearly than Peirce who was uniquely qualified to do so by being a close student both of Duns Scotus and of modern scientific methods.

It is instructive in this respect to contrast the views of Peirce and James. James, who so generously indicated his indebtedness to Peirce for his pragmatism, was also largely indebted to Peirce for his doctrine of radical empiricism.[5] The latter doctrine seeks to rescue the continuity and fluidity of experience from the traditional British empiricism or nominalism, which had resolved everything into a number of mutually exclusive mental states. It is curious, however, that while in his psychology James made extensive use of the principle of continuity, he could not free himself

[5] James, *Pluralistic Universe*, pp. 398–400.

from British nominalism in his philosophy — witness the extreme individualism of his social philosophy or the equally extreme anthropomorphism of his religion. Certain of Peirce's suggestions as to the use of continuity in social philosophy have been developed by Royce in his theory of social consciousness and the nature of the community;[6] but much remains to be worked out and we can but repeat Peirce's own hope: "May some future student go over this ground again and have the leisure to give his results to the world."

It is well to note, however, that after writing the papers included in this volume Peirce continued to be occupied with the issues here raised. This he most significantly indicated in the articles on logical topics contributed to Baldwin's Dictionary of Philosophy.[7]

In these articles it is naturally the logical bearing of the principles of tychism (chance), synechism (continuity), and agapism (love) that is stressed. To use the Kantian terminology, almost native to Peirce, the regulative rather than the constitutive aspect of these principles is emphasized. Thus the doctrine of chance is not only what it was for James' radical empiricism, a release from the blind necessity of a "block universe," but also a method of keep-

[6] Royce, *Studies in Good and Evil*, and *The Problem of Christianity*, esp. Vol. 2. Baldwin (*Mental Development*) is heavily indebted to Royce in this respect.

[7] These articles are by-products or fragments of a comprehensive work on *Logic* on which Peirce was engaged for many years. For the writing of this book, Royce declared, no greater mind or greater erudition has appeared in America. Only several chapters seem to have been finished, and will doubtless be included with other hitherto unpublished manuscripts in the complete edition of Peirce's writings that is now being prepared by Harvard University.

ing open a possible explanation of the genesis of the laws of nature and an interpretation of them in accordance with the theorems of probability, so fruitful in physical science as well as in practical life. So the doctrine of love is not only a cosmologic one, showing how chance feeling generates order or rational diversity through the habit of generality or continuity, but it also gives us the meaning of truth in social terms, in showing that the test as to whether any proposition is true postulates an indefinite number of co-operating investigators. On its logical side the doctrine of love (agapism) also recognized the important fact that general ideas have a certain attraction which makes us divine their nature even though we cannot clearly determine their precise meaning before developing their possible consequences.

Of the doctrine of continuity we are told expressly [8] that "synechism is not an ultimate absolute metaphysical doctrine. It is a regulative principle of logic," seeking the thread of identity in diverse cases and avoiding hypotheses that this or that is ultimate and, therefore, inexplicable. (Examples of such hypotheses are: the existence of absolutely accurate or uniform laws of nature, the eternity and absolute likeness of all atoms, etc.) To be sure, the synechist cannot deny that there is an element of the inexplicable or ultimate, since it is directly forced upon him. But he cannot regard it as a source of explanation. The assumption of an inexplicability is a barrier on the road to science. "The form under which alone anything can be understood is the form of generality which is the same thing

[8] Baldwin's *Dictionary,* article Synechism.

as continuity."[9] This insistence on the generality of intelligible form is perfectly consistent with due emphases on the reality of the individual, which to a Scotist realist connotes an element of will or will-resistence, but in logical procedure means that the test of the truth or falsity of any proposition refers us to particular perceptions.[10] But as no multitude of individuals can exhaust the meaning of a continuum, which includes also organizing relations of order, the full meaning of a concept cannot be in any individual reaction, but is rather to be sought in the manner in which all such reactions contribute to the development of the concrete reasonableness of the whole evolutionary process. In scientific procedure this means that integrity of belief in general is more important than, because it is the condition of, particular true beliefs.

II

This insistence on the continuity so effectually used as a heuristic principle in natural and mathematical science, distinguishes the pragmatism of Peirce from that of his follower James. Prof. Dewey has developed this point authoritatively in the supplementary essay; but in view of the general ignorance as to the sources of pragmatism which prevails in this incurious age, some remarks on the actual historical origin of pragmatism may be in order.

There can be little doubt that Peirce was led to the formulation of the principle of pragmatism through the influence

[9] *Ib.*

[10] Baldwin's *Dictionary*, art. Individual: "Everything whose identity consists in a continuity of reactions will be a single logical individual."

of Chauncey Wright.[11] Wright who had first hand acquaintance with creative scientific work in mathematics, physics, and botany was led by the study of Mill and Bain to reflect on the characteristics of scientific method. This reflection led him to draw a distinction between the use of popular scientific material, by men like Spencer, to construct a myth or picture of the world, and the scientific use of laws by men like Newton as means for extending our knowledge of phenomena. Gravitation as a general fact had interested metaphysicians long before Newton. What made Newton's contribution scientific was the formulation of a mathematical law which has enabled us to deduce all the then known facts of the solar system and to anticipate or predict many more facts the existence of which would not otherwise be even suspected, e.g., the existence of the planet Neptune. Wright insists, therefore, that the principles of modern mathematical and physical science are the means through which nature is discovered, that scientific

[11] The personal relations between Peirce and Wright were thus described by Peirce in a letter to Mrs. Ladd-Franklin (*Journal of Philosophy* Vol. 13, p. 719): "It must have been about 1857 when I first made the acquaintance of Chauncey Wright, a mind about on the level of J. S. Mill. He was a thorough mathematician. He had a most penetrating intellect. — He and I used to have long and very lively and close disputations lasting two or three hours daily for many years. In the sixties I started a little club called 'The Metaphysical Club.' — Wright was the strongest member and probably I was next. — Then there were Frank Abbott, William James and others." "It was there that the name and the doctrine of pragmatism saw the light." It might be added that Peirce's tychism is indebted to Wright's doctrine of accidents and "cosmic weather," a doctrine which maintained against LaPlace that a mind knowing nature from moment to moment is bound to encounter genuine novelty in phenomena, which no amount of knowledge would enable us to foresee. See Wright's *Philosophical Discussions* — 1876, also Cambridge *Hist. of American Literature*, Vol. 3, p. 234.

laws are the finders rather than merely the summaries of factual truths. This conception of the experimental scientist as translating general propositions into prescriptions for attaining new experimental truths, is the starting point of Peirce's pragmatism. The latter is embodied in the principle that the meaning of a concept is to be found in "all the conceivable experimental phenomena which the affirmation or denial of the concept could imply." [12]

In the earlier statement of the pragmatic maxim,[13] Peirce emphasized the consequences for conduct that follow from the acceptance or rejection of an idea; but the stoical maxim that the end of man is action did not appeal to him as much at sixty as it did at thirty.[14] Naturally also Peirce could not follow the development of pragmatism by Wm. James who, like almost all modern psychologists, was a thorough nominalist and always emphasized particular sensible experience.[15] It seemed to Peirce that such em-

[12] *Monist,* Vol. 15, p. 180.

[13] This volume, pp. 43-45.

[14] "To say that we live for the sake of action would be to say that there is no such thing as a rational purport." *Monist,* Vol. XV, p. 175.

[15] The letter to Mrs. Ladd-Franklin quoted before, explains why James, though always loyal to Peirce and anxious to give him credit whenever possible, could not understand the latter's lectures on pragmatism. Peirce's incidental judgments on others is worth quoting here:

"Modern psycholoigsts are so soaked with sensationalism that they cannot understand anything that does not mean that. How can I, to whom nothing seems so thoroughly real as generals, and who regards Truth and Justice as *literally* the most powerful powers in the world, expect to be understood by the thoroughgoing Wundtian? But the curious thing is to see absolute idealists tainted with this disease, — or men who, like John Dewey, hover between Absolute Idealism and Sensationalism. Royce's opinions as developed in his *World and Individualism* are extremely near to mine. His insistence on the elements of purpose in intellectual concepts is essentially the pragmatic position."

phasis on particular experiences endangered the principle of continuity which in the hands of men like Weierstrass had reformed modern mathematics. For this reason he began to call his own doctrine pragmaticism, a sufficiently unattractive name, he thought, to save it from kidnappers and from popularity. He never, however, abandoned the principle of pragmatism, that the meaning of an idea is clarified (because constituted) by its conceivable experimental consequences. Indeed, if we want to clarify the meaning of the idea of pragmatism, let us apply the pragmatic test to it. What will be the effect of accepting it? Obviously it will be to develop certain general ideas or habits of looking at things.

Peirce's pragmatism has, therefore, a decidedly intellectual cast. The meaning of an idea or proposition is found not by an intuition of it but by working out its implications. It admits that thought does not constitute reality. Categories can have no concrete being without action or immediate feeling. But thought is none the less an essential ingredient of reality; thought is "the melody running through the succession of our sensations." Pragmatism, according to Peirce, seeks to define the rational purport, not the sensuous quality. It is interested not in the effect of our practical occupations or desires on our ideas, but in the function of ideas as guides of action. Whether a man is to pay damages in a certain lawsuit may depend, in fact, on a term in the Aristotelian logic such as proximate cause.

It is of interest to observe that though Peirce is an ardent admirer of Darwin's method, his scientific caution makes him refuse to apply the analogy of biologic natural selection to the realm of ideas, in the wholesale and uncritical manner that has lately become fashionable. Natural selection may well favor the triumph of views which directly influence biclogic survival. But the pleasure of entertaining congenial illusions may overbalance the inconvenience resulting from their deceptive character. Thus rhetorical appeals may long prevail over scientific evidence.

III

Peirce preferred to call himself a logician, and his contributions to logic have so far proved his most generally recognized achievement. For a right perspective of these contributions we may well begin with the observation that though few branches of philosophy have been cultivated as continuously as logic, Kant was able to affirm that the science of logic had made no substantial progress since the time of Aristotle. The reason for this is that Aristotle's logic, the logic of classes, was based on his own scientific procedure as a zoologist, and is still in essence a valid method so far as classification is part of all rational procedure. But when we come to describe the mathematical method of physical science, we cannot cast it into the Aristotelian form without involving ourselves in such complicated artificialities as to reduce almost to nil the value of Aristotle's logic as an organon. Aristotle's logic enables us to make a single inference from two premises. But the vast multitude of theorems that modern mathematics has derived from a few premises as to the nature of number, shows the need of formulating a logic or theory of inference that shall correspond to the modern, more complicated, practice as Aristotle's logic did to simple classificatory zoology. To do this effectively would require the highest constructive logical genius, together with an intimate knowledge of the methods of the great variety of modern sciences. This is in the nature of the case a very rare combination, since great investigators are not as critical in examining their own procedure as they are in examining the subject matter which is their primary scientific interest. Hence, when great investigators like Poincaré come to describe their own work, they fall back on the uncritical assumptions of the traditional logic which they learned in their school days. Moreover, "For the last three centuries thought has been conducted in laboratories, in the field, or otherwise in the face of the facts, while chairs of logic have been filled by men who breathe the air of the seminary."[16] The great Leibnitz had the qualifications, but here, as elsewhere, his worldly occupations left him no opportunity except for very fragmentary contributions. It was not until the middle of the 19th century that two mathematicians, Boole and DeMorgan, laid the foundations for a more generalized logic. Boole developed a general logical algorithm or calculus, while DeMorgan called attention to non-syllogistic inference and especially to the importance of the logic of relations. Peirce's great achievement is to have recognized the possibilities of both and to have generalized and developed them into a general theory of scientific inference. The extent and thoroughness of his achievement has been obscured by his fragmentary way of writing and by a rather

[16] Baldwin's *Dictionary*, art. Method.

unwieldy symbolism. Still, modern mathematical logic, such as that of Russell's *Principles of Mathematics*, is but a development of Peirce's logic of relatives.

This phase of Peirce's work is highly technical and an account of it is out of place here. Such an account will be found in Lewis' *Survey of Symbolic Logic*.[17] I refer to it here only to remind the reader that the *Illustrations of the Logic of the Sciences* (Part I of this volume) have a background of patient detailed work which is still being developed to-day.

Symbolic logic has been held in rather low esteem by the followers of the old classical methods in philosophy. Their stated objection to it has been mainly that it is concerned with the minutiae of an artificial language and is of no value as a guide to the interpretation of reality. Now it should be readily admitted that preoccupation with symbolic logic is rather apt to retard the irresponsible flight of philosophic fancy. Yet this is by no means always an evil. By insisting on an accuracy that is painful to those impatient to obtain sweeping and comforting, though hasty, conclusions, symbolic logic is well calculated to remove the great scandal of traditional philosophy — the claim of absolutely certain results in fields where there is the greatest conflict of opinion. This scandalous situation arises in part from the fact that in popular exposition we do not have to make our premises or assumptions explicit; hence all sorts of dubious prejudices are implicitly appealed to as abso-

[17] "Peirce anticipated the most important procedures of his successors even when he did not work them out himself. Again and again one finds the clue to the most recent developments in the writings of Peirce," Lewis' *Survey of Symbolic Logic*, p. 79.

lutely necessary principles. Also, by the use of popular terms which have a variety of meanings, one easily slides from one meaning to another, so that the most improbable conclusions are thus derived from seeming truisms. By making assumptions and rules explicit, and by using technical terms that do not drag wide penumbras of meaning with them, the method of symbolic logic may cruelly reduce the sweeping pretensions of philosophy. But there is no reason for supposing that pretentiousness rather than humility is the way to philosophic salvation. Man is bound to speculate about the universe beyond the range of his knowledge, but he is not bound to indulge the vanity of setting up such speculations as absolutely certain dogmas.

There is, however, no reason for denying that greater rigor and accuracy of exposition can really help us to discern new truth. Modern mathematics since Gauss and Weierstrass has actually been led to greater fruitfulness by increased rigor which makes such procedure as the old proofs of Taylor's theorem no longer possible. The substitution of rigorous analytic procedures for the old Euclidean proofs based on intuition, has opened up vast fields of geometry. Nor has this been without any effect on philosophy. Where formerly concepts like infinity and continuity were objects of gaping awe or the recurrent occasions for intellectual violence,[18] we are now beginning to use them, thanks to Peirce and Royce, in accurate and definable senses. Consider, for instance, the amount of a priori nonsense which Peirce eliminates by pointing out

[18] Hans Breitmann is symbolic of those who "solved the infinite as one eternal sphere."

that the application of the concept of continuity to a span of consciousness removes the necessity for assuming a first or last moment; so likewise the range of vision on a large unobstructed ground has no line between the visible and the invisible. These considerations will be found utterly destructive of the force of the old arguments (fundamental to Kant and others) as to the necessary infinity of time and space. Similar enlightenment is soon likely to result from the more careful use of terms like relative and absolute, which are bones of contention in philosophy but Ariadne threads of exploration in theoretical physics, because of the definite symbolism of mathematics. Other important truths made clear by symbolic logic is the hypothetical character of universal propositions and the consequent insight that no particulars can be deduced from universals alone, since no number of hypotheses can without given data establish an existing fact.

There is, however, an even more positive direction in which symbolic logic serves the interest of philosophy, and that is in throwing light on the nature of symbols and on the relation of meaning. Philosophers have light-heartedly dismissed questions as to the nature of significant signs as 'merely' (most fatal word!) a matter of language. But Peirce in the paper on Man's Glassy [Shakespearian for Mirror-Like] Essence, endeavors to exhibit man's whole nature as symbolic.[19] This is closely connected with his logical doctrine which regards signs or symbols as one of

[19] See *Journal of Speculative Philosophy*, Vol. 2, pp. 155–157, article on A New List of Categories in the Proceedings of the American Academy of Arts and Sciences, Vol. 7, 287–298 and article on *Sign*, in Baldwin's *Dictionary*.

the fundamental categories or aspects of the universe (Thoughts and things are the other two). Independently of Peirce but in line with his thought another great and neglected thinker, Santayana, has shown that the whole life of man that is bound up with the institutions of civilization, is concerned with symbols.

It is not altogether accidental that, since Boole and DeMorgan, those who have occupied themselves with symbolic logic have felt called upon to deal with the problem of probability. The reason is indicated by Peirce when he formulates the problem of probable inference in such a way as to make the old classic logic of absolutely true or false conclusions, a limiting case (i.e., of values 1 and 0) of the logic of probable inference whose values range all the way between these two limits. This technical device is itself the result of applying the principle of continuity to throw two hitherto distinct types of reasoning into the same class. The result is philosophically significant.

Where the classical logic spoke of major and minor premises without establishing any really important difference between the two, Peirce draws a distinction between the premises and the guiding principle of our argument. All reasoning is from some concrete situation to another. The propositions which represent the first are the premises in the strict sense of the word. But the feeling that certain conclusions follow from these premises is conditioned by an implicit or explicit belief in some guiding principle which connects the premises and the conclusions. When such a leading principle results in true conclusions in all cases of true premises, we have logical deduction of the orthodox type. If, however, such a principle brings about a true conclusion only in a certain proportion of cases, then we have probability.

This reduction of probability to the relative frequency of true propositions in a class of propositions, was suggested to Peirce by Venn's *Logic of Chance.* Peirce uses it to establish some truths of greatest importance to logic and philosophy.

He eliminates the difficulties of the old conceptualist view, which made probability a measure of our ignorance and yet had to admit that almost all fruitfulness of our practical and scientific reasoning depended on the theorems of probability. How could we safely predict phenomena by measuring our ignorance?

Probability being reduced to a matter of the relative frequency of a class in a larger class or genus, it becomes, strictly speaking, inapplicable to single cases by themselves. A single penny will fall head or it will fall tail every time; to-morrow it will rain, or it will not rain at all. The probability of $\frac{1}{2}$ or any other fraction means nothing in the single case. It is only because we feel the single event as representative of a class, as something which repeats itself, that we speak elliptically of the probability of a single event. Hence follows the important corollary that reasoning with respect to the probability of this or that arrangement of the universe would be valid only if universes were as plentiful as blackberries.

To be useful at all, theories must be simpler than the complex facts which they seek to explain. Hence, it is often convenient to employ a principle of certainty where the facts justify only a principle of some degree of probability. In such cases we must be cautious in accepting any extreme consequence of these principles, and also be on guard against apparent refutations based on such extreme consequences.

Finally I should like to emphasize the value of Peirce's theory of inference for a philosophy of civilization. To the old argument that logic is of no importance because people learn to reason, as to walk, by instinct and habit and not by scientific instruction, Peirce admits [20] that "all human knowledge up to the highest flights of science is but the development of our inborn animal instincts." But though logical rules are first felt implicitly, bringing them into explicit consciousness helps the process of analysis and thus makes possible the recognition of old principles in novel situations. This increases our range of adaptability to such an extent as to justify a general distinction between the slave of routine or habit and the freeman who can anticipate and control nature through knowledge of principles. Peirce's analysis of the method of science as a method of attaining stability of beliefs by free inquiry inviting all possible doubt, in contrast with the methods of iteration ("will to believe") and social authority, is one of the best introductions to a theory of liberal or Hellenic civilization, as opposed to those of despotic societies. Authority has its roots in the force of habit, but it cannot prevent new and unorthodox ideas from arising; and in the effort to defend authoritative social views men are apt to be far more ruthless than in defending their own personal convictions.

[20] *Studies in Logic*, p. 181.

IV

Not only the pragmatism and the radical empiricism of James, but the idealism of Royce and the more recent movement of neo-realism are largely indebted to Peirce.

It may seem strange that the same thinker should be claimed as foster-father of both recent idealism and realism, and some may take it as another sign of his lack of consistency. But this seeming strangeness is really due to the looseness with which the antithesis between realism and idealism has generally been put. If by idealism we denote the nominalistic doctrine of Berkeley, then Peirce is clearly not an idealist; and his work in logic as a study of types of order (in which Royce followed him) is fundamental for a logical realism. But if idealism means the old Platonic doctrine that "ideas," genera, or forms are not merely mental but the real conditions of existence, we need not wonder that Peirce was both idealist and realist.

Royce's indebtedness to Peirce is principally in the use of modern mathematical material, such as the recent development of the concepts of infinity and continuity, to throw light on fundamental questions of philosophy, such as relation of the individual to God or the Universe. At the end of the nineteenth century mathematics had almost disappeared from the repertory of philosophy (cf. Külpe's *Introduction to Philosophy*), and Peirce's essay on the *Law of Mind* opened a new way which Royce followed in his *World and the Individual,* to the great surprise of his idealistic brethren. In his *Problem of Christianity* Royce has also indicated his indebtedness to Peirce for his doctrine of social consciousness, the mind of the community, and the process of interpretation. It may be that a great deal of the similarity between the thoughts of these two men is due to common sources, such as the works of Kant and Schelling; but it is well to note that not only in his later writings but also in his lectures and seminars Royce continually referred to Peirce's views.

The ground for the neo-realist movement in American philosophy was largely prepared by the mathematical work of Russell and by the utilization of mathematics to which Royce was led by Peirce. The logic of Mr. Russell is based, as he himself has pointed out, on a combination of the work of Peirce and Peano. In this combination the notation of Peano has proved of greater technical fluency, but all of Peano's results can also be obtained by Peirce's method as developed by Schroeder and Mrs. Ladd-Franklin. But philosophically Peirce's influence is far greater in insisting that logic is not a branch of psychology, that it is not concerned with merely mental processes, but with objective relations. To the view that the laws of logic represent "the necessities of thought," that propositions are true because "we can not help thinking so," he answers: "Exact logic will say that *C*'s following logically from *A* is a state of things which no impotence of thought alone can bring about."[21] "The question of validity is purely one of fact and not of thinking. . . . It is not in the least the question whether, when the premises are accepted by the mind, we feel an impulse to accept the conclusion also.

[21] *Monist,* Vol. 7, p. 27. *Cf. Journal of Speculative Philosophy,* Vol. 2, p. 207; *Popular Science Monthly,* Vol. 58, pp. 305-306.

The true conclusion would remain true if we had no impulse to accept it, and the false one would remain false though we could not resist the tendency to believe in it." [22]

Since the days of Locke modern philosophy has been almost entirely dominated by the assumption that one must study the process of knowing before one can find out the nature of things known; in other words, that psychology is *the* central philosophic science. The result of this has been an almost complete identification of philosophy with mental science. Nor did the influence of biologic studies of the middle of the nineteenth century shake the belief in that banal dictum of philosophic mediocrity: "The proper study of mankind is man." The recent renaissance of logical studies, and the remarkable progress of physics in our own day bid fair to remind us that while the Lockian way has brought some gains to philosophy, the more ancient way of philosophy is by no means exhausted of promise. Man cannot lose his interest in the great cosmic play. Those who have faith in the ancient and fruitful approach to philosophy through the doors of mathematics and physics will find the writings of Charles S. Peirce full of suggestions. That such an approach can also throw light on the vexed problem of knowledge needs no assurance to those acquainted with Plato and Aristotle. But I may conclude by referring to Peirce's doctrine of ideal as opposed to sensible experiment,[23] and to his treatment of the question

[22] This vol., p. 15.

[23] Suggestive for a theory of the metaphysics of fictions is the suggestion (p. 46) "that the question of what would occur under circumstances which do not actually arise, is not a question of fact, but only of the most perspicuous arrangement of them." This arrangement is, of course, not merely subjective.

how it is that in spite of an infinity of possible hypotheses, mankind has managed to make so many successful inductions.[24] And for the bearing of mathematical studies on the wisdom of life, the following is certainly worth serious reflection: "All human affairs rest upon probabilities. If man were immortal [on earth] he could be perfectly sure of seeing the day when everything in which he had trusted should betray his trust. He would break down, at last, as every great fortune, as every dynasty, as every civilization does. In place of this we have death." The recognition that the death of the individual does not destroy the logical meaning of his utterances, that this meaning involves the ideal of an unlimited community, carries us into the heart of pure religion.

[24] Pp. 128–129, *cf. Monist,* Vol. 7, p. 206, and *Logical Studies,* pp. 175 ff.

CHANCE, LOVE, AND LOGIC

PROEM

THE RULES OF PHILOSOPHY[1]

DESCARTES is the father of modern philosophy, and the spirit of Cartesianism — that which principally distinguishes it from the scholasticism which it displaced — may be compendiously stated as follows:

1. It teaches that philosophy must begin with universal doubt; whereas scholasticism had never questioned fundamentals.

2. It teaches that the ultimate test of certainty is to be found in the individual consciousness; whereas scholasticism had rested on the testimony of sages and of the Catholic Church.

3. The multiform argumentation of the middle ages is replaced by a single thread of inference depending often upon inconspicuous premises.

4. Scholasticism had its mysteries of faith, but undertook to explain all created things. But there are many facts which Cartesianism not only does not explain but renders absolutely inexplicable, unless to say that "God makes them so" is to be regarded as an explanation.

In some, or all of these respects, most modern philosophers have been, in effect, Cartesians. Now without wishing

[1] From the *Journal of Speculative Philosophy*, vol. 2, p. 140.

to return to scholasticism, it seems to me that modern science and modern logic require us to stand upon a very different platform from this.

1. We cannot begin with complete doubt. We must begin with all the prejudices which we actually have when we enter upon the study of philosophy. These prejudices are not to be dispelled by a maxim, for they are things which it does not occur to us can be questioned. Hence this initial skepticism will be a mere self-deception, and not real doubt; and no one who follows the Cartesian method will ever be satisfied until he has formally recovered all those beliefs which in form he has given up. It is, therefore, as useless a preliminary as going to the North Pole would be in order to get to Constantinople by coming down regularly upon a meridian. A person may, it is true, in the course of his studies, find reason to doubt what he began by believing; but in that case he doubts because he has a positive reason for it, and not on account of the Cartesian maxim. Let us not pretend to doubt in philosophy what we do not doubt in our hearts.

2. The same formalism appears in the Cartesian criterion, which amounts to this: "Whatever I am clearly convinced of, is true." If I were really convinced, I should have done with reasoning and should require no test of certainty. But then to make single individuals absolute judges of truth is most pernicious. The result is that metaphysics has reached a pitch of certainty far beyond that of the physical sciences; — only they can agree upon nothing else. In sciences in which men come to agreement, when a theory

has been broached it is considered to be on probation until this agreement is reached. After it is reached, the question of certainty becomes an idle one, because there is no one left who doubts it. We individually cannot reasonably hope to attain the ultimate philosophy which we pursue; we can only seek it, therefore, for the community of philosophers. Hence, if disciplined and candid minds carefully examine a theory and refuse to accept it, this ought to create doubts in the mind of the author of the theory himself.

3. Philosophy ought to imitate the successful sciences in its methods, so far as to proceed only from tangible premises which can be subjected to careful scrutiny, and to trust rather to the multitude and variety of its arguments than to the conclusiveness of any one. Its reasoning should not form a chain which is no stronger than its weakest link, but a cable whose fibers may be ever so slender, provided they are sufficiently numerous and intimately connected.

4. Every unidealistic philosophy supposes some absolutely inexplicable, unanalyzable ultimate; in short, something resulting from mediation itself not susceptible of mediation. Now that anything *is* thus inexplicable, can only be known by reasoning from signs. But the only justification of an inference from signs is that the conclusion explains the fact. To suppose the fact absolutely inexplicable, is not to explain it, and hence this supposition is never allowable.

PART I

CHANCE AND LOGIC

(ILLUSTRATIONS OF THE LOGIC OF SCIENCE)

CHANCE AND LOGIC

FIRST PAPER

THE FIXATION OF BELIEF[1]

I

Few persons care to study logic, because everybody conceives himself to be proficient enough in the art of reasoning already. But I observe that this satisfaction is limited to one's own ratiocination, and does not extend to that of other men.

We come to the full possession of our power of drawing inferences the last of all our faculties, for it is not so much a natural gift as a long and difficult art. The history of its practice would make a grand subject for a book. The medieval schoolman, following the Romans, made logic the earliest of a boy's studies after grammar, as being very easy. So it was as they understood it. Its fundamental principle, according to them, was, that all knowledge rests on either authority or reason; but that whatever is deduced by reason depends ultimately on a premise derived from authority. Accordingly, as soon as a boy was perfect in the syllogistic procedure, his intellectual kit of tools was held to be complete.

[1] *Popular Science Monthly*, November, 1877.

To Roger Bacon, that remarkable mind who in the middle of the thirteenth century was almost a scientific man, the schoolmen's conception of reasoning appeared only an obstacle to truth. He saw that experience alone teaches anything — a proposition which to us seems easy to understand, because a distinct conception of experience has been handed down to us from former generations; which to him also seemed perfectly clear, because its difficulties had not yet unfolded themselves. Of all kinds of experience, the best, he thought, was interior illumination, which teaches many things about Nature which the external senses could never discover, such as the transubstantiation of bread.

Four centuries later, the more celebrated Bacon, in the first book of his "Novum Organum," gave his clear account of experience as something which must be open to verification and reëxamination. But, superior as Lord Bacon's conception is to earlier notions, a modern reader who is not in awe of his grandiloquence is chiefly struck by the inadequacy of his view of scientific procedure. That we have only to make some crude experiments, to draw up briefs of the results in certain blank forms, to go through these by rule, checking off everything disproved and setting down the alternatives, and that thus in a few years physical science would be finished up — what an idea! "He wrote on science like a Lord Chancellor,"[2] indeed.

The early scientists, Copernicus, Tycho, Brahe, Kepler, Galileo and Gilbert, had methods more like those of their modern brethren. Kepler undertook to draw a curve

[2] [This is substantially the dictum of Harvey to John Aubrey. See the latter's *Brief Lives* (Oxford ed. 1898) I 299].

through the places of Mars;[3] and his greatest service to science was in impressing on men's minds that this was the thing to be done if they wished to improve astronomy; that they were not to content themselves with inquiring whether one system of epicycles was better than another but that they were to sit down by the figures and find out what the curve, in truth, was. He accomplished this by his incomparable energy and courage, blundering along in the most inconceivable way (to us), from one irrational hypothesis to another, until, after trying twenty-two of these, he fell, by the mere exhaustion of his invention, upon the orbit which a mind well furnished with the weapons of modern logic would have tried almost at the outset.[4]

In the same way, every work of science great enough to be remembered for a few generations affords some exemplification of the defective state of the art of reasoning of the time when it was written; and each chief step in science has been a lesson in logic. It was so when Lavoisier and his contemporaries took up the study of Chemistry. The old chemist's maxim had been, "Lege, lege, lege, labora, ora, et relege." Lavoisier's method was not to read and pray, not to dream that some long and complicated chemical process would have a certain effect, to put it into practice with dull patience, after its inevitable failure to dream that with some modification it would have another result, and to end by publishing the last dream as a fact: his way was to carry his mind into his laboratory, and to make of his alembics and cucurbits instruments of thought,

[3] Not quite so, but as nearly so as can be told in a few words.

[4] [This modern logic, however, is largely the outcome of Kepler's work.]

giving a new conception of reasoning as something which was to be done with one's eyes open, by manipulating real things instead of words and fancies.

The Darwinian controversy is, in large part, a question of logic. Mr. Darwin proposed to apply the statistical method to biology. The same thing has been done in a widely different branch of science, the theory of gases. Though unable to say what the movement of any particular molecule of gas would be on a certain hypothesis regarding the constitution of this class of bodies, Clausius and Maxwell were yet able, by the application of the doctrine of probabilities, to predict that in the long run such and such a proportion of the molecules would, under given circumstances, acquire such and such velocities; that there would take place, every second, such and such a number of collisions, etc.; and from these propositions they were able to deduce certain properties of gases, especially in regard to their heat-relations. In like manner, Darwin, while unable to say what the operation of variation and natural selection in every individual case will be, demonstrates that in the long run they will adapt animals to their circumstances. Whether or not existing animal forms are due to such action, or what position the theory ought to take, forms the subject of a discussion in which questions of fact and questions of logic are curiously interlaced.

II

The object of reasoning is to find out, from the consideration of what we already know, something else which we do not know. Consequently, reasoning is good if it be such as to give a true conclusion from true premises, and not otherwise. Thus, the question of validity is purely one of fact and not of thinking. A being the premises and B being the conclusion, the question is, whether these facts are really so related that if A is B is. If so, the inference is valid; if not, not. It is not in the least the question whether, when the premises are accepted by the mind, we feel an impulse to accept the conclusion also. It is true that we do generally reason correctly by nature. But that is an accident; the true conclusion would remain true if we had no impulse to accept it; and the false one would remain false, though we could not resist the tendency to believe in it.

We are, doubtless, in the main logical animals, but we are not perfectly so. Most of us, for example, are naturally more sanguine and hopeful than logic would justify. We seem to be so constituted that in the absence of any facts to go upon we are happy and self-satisfied; so that the effect of experience is continually to counteract our hopes and aspirations. Yet a lifetime of the application of this corrective does not usually eradicate our sanguine disposition. Where hope is unchecked by any experience, it is likely that our optimism is extravagant. Logicality in regard to practical matters is the most useful quality an animal can possess, and might, therefore, result from the action of natural selection; but outside of these it is probably of more advantage to the animal to have his mind filled with pleasing and encouraging visions, independently of their truth; and thus, upon unpractical subjects, natural selection might occasion a fallacious tendency of thought.

That which determines us, from given premises, to draw one inference rather than another, is some habit of mind, whether it be constitutional or acquired. The habit is good or otherwise, according as it produces true conclusions from true premises or not; and an inference is regarded as valid or not, without reference to the truth or falsity of its conclusion specially, but according as the habit which determines it is such as to produce true conclusions in general or not. The particular habit of mind which governs this or that inference may be formulated in a proposition whose truth depends on the validity of the inferences which the habit determines; and such a formula is called a *guiding principle* of inference. Suppose, for example, that we observe that a rotating disk of copper quickly comes to rest when placed between the poles of a magnet, and we infer that this will happen with every disk of copper. The guiding principle is, that what is true of one piece of copper is true of another. Such a guiding principle with regard to copper would be much safer than with regard to many other substances — brass, for example.

A book might be written to signalize all the most important of these guiding principles of reasoning. It would probably be, we must confess, of no service to a person whose thought is directed wholly to practical subjects, and whose activity moves along thoroughly beaten paths. The problems which present themselves to such a mind are matters of routine which he has learned once for all to handle in learning his business. But let a man venture into an unfamiliar field, or where his results are not continually checked by experience, and all history shows that the most masculine intellect will ofttimes lose his orientation and waste his efforts in directions which bring him no nearer to his goal, or even carry him entirely astray. He is like a ship on the open sea, with no one on board who understands the rules of navigation. And in such a case some general study of the guiding principles of reasoning would be sure to be found useful.

The subject could hardly be treated, however, without being first limited; since almost any fact may serve as a guiding principle. But it so happens that there exists a division among facts, such that in one class are all those which are absolutely essential as guiding principles, while in the other are all those which have any other interest as objects of research. This division is between those which are necessarily taken for granted in asking whether a certain conclusion follows from certain premises, and those which are not implied in that question. A moment's thought will show that a variety of facts are already assumed when the logical question is first asked. It is implied, for instance, that there are such states of mind as doubt and belief — that a passage from one to the other is possible, the object of thought remaining the same, and that this transition is subject to some rules which all minds are alike bound by. As these are facts which we must already know before we can have any clear conception of reasoning at all, it cannot be supposed to be any longer of much interest to inquire into their truth or falsity. On the other hand, it is easy to believe that those rules of reasoning which are deduced from the very idea of the process are the ones which are the most essential; and, indeed, that so long as it conforms to these it will, at least, not lead to false conclusions from true premises. In point of fact, the importance of what may be deduced from the assumptions involved in the logical question turns out to be greater than might be supposed, and this for reasons which it is difficult to exhibit at the outset. The only one which I shall here mention is, that conceptions which are really products of logical reflections, without being readily seen to be so, mingle with our ordinary thoughts, and are frequently the causes of great confusion. This is the case, for example, with the conception of quality. A quality as such is never an object of observation. We can see that a thing is blue or green, but the quality of being blue and the quality of being green are not things which we see; they are products of logical reflections. The truth is, that common-sense, or thought as it first emerges above the level of the narrowly practical, is deeply imbued with that bad logical quality to which the epithet *metaphysical* is commonly applied; and nothing can clear it up but a severe course of logic.

III

We generally know when we wish to ask a question and when we wish to pronounce a judgment, for there is a dissimilarity between the sensation of doubting and that of believing.

But this is not all which distinguishes doubt from belief. There is a practical difference. Our beliefs guide our desires and shape our actions. The Assassins, or followers of the Old Man of the Mountain, used to rush into death at his least command, because they believed that obedience to him would insure everlasting felicity. Had they doubted this, they would not have acted as they did. So it is with every belief, according to its degree. The feeling of believing is a more or less sure indication of there being established in our nature some habit which will determine our actions. Doubt never has such an effect.

Nor must we overlook a third point of difference. Doubt is an uneasy and dissatisfied state from which we struggle to free ourselves and pass into the state of belief; while the latter is a calm and satisfactory state which we do not wish to avoid, or to change to a belief in anything else.[5] On the contrary, we cling tenaciously, not merely to believing, but to believing just what we do believe.

Thus, both doubt and belief have positive effects upon us, though very different ones. Belief does not make us act at once, but puts us into such a condition that we shall behave in a certain way, when the occasion arises. Doubt has not the least effect of this sort, but stimulates us to action until it is destroyed. This reminds us of the irritation of a nerve and the reflex action produced thereby; while for the analogue of belief, in the nervous system, we must look to what are called nervous associations — for example, to that habit of the nerves in consequence of which the smell of a peach will make the mouth water.

[5] I am not speaking of secondary effects occasionally produced by the interference of other impulses.

IV

The irritation of doubt causes a struggle to attain a state of belief. I shall term this struggle *inquiry*, though it must be admitted that this is sometimes not a very apt designation.

The irritation of doubt is the only immediate motive for the struggle to attain belief. It is certainly best for us that our beliefs should be such as may truly guide our actions so as to satisfy our desires; and this reflection will make us reject any belief which does not seem to have been so formed as to insure this result. But it will only do so by creating a doubt in the place of that belief. With the doubt, therefore, the struggle begins, and with the cessation of doubt it ends. Hence, the sole object of inquiry is the settlement of opinion. We may fancy that this is not enough for us, and that we seek not merely an opinion, but a true opinion. But put this fancy to the test, and it proves groundless; for as soon as a firm belief is reached we are entirely satisfied, whether the belief be false or true. And it is clear that nothing out of the sphere of our knowledge can be our object, for nothing which does not affect the mind can be a motive for a mental effort. The most that can be maintained is, that we seek for a belief that we shall *think* to be true. But we think each one of our beliefs to be true, and, indeed, it is mere tautology to say so.

That the settlement of opinion is the sole end of inquiry is a very important proposition. It sweeps away, at once, various vague and erroneous conceptions of proof. A few of these may be noticed here.

1. Some philosophers have imagined that to start an inquiry it was only necessary to utter or question or set it down on paper, and have even recommended us to begin our studies with questioning everything! But the mere putting of a proposition into the interrogative form does not stimulate the mind to any struggle after belief. There must be a real and living doubt, and without all this discussion is idle.

2. It is a very common idea that a demonstration must rest on some ultimate and absolutely indubitable propositions. These, according to one school, are first principles of a general nature; according to another, are first sensations. But, in point of fact, an inquiry, to have that completely satisfactory result called demonstration, has only to start with propositions perfectly free from all actual doubt. If the premises are not in fact doubted at all, they cannot be more satisfactory than they are.

3. Some people seem to love to argue a point after all the world is fully convinced of it. But no further advance can be made. When doubt ceases, mental action on the subject comes to an end; and, if it did go on, it would be without a purpose.

V

If the settlement of opinion is the sole object of inquiry, and if belief is of the nature of a habit, why should we not attain the desired end, by taking any answer to a question, which we may fancy, and constantly reiterating it to ourselves, dwelling on all which may conduce to that belief, and learning to turn with contempt and hatred from anything which might disturb it? This simple and direct method is really pursued by many men. I remember once being entreated not to read a certain newspaper lest it might change my opinion upon free-trade. "Lest I might be entrapped by its fallacies and misstatements," was the form of expression. "You are not," my friend said, "a special student of political economy. You might, therefore, easily be deceived by fallacious arguments upon the subject. You might, then, if you read this paper, be led to believe in protection. But you admit that free-trade is the true doctrine; and you do not wish to believe what is not true." I have often known this system to be deliberately adopted. Still oftener, the instinctive dislike of an undecided state of mind, exaggerated into a vague dread of doubt, makes men cling spasmodically to the views they already take. The man feels that, if he only holds to his belief without wavering, it will be entirely satisfactory. Nor can it be denied that a steady and immovable faith yields great peace of mind. It may, indeed, give rise to inconveniences, as if a man should resolutely continue to believe that fire would not burn him, or that he would be eternally damned if he received his *ingesta* otherwise than through a stomach-pump. But then the man who adopts this method will not allow that its inconveniences are greater than its advantages. He will say, "I hold steadfastly to the truth and the truth is always wholesome." And in many cases it may very well be that the pleasure he derives from his calm faith overbalances any inconveniences resulting from its deceptive character. Thus, if it be true that death is annihilation, then the man who believes that he will certainly go straight to heaven when he dies, provided he have fulfilled certain simple observances in this life, has a cheap pleasure which will not be followed by the least disappointment. A similar consideration seems to have weight with many persons in religious topics, for we frequently hear it said, "Oh, I could not believe so-and-so, because I should be wretched if I did." When an ostrich buries its head in the sand as danger approaches, it very likely takes the happiest course. It hides the danger, and then calmly says there is no danger; and, if it feels perfectly sure there is none, why should it raise its head to see? A man may go through life, systematically keeping out of view all that might cause a change in his opinions, and if he only succeeds — basing his method, as he does, on two fundamental psychological laws — I do not see what can be said against his doing so. It would be an egotistical impertinence to object that his procedure is irrational, for that only amounts to saying that his method of settling belief is not ours. He does not propose to himself to be rational, and indeed, will often talk with scorn of man's weak and illusive reason. So let him think as he pleases.

But this method of fixing belief, which may be called the method of tenacity, will be unable to hold its ground in practice. The social impulse is against it. The man who adopts it will find that other men think differently from him, and it will be apt to occur to him in some saner moment that their opinions are quite as good as his own, and this will shake his confidence in his belief. This conception, that another man's thought or sentiment may be equivalent to one's own, is a distinctly new step, and a highly important one. It arises from an impulse too strong in man to be suppressed, without danger of destroying the human species. Unless we make ourselves hermits, we shall necessarily influence each other's opinions; so that the problem becomes how to fix belief, not in the individual merely, but in the community.

Let the will of the state act, then, instead of that of the individual. Let an institution be created which shall have for its object to keep correct doctrines before the attention of the people, to reiterate them perpetually, and to teach them to the young; having at the same time power to prevent contrary doctrines from being taught, advocated, or expressed. Let all possible causes of a change of mind be removed from men's apprehensions. Let them be kept ignorant, lest they should learn of some reason to think otherwise than they do. Let their passions be enlisted, so that they may regard private and unusual opinions with hatred and horror. Then, let all men who reject the established belief be terrified into silence. Let the people turn out and tar-and-feather such men, or let inquisitions be made into the manner of thinking of suspected persons, and, when they are found guilty of forbidden beliefs, let them be subjected to some signal punishment. When complete agreement could not otherwise be reached, a general massacre of all who have not thought in a certain way has proved a very effective means of settling opinion in a country. If the power to do this be wanting, let a list of opinions be drawn up, to which no man of the least independence of thought can assent, and let the faithful be required to accept all these propositions, in order to segregate them as radically as possible from the influence of the rest of the world.

This method has, from the earliest times, been one of the chief means of upholding correct theological and political doctrines, and of preserving their universal or catholic character. In Rome, especially, it has been practiced from the days of Numa Pompilius to those of Pius Nonus. This is the most perfect example in history; but wherever there is a priesthood — and no religion has been without one — this method has been more or less made use of. Wherever there is aristocracy, or a guild, or any association of a class of men whose interests depend or are supposed to depend on certain propositions, there will be inevitably found some traces of this natural product of social feeling. Cruelties always accompany this system; and when it is consistently carried out, they become atrocities of the most horrible kind in the eyes of any rational man. Nor should this occasion surprise, for the officer of a society does not feel justified in surrendering the interests of that society for the sake of mercy, as he might his own private interests. It is natural, therefore, that sympathy and fellowship should thus produce a most ruthless power.

In judging this method of fixing belief, which may be called the method of authority, we must in the first place, allow its immeasurable mental and moral superiority to the method of tenacity. Its success is proportionally greater; and in fact it has over and over again worked the most majestic results. The mere structures of stone which it has caused to be put together — in Siam, for example, in Egypt, and in Europe — have many of them a sublimity hardly more than rivaled by the greatest works of Nature. And, except the geological epochs, there are no periods of time so vast as those which are measured by some of these organized faiths. If we scrutinize the matter closely, we shall find that there has not been one of their creeds which has remained always the same; yet the change is so slow as to be imperceptible during one person's life, so that individual belief remains sensibly fixed. For the mass of mankind, then, there is perhaps no better method than this. If it is their highest impulse to be intellectual slaves, then slaves they ought to remain.

But no institution can undertake to regulate opinions upon every subject. Only the most important ones can be attended to, and on the rest men's minds must be left to the action of natural causes. This imperfection will be no source of weakness so long as men are in such a state of culture that one opinion does not influence another — that is, so long as they cannot put two and two together. But in the most priest-ridden states some individuals will be found who are raised above that condition. These men possess a wider sort of social feeling; they see that men in other countries and in other ages have held to very different doctrines from those which they themselves have been brought up to believe; and they cannot help seeing that it is the mere accident of their having been taught as they have, and of their having been surrounded with the manners and associations they have, that has caused them to believe as they do and not far differently. And their candor cannot resist the reflection that there is no reason to rate their own views at a higher value than those of other nations and other centuries; and this gives rise to doubts in their minds.

They will further perceive that such doubts as these must exist in their minds with reference to every belief which seems to be determined by the caprice either of themselves or of those who originated the popular opinions. The willful adherence to a belief, and the arbitrary forcing of it upon others, must, therefore, both be given up and a new method of settling opinions must be adopted, which shall not only produce an impulse to believe, but shall also decide what proposition it is which is to be believed. Let the action of natural preferences be unimpeded, then, and under their influence let men conversing together and regarding matters in different lights, gradually develop beliefs in harmony with natural causes. This method resembles that by which conceptions of art have been brought to maturity. The most perfect example of it is to be found in the history of metaphysical philosophy. Systems of this sort have not usually rested upon observed facts, at least not in any great degree. They have been chiefly adopted because their fundamental propositions seemed "agreeable to reason." This is an apt expression; it does not mean that which agrees with experience, but that which we find ourselves inclined to believe. Plato, for example, finds it agreeable to reason that the distances of the celestial spheres from one another should be proportional to the different lengths of strings which produce harmonious chords. Many philosophers have been led to their main conclusions by considerations like this; but this is the lowest and least developed form which the method takes, for it is clear that another man might find Kepler's [earlier] theory, that the celestial spheres are proportional to the inscribed and circumscribed spheres of the different regular solids, more agreeable to *his* reason. But the shock of opinions will soon lead men to rest on preferences of a far more universal nature. Take, for example, the doctrine that man only acts selfishly — that is, from the consideration that acting in one way will afford him more pleasure than acting in another. This rests on no fact in the world, but it has had a wide acceptance as being the only reasonable theory.

This method is far more intellectual and respectable from the point of view of reason than either of the others which we have noticed. But its failure has been the most manifest. It makes of inquiry something similar to the development of taste; but taste, unfortunately, is always more or less a matter of fashion, and accordingly, metaphysicians have never come to any fixed agreement, but the pendulum has swung backward and forward between a more material and a more spiritual philosophy, from the earliest times to the latest. And so from this, which has been called the *a priori* method, we are driven, in Lord Bacon's phrase, to a true induction. We have examined into this *a priori* method as something which promised to deliver our opinions from their accidental and capricious element. But development, while it is a process which eliminates the effect of some casual circumstances, only magnifies that of others. This method, therefore, does not differ in a very essential way from that of authority. The government may not have lifted its finger to influence my convictions; I may have been left outwardly quite free to choose, we will say, between monogamy and polygamy, and appealing to my conscience only, I may have concluded that the latter practice is in itself licentious. But when I come to see that the chief obstacle to the spread of Christianity among a people of as high culture as the Hindoos has been a conviction of the immorality of our way of treating women, I cannot help seeing that, though governments do not interfere, sentiments in their development will be very greatly determined by accidental causes. Now, there are some people, among whom I must suppose that my reader is to be found, who, when they see that any belief of theirs is determined by any circumstance extraneous to the facts, will from that moment not merely admit in words that that belief is doubtful, but will experience a real doubt of it, so that it ceases to be a belief.

To satisfy our doubts, therefore, it is necessary that a method should be found by which our beliefs may be caused by nothing human, but by some external permanency — by something upon which our thinking has no effect. Some mystics imagine that they have such a method in a private inspiration from on high. But that is only a form of the method of tenacity, in which the conception of truth as something public is not yet developed. Our external permanency would not be external, in our sense, if it was restricted in its influence to one individual. It must be something which affects, or might affect, every man. And, though these affections are necessarily as various as are individual conditions, yet the method must be such that the ultimate conclusion of every man shall be the same.

Such is the method of science. Its fundamental hypothesis, restated in more familiar language, is this: There are real things, whose characters are entirely independent of our opinions about them; whose realities affect our senses according to regular laws, and, though our sensations are as different as our relations to the objects, yet, by taking advantage of the laws of perception, we can ascertain by reasoning how things really are, and any man, if he have sufficient experience and reason enough about it, will be led to the one true conclusion. The new conception here involved is that of reality. It may be asked how I know that there are any realities. If this hypothesis is the sole support of my method of inquiry, my method of inquiry must not be used to support my hypothesis. The reply is this: 1. If investigation cannot be regarded as proving that there are real things, it at least does not lead to a contrary conclusion; but the method and the conception on which it is based remain ever in harmony. No doubts of the method, therefore, necessarily arise from its practice, as is the case with all the others. 2. The feeling which gives rise to any method of fixing belief is a dissatisfaction at two repugnant propositions. But here already is a vague concession that there is some *one* thing to which a proposition should conform. Nobody, therefore, can really doubt that there are realities, or, if he did, doubt would not be a source of dissatisfaction. The hypothesis, therefore, is one which every mind admits. So that the social impulse does not cause me to doubt it. 3. Everybody uses the scientific method about a great many things, and only ceases to use it when he does not know how to apply it. 4. Experience of the method has not led me to doubt it, but, on the contrary, scientific investigation has had the most wonderful triumphs in the way of settling opinion. These afford the explanation of my not doubting the method or the hypothesis which it supposes; and not having any doubt, nor believing that anybody else whom I could influence has, it would be the merest babble for me to say more about it. If there be anybody with a living doubt upon the subject, let him consider it.

To describe the method of scientific investigation is the object of this series of papers. At present I have only room to notice some points of contrast between it and other methods of fixing belief.

This is the only one of the four methods which presents any distinction of a right and a wrong way. If I adopt the method of tenacity and shut myself out from all influences, whatever I think necessary to doing this is necessary according to that method. So with the method of authority: the state may try to put down heresy by means which, from a scientific point of view, seems very ill-calculated to accomplish its purposes; but the only test *on that method* is what the state thinks, so that it cannot pursue the method wrongly. So with the *a priori* method. The very essence of it is to think as one is inclined to think. All metaphysicians will be sure to do that, however they may be inclined to judge each other to be perversely wrong. The Hegelian system recognizes every natural tendency of thought as logical, although it is certain to be abolished by counter-tendencies. Hegel thinks there is a regular system in the succession of these tendencies, in consequence of which, after drifting one way and the other for a long time, opinion will at last go right. And it is true that metaphysicians get the right ideas at last; Hegel's system of Nature represents tolerably the science of that day; and one may be sure that whatever scientific investigation has put out of doubt will presently receive *a priori* demonstration on the part of the metaphysicians. But with the scientific method the case is different. I may start with known and observed facts to proceed to the unknown; and yet the rules which I follow in doing so may not be such as investigation would approve. The test of whether I am truly following the method is not an immediate appeal to my feelings and purposes, but, on the contrary, itself involves the application of the method. Hence it is that bad reasoning as well as good reasoning is possible; and this fact is the foundation of the practical side of logic.

It is not to be supposed that the first three methods of settling opinion present no advantage whatever over the scientific method. On the contrary, each has some peculiar convenience of its own. The *a priori* method is distinguished for its comfortable conclusions. It is the nature of the process to adopt whatever belief we are inclined to, and there are certain flatteries to one's vanities which we all believe by nature, until we are awakened from our pleasing dream by rough facts. The method of authority will always govern the mass of mankind; and those who wield the various forms of organized force in the state will never be convinced that dangerous reasoning ought not to be suppressed in some way. If liberty of speech is to be untrammeled from the grosser forms of constraint, then uniformity of opinion will be secured by a moral terrorism to which the respectability of society will give its thorough approval. Following the method of authority is the path of peace. Certain non-conformities are permitted; certain others (considered unsafe) are forbidden. These are different in different countries and in different ages; but, wherever you are let it be known that you seriously hold a tabooed belief, and you may be perfectly sure of being treated with a cruelty no less brutal but more refined than hunting you like a wolf. Thus, the greatest intellectual benefactors of mankind have never dared, and dare not now, to utter the whole of their thought; and thus a shade of *prima facie* doubt is cast upon every proposition which is considered essential to the security of society. Singularly enough, the persecution does not all come from without; but a man torments himself and is oftentimes most distressed at finding himself believing propositions which he has been brought up to regard with aversion. The peaceful and sympathetic man will, therefore, find it hard to resist the temptation to submit his opinions to authority. But most of all I admire the method of tenacity for its strength, simplicity, and directness. Men who pursue it are distinguished for their decision of character, which becomes very easy with such a mental rule. They do not waste time in trying to make up their minds to what they want, but, fastening like lightning upon whatever alternative comes first, they hold to it to the end, whatever happens, without an instant's irresolution. This is one of the splendid qualities which generally accompany brilliant, unlasting success. It is impossible not to envy the man who can dismiss reason, although we know how it must turn out at last.

Such are the advantages which the other methods of settling opinions have over scientific investigation. A man should consider well of them; and then he should consider that, after all, he wishes his opinions to coincide with the fact, and that there is no reason why the results of these three methods should do so. To bring about this effect is the prerogative of the method of science. Upon such considerations he has to make his choice — a choice which is far more than the adoption of any intellectual opinion, which is one of the ruling decisions of his life, to which when once made he is bound to adhere. The force of habit will sometimes cause a man to hold on to old beliefs, after he is in a condition to see that they have no sound basis. But reflection upon the state of the case will overcome these habits, and he ought to allow reflection full weight. People sometimes shrink from doing this, having an idea that beliefs are wholesome which they cannot help feeling rest on nothing. But let such persons suppose an analogous though different case from their own. Let them ask themselves what they would say to a reformed Mussulman who should hesitate to give up his old notions in regard to the relations of the sexes; or to a reformed Catholic who should still shrink from the Bible. Would they not say that these persons ought to consider the matter fully, and clearly understand the new doctrine, and then ought to embrace it in its entirety? But, above all, let it be considered that what is more wholesome than any particular belief, is integrity of belief; and that to avoid looking into the support of any belief from a fear that it may turn out rotten is quite as immoral as it is disadvantageous. The person who confesses that there is such a thing as truth, which is distinguished from falsehood simply by this, that if acted on it will carry us to the point we aim at and not astray, and then though convinced of this, dares not know the truth and seeks to avoid it, is in a sorry state of mind, indeed.

Yes, the other methods do have their merits: a clear logical conscience does cost something — just as any virtue, just as all that we cherish, costs us dear. But, we should not desire it to be otherwise. The genius of a man's logical method should be loved and reverenced as his bride, whom he has chosen from all the world. He need not condemn the others; on the contrary, he may honor them deeply, and in doing so he only honors her the more. But she is the one that he has chosen, and he knows that he was right in making that choice. And having made it, he will work and fight for her, and will not complain that there are blows to take, hoping that there may be as many and as hard to give, and will strive to be the worthy knight and champion of her from the blaze of whose splendors he draws his inspiration and his courage.

SECOND PAPER

HOW TO MAKE OUR IDEAS CLEAR[1]

I

WHOEVER has looked into a modern treatise on logic of the common sort, will doubtless remember the two distinctions between *clear* and *obscure* conceptions, and between *distinct* and *confused* conceptions. They have lain in the books now for nigh two centuries, unimproved and unmodified, and are generally reckoned by logicians as among the gems of their doctrine.

A clear idea is defined as one which is so apprehended that it will be recognized wherever it is met with, and so that no other will be mistaken for it. If it fails of this clearness, it is said to be obscure.

This is rather a neat bit of philosophical terminology; yet, since it is clearness that they were defining, I wish the logicians had made their definition a little more plain. Never to fail to recognize an idea, and under no circumstances to mistake another for it, let it come in how recondite a form it may, would indeed imply such prodigious force and clearness of intellect as is seldom met with in this world. On the other hand, merely to have such an acquaintance with the idea as to have become familiar with it, and to have lost all hesitancy in recognizing it in ordinary

[1] *Popular Science Monthly*, January, 1878.

cases, hardly seems to deserve the name of clearness of apprehension, since after all it only amounts to a subjective feeling of mastery which may be entirely mistaken. I take it, however, that when the logicians speak of "clearness," they mean nothing more than such a familiarity with an idea, since they regard the quality as but a small merit, which needs to be supplemented by another, which they call *distinctness*.

A distinct idea is defined as one which contains nothing which is not clear. This is technical language; by the *contents* of an idea logicians understand whatever is contained in its definition. So that an idea is *distinctly* apprehended, according to them, when we can give a precise definition of it, in abstract terms. Here the professional logicians leave the subject; and I would not have troubled the reader with what they have to say, if it were not such a striking example of how they have been slumbering through ages of intellectual activity, listlessly disregarding the enginery of modern thought, and never dreaming of applying its lessons to the improvement of logic. It is easy to show that the doctrine that familiar use and abstract distinctness make the perfection of apprehension, has its only true place in philosophies which have long been extinct; and it is now time to formulate the method of attaining to a more perfect clearness of thought, such as we see and admire in the thinkers of our own time.

When Descartes set about the reconstruction of philosophy, his first step was to (theoretically) permit skepticism and to discard the practice of the schoolmen of looking to authority as the ultimate source of truth. That done, he sought a more natural fountain of true principles, and professed to find it in the human mind; thus passing, in the directest way, from the method of authority to that of apriority, as described in my first paper. Self-consciousness was to furnish us with our fundamental truths, and to decide what was agreeable to reason. But since, evidently, not all ideas are true, he was led to note, as the first condition of infallibility, that they must be clear. The distinction between an idea *seeming* clear and really being so, never occurred to him. Trusting to introspection, as he did, even for a knowledge of external things, why should he question its testimony in respect to the contents of our own minds? But then, I suppose, seeing men, who seemed to be quite clear and positive, holding opposite opinions upon fundamental principles, he was further led to say that clearness of ideas is not sufficient, but that they need also to be distinct, i.e., to have nothing unclear about them. What he probably meant by this (for he did not explain himself with precision) was, that they must sustain the test of dialectical examination; that they must not only seem clear at the outset, but that discussion must never be able to bring to light points of obscurity connected with them.

Such was the distinction of Descartes, and one sees that it was precisely on the level of his philosophy. It was somewhat developed by Leibnitz. This great and singular genius was as remarkable for what he failed to see as for what he saw. That a piece of mechanism could not do work perpetually without being fed with power in some form, was a thing perfectly apparent to him; yet he did not understand that the machinery of the mind can only transform knowledge, but never originate it, unless it be fed with facts of observation. He thus missed the most essential point of the Cartesian philosophy, which is, that to accept propositions which seem perfectly evident to us is a thing which, whether it be logical or illogical, we cannot help doing. Instead of regarding the matter in this way, he sought to reduce the first principles of science to formulas which cannot be denied without self-contradiction, and was apparently unaware of the great difference between his position and that of Descartes. So he reverted to the old formalities of logic, and, above all, abstract definitions played a great part in his philosophy. It was quite natural, therefore, that on observing that the method of Descartes labored under the difficulty that we may seem to ourselves to have clear apprehensions of ideas which in truth are very hazy, no better remedy occurred to him than to require an abstract definition of every important term. Accordingly, in adopting the distinction of *clear* and *distinct* notions, he described the latter quality as the clear apprehension of everything contained in the definition; and the books have ever since copied his words. There is no danger that his chimerical scheme will ever again be over-valued. Nothing new can ever be learned by analyzing definitions. Nevertheless, our existing beliefs can be set in order by this process, and order is an essential element of intellectual economy, as of every other. It may be acknowledged, therefore, that the books are right in making familiarity with a notion the first step toward clearness of apprehension, and the defining of it the second. But in omitting all mention of any higher perspicuity of thought, they simply mirror a philosophy which was exploded a hundred years ago. That much-admired "ornament of logic" — the doctrine of clearness and distinctness — may be pretty enough, but it is high time to relegate to our cabinet of curiosities the antique *bijou,* and to wear about us something better adapted to modern uses.

The very first lesson that we have a right to demand that logic shall teach us is, how to make our ideas clear; and a most important one it is, depreciated only by minds who stand in need of it. To know what we think, to be masters of our own meaning, will make a solid foundation for great and weighty thought. It is most easily learned by those whose ideas are meagre and restricted; and far happier they than such as wallow helplessly in a rich mud of conceptions. A nation, it is true, may, in the course of generations, overcome the disadvantage of an excessive wealth of language and its natural concomitant, a vast, unfathomable deep of ideas. We may see it in history, slowly perfecting its literary forms, sloughing at length its metaphysics, and, by virtue of the untirable patience which is often a compensation, attaining great excellence in every branch of mental acquirement. The page of history is not yet unrolled which is to tell us whether such a people will or will not in the long run prevail over one whose ideas (like the words of their language) are few, but which possesses a wonderful mastery over those which it has. For an individual, however, there can be no question that a few clear ideas are worth more than many confused ones. A young man would hardly be persuaded to sacrifice the greater part of his thoughts to save the rest; and the muddled head is the least apt to see the necessity of such a sacrifice. Him we can usually only commiserate, as a person with a congenital defect. Time will help him, but intellectual maturity with regard to clearness comes rather late, an unfortunate arrangement of Nature, inasmuch as clearness is of less use to a man settled in life, whose errors have in great measure had their effect, than it would be to one whose path lies before him. It is terrible to see how a single unclear idea, a single formula without meaning, lurking in a young man's head, will sometimes act like an obstruction of inert matter in an artery, hindering the nutrition of the brain, and condemning its victim to pine away in the fullness of his intellectual vigor and in the midst of intellectual plenty. Many a man has cherished for years as his hobby some vague shadow of an idea, too meaningless to be positively false; he has, nevertheless, passionately loved it, has made it his companion by day and by night, and has given to it his strength and his life, leaving all other occupations for its sake, and in short has lived with it and for it, until it has become, as it were, flesh of his flesh and bone of his bone; and then he has waked up some bright morning to find it gone, clean vanished away like the beautiful Melusina of the fable, and the essence of his life gone with it. I have myself known such a man; and who can tell how many histories of circle-squarers, metaphysicians, astrologers, and what not, may not be told in the old German story?

II

The principles set forth in the first of these papers lead, at once, to a method of reaching a clearness of thought of a far higher grade than the "distinctness" of the logicians. We have there found that the action of thought is excited by the irritation of doubt, and ceases when belief is attained; so that the production of belief is the sole function of thought. All these words, however, are too strong for my purpose. It is as if I had described the phenomena as they appear under a mental microscope. Doubt and Belief, as the words are commonly employed, relate to religious or other grave discussions. But here I use them to designate the starting of any question, no matter how small or how great, and the resolution of it. If, for instance, in a horse-car, I pull out my purse and find a five-cent nickel and five coppers, I decide, while my hand is going to the purse, in which way I will pay my fare. To call such a question Doubt, and my decision Belief, is certainly to use words very disproportionate to the occasion. To speak of such a doubt as causing an irritation which needs to be appeased, suggests a temper which is uncomfortable to the verge of insanity. Yet, looking at the matter minutely, it must be admitted that, if there is the least hesitation as to whether I shall pay the five coppers or the nickel (as there will be sure to be, unless I act from some previously contracted habit in the matter), though irritation is too strong a word, yet I am excited to such small mental activity as may be necessary to deciding how I shall act. Most frequently doubts arise from some indecision, however momentary, in our action. Sometimes it is not so. I have, for example, to wait in a railway-station, and to pass the time I read the advertisements on the walls, I compare the advantages of different trains and different routes which I never expect to take, merely fancying myself to be in a state of hesitancy, because I am bored with having nothing to trouble me. Feigned hesitancy, whether feigned for mere amusement or with a lofty purpose, plays a great part in the production of scientific inquiry. However the doubt may originate, it stimulates the mind to an activity which may be slight or energetic, calm or turbulent. Images pass rapidly through consciousness, one incessantly melting into another, until at last, when all is over — it may be in a fraction of a second, in an hour, or after long years — we find ourselves decided as to how we should act under such circumstances as those which occasioned our hesitation. In other words, we have attained belief.

In this process we observe two sorts of elements of consciousness, the distinction between which may best be made clear by means of an illustration. In a piece of music there are the separate notes, and there is the air. A single tone may be prolonged for an hour or a day, and it exists as perfectly in each second of that time as in the whole taken together; so that, as long as it is sounding, it might be present to a sense from which everything in the past was as completely absent as the future itself. But it is different with the air, the performance of which occupies a certain time, during the portions of which only portions of it are played. It consists in an orderliness in the succession of sounds which strike the ear at different times; and to perceive it there must be some continuity of consciousness which makes the events of a lapse of time present to us. We certainly only perceive the air by hearing the separate notes; yet we cannot be said to directly hear it, for we hear only what is present at the instant, and an orderliness of succession cannot exist in an instant. These two sorts of objects, what we are *immediately* conscious of and what we are *mediately* conscious of, are found in all consciousness. Some elements (the sensations) are completely present at every instant so long as they last, while others (like thought) are actions having beginning, middle, and end, and consist in a congruence in the succession of sensations which flow through the mind. They cannot be immediately present to us, but must cover some portion of the past or future. Thought is a thread of melody running through the succession of our sensations.

We may add that just as a piece of music may be written in parts, each part having its own air, so various systems of relationship of succession subsist together between the same sensations. These different systems are distinguished by having different motives, ideas, or functions. Thought is only one such system; for its sole motive, idea, and function is to produce belief, and whatever does not concern that purpose belongs to some other system of relations. The action of thinking may incidentally have other results. It may serve to amuse us, for example, and among *dilettanti* it is not rare to find those who have so perverted thought to the purposes of pleasure that it seems to vex them to think that the questions upon which they delight to exercise it may ever get finally settled; and a positive discovery which takes a favorite subject out of the arena of literary debate is met with ill-concealed dislike. This disposition is the very debauchery of thought. But the soul and meaning of thought, abstracted from the other elements which accompany it, though it may be voluntarily thwarted, can never be made to direct itself toward anything but the production of belief. Thought in action has for its only possible motive the attainment of thought at rest; and whatever does not refer to belief is no part of the thought itself.

And what, then, is belief? It is the demi-cadence which closes a musical phrase in the symphony of our intellectual life. We have seen that it has just three properties: First, it is something that we are aware of; second, it appeases the irritation of doubt; and, third, it involves the establishment in our nature of a rule of action, or, say for short, a *habit*. As it appeases the irritation of doubt, which is the motive for thinking, thought relaxes, and comes to rest for a moment when belief is reached. But, since belief is a rule for action, the application of which involves further doubt and further thought, at the same time that it is a stopping-place, it is also a new starting-place for thought. That is why I have permitted myself to call it thought at rest, although thought is essentially an action. The *final* upshot of thinking is the exercise of volition, and of this thought no longer forms a part; but belief is only a stadium of mental action, an effect upon our nature due to thought, which will influence future thinking.

The essence of belief is the establishment of a habit, and different beliefs are distinguished by the different modes of action to which they give rise. If beliefs do not differ in this respect, if they appease the same doubt by producing the same rule of action, then no mere differences in the manner of consciousness of them can make them different beliefs, any more than playing a tune in different keys is playing different tunes. Imaginary distinctions are often drawn between beliefs which differ only in their mode of expression; — the wrangling which ensues is real enough, however. To believe that any objects are arranged as in Fig. 1, and to believe that they are arranged as in Fig. 2, are

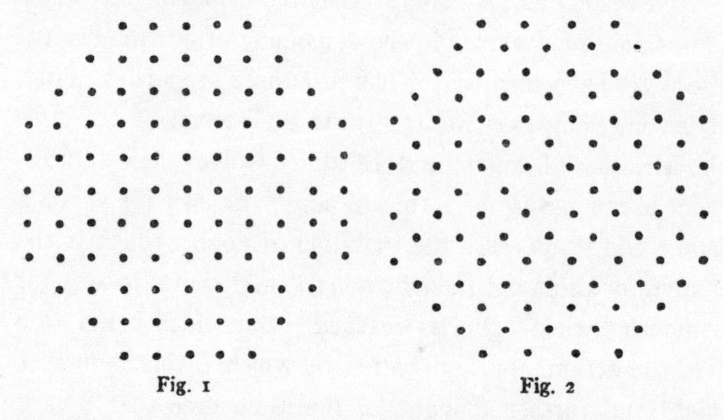

Fig. 1 Fig. 2

one and the same belief; yet it is conceivable that a man should assert one proposition and deny the other. Such false distinctions do as much harm as the confusion of beliefs really different, and are among the pitfalls of which we ought constantly to beware, especially when we are upon metaphysical ground. One singular deception of this sort, which often occurs, is to mistake the sensation produced by our own unclearness of thought for a character of the object we are thinking. Instead of perceiving that the obscurity is purely subjective, we fancy that we contemplate a quality of the object which is essentially mysterious; and if our conception be afterward presented to us in a clear form we do not recognize it as the same, owing to the absence of the feeling of unintelligibility. So long as this deception lasts, it obviously puts an impassable barrier in the way of perspicuous thinking; so that it equally interests the opponents of rational thought to perpetuate it, and its adherents to guard against it.

Another such deception is to mistake a mere difference in the grammatical construction of two words for a distinction between the ideas they express. In this pedantic age, when the general mob of writers attend so much more to words than to things, this error is common enough. When I just said that thought is an *action,* and that it consists in a *relation,* although a person performs an action but not a relation, which can only be the result of an action, yet there was no inconsistency in what I said, but only a grammatical vagueness.

From all these sophisms we shall be perfectly safe so long as we reflect that the whole function of thought is to produce habits of action; and that whatever there is connected with a thought, but irrelevant to its purpose, is an accretion to it, but no part of it. If there be a unity among our sensations which has no reference to how we shall act on a given occasion, as when we listen to a piece of music, why we do not call that thinking. To develop its meaning, we have, therefore, simply to determine what habits it produces, for what a thing means is simply what habits it involves. Now, the identity of a habit depends on how it might lead us to act, not merely under such circumstances as are likely to arise, but under such as might possibly occur, no matter how improbable they may be. What the habit is depends on *when* and *how* it causes us to act. As for the *when*, every stimulus to action is derived from perception; as for the *how*, every purpose of action is to produce some sensible result. Thus, we come down to what is tangible and practical, as the root of every real distinction of thought, no matter how subtile it may be; and there is no distinction of meaning so fine as to consist in anything but a possible difference of practice.

To see what this principle leads to, consider in the light of it such a doctrine as that of transubstantiation. The Protestant churches generally hold that the elements of the sacrament are flesh and blood only in a tropical sense; they nourish our souls as meat and the juice of it would our bodies. But the Catholics maintain that they are literally just that; although they possess all the sensible qualities of wafer-cakes and diluted wine. But we can have no conception of wine except what may enter into a belief, either —

1. That this, that, or the other, is wine; or,
2. That wine possesses certain properties.

Such beliefs are nothing but self-notifications that we should, upon occasion, act in regard to such things as we believe to be wine according to the qualities which we believe wine to possess. The occasion of such action would be some sensible perception, the motive of it to produce some sensible result. Thus our action has exclusive reference to what affects the senses, our habit has the same bearing as our action, our belief the same as our habit, our conception the same as our belief; and we can consequently mean nothing by wine but what has certain effects, direct or indirect, upon our senses; and to talk of something as having all the sensible characters of wine, yet being in reality blood, is senseless jargon. Now, it is not my object to pursue the theological question; and having used it as a logical example I drop it, without caring to anticipate the theologian's reply. I only desire to point out how impossible it is that we should have an idea in our minds which relates to anything but conceived sensible effects of things. Our idea of anything *is* our idea of its sensible effects; and if we fancy that we have any other we deceive ourselves, and mistake a mere sensation accompanying the thought for a part of the thought itself. It is absurd to say that thought has any meaning unrelated to its only function. It is foolish for Catholics and Protestants to fancy themselves in disagreement about the elements of the sacrament, if they agree in regard to all their sensible effects, here or hereafter.

It appears, then, that the rule for attaining the third grade of clearness of apprehension is as follows: Consider what effects, which might conceivably have practical bearings, we conceive the object of our conception to have. Then, our conception of these effects is the whole of our conception of the object.

III

Let us illustrate this rule by some examples; and, to begin with the simplest one possible, let us ask what we mean by calling a thing *hard*. Evidently that it will not be scratched by many other substances. The whole conception of this quality, as of every other, lies in its conceived effects. There is absolutely no difference between a hard thing and a soft thing so long as they are not brought to the test. Suppose, then, that a diamond could be crystallized in the midst of a cushion of soft cotton, and should remain there until it was finally burned up. Would it be false to say that that diamond was soft? This seems a foolish question, and would be so, in fact, except in the realm of logic. There such questions are often of the greatest utility as serving to bring logical principles into sharper relief than real discussions ever could. In studying logic we must not put them aside with hasty answers, but must consider them with attentive care, in order to make out the principles involved. We may, in the present case, modify our question, and ask what prevents us from saying that all hard bodies remain perfectly soft until they are touched, when their hardness increases with the pressure until they are scratched. Reflection will show that the reply is this: there would be no *falsity* in such modes of speech. They would involve a modification of our present usage of speech with regard to the words hard and soft, but not of their meanings. For they represent no fact to be different from what it is; only they involve arrangements of facts which would be exceedingly maladroit. This leads us to remark that the question of what would occur under circumstances which do not actually arise is not a question of fact, but only of the most perspicuous arrangement of them. For example, the question of free-will and fate in its simplest form, stripped of verbiage, is something like this: I have done something of which I am ashamed; could I, by an effort of the will, have resisted the temptation, and done otherwise? The philosophical reply is, that this is not a question of fact, but only of the arrangement of facts. Arranging them so as to exhibit what is particularly pertinent to my question — namely, that I ought to blame myself for having done wrong — it is perfectly true to say that, if I had willed to do otherwise than I did, I should have done otherwise. On the other hand, arranging the facts so as to exhibit another important consideration, it is equally true that, when a temptation has once been allowed to work, it will, if it has a certain force, produce its effect, let me struggle how I may. There is no objection to a contradiction in what would result from a false supposition. The *reductio ad absurdum* consists in showing that contradictory results would follow from a hypothesis which is consequently judged to be false. Many questions are involved in the free-will discussion, and I am far from desiring to say that both sides are equally right. On the contrary, I am of opinion that one side denies important facts, and that the other does not. But what I do say is, that the above single question was the origin of the whole doubt; that, had it not been for this question, the controversy would never have arisen; and that this question is perfectly solved in the manner which I have indicated.

Let us next seek a clear idea of Weight. This is another very easy case. To say that a body is heavy means simply that, in the absence of opposing force, it will fall. This (neglecting certain specifications of how it will fall, etc., which exist in the mind of the physicist who uses the word) is evidently the whole conception of weight. It is a fair question whether some particular facts may not *account* for gravity; but what we mean by the force itself is completely involved in its effects.

This leads us to undertake an account of the idea of Force in general. This is the great conception which, developed in the early part of the seventeenth century from the rude idea of a cause, and constantly improved upon since, has shown us how to explain all the changes of motion which bodies experience, and how to think about all physical phenomena; which has given birth to modern science, and changed the face of the globe; and which, aside from its more special uses, has played a principal part in directing the course of modern thought, and in furthering modern social development. It is, therefore, worth some pains to comprehend it. According to our rule, we must begin by asking what is the immediate use of thinking about force; and the answer is, that we thus account for changes of motion. If bodies were left to themselves, without the intervention of forces, every motion would continue unchanged both in velocity and in direction. Furthermore, change of motion never takes place abruptly; if its direction is changed, it is always through a curve without angles; if its velocity alters, it is by degrees. The gradual changes which are constantly taking place are conceived by geometers to be compounded together according to the rules of the parallelogram of forces. If the reader does not already know what this is, he will find it, I hope, to his advantage to endeavor to follow the following explanation; but if mathematics are insupportable to him, pray let him skip three paragraphs rather than that we should part company here.

A *path* is a line whose beginning and end are distinguished. Two paths are considered to be equivalent, which, beginning at the same point, lead to the same point. Thus the two paths, *A B C D E* and *A F G H E* (Fig. 3), are equivalent. Paths which do *not* begin at the same point are considered to be equivalent, provided that, on moving either of them without turning it, but keeping it always parallel to its original position, [so that] when its beginning coincides with that of the other path, the ends also coincide. Paths are considered as geometrically added together, when one begins where the other ends; thus the path *A E* is conceived to be a sum of *A B, B C, C D,* and *D E.* In the parallelogram of Fig. 4 the diagonal *A C* is the sum of *A B* and *B C;* or, since *A D* is geometrically equivalent to *B C, A C* is the geometrical sum of *A B* and *A D.*

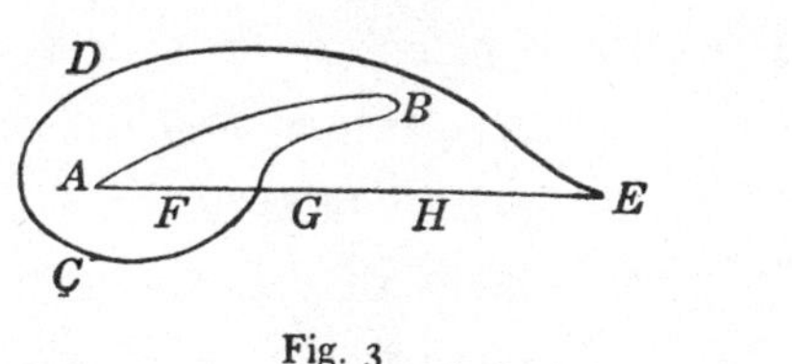

Fig. 3

Fig. 4

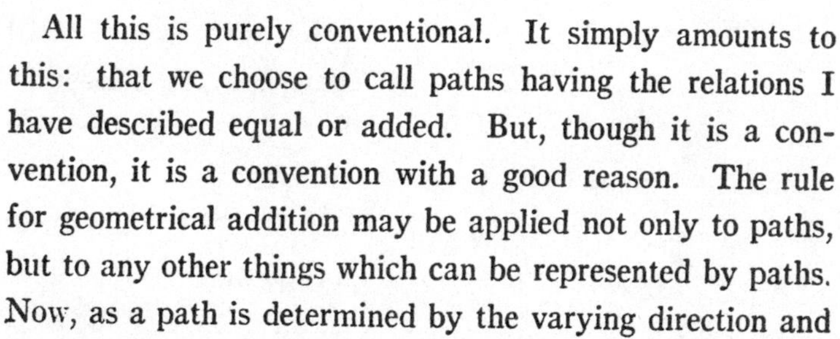

All this is purely conventional. It simply amounts to this: that we choose to call paths having the relations I have described equal or added. But, though it is a convention, it is a convention with a good reason. The rule for geometrical addition may be applied not only to paths, but to any other things which can be represented by paths. Now, as a path is determined by the varying direction and distance of the point which moves over it from the starting-point, it follows that anything which from its beginning to its end is determined by a varying direction and a varying magnitude is capable of being represented by a line. Accordingly, *velocities* may be represented by lines, for they have only directions and rates. The same thing is true of *accelerations,* or changes of velocities. This is evident enough in the case of velocities; and it becomes evident for accelerations if we consider that precisely what velocities are to positions — namely, states of change of them — that accelerations are to velocities.

The so-called "parallelogram of forces" is simply a rule for compounding accelerations. The rule is, to represent the accelerations by paths, and then to geometrically add the paths. The geometers, however, not only use the "parallelogram of forces" to compound different accelerations, but also to resolve one acceleration into a sum of several. Let *A B* (Fig. 5) be the path which represents a certain acceleration — say, such a change in the motion of a body that at the end of one second the body will, under the influence of that change, be in a position different from what it would have had if its motion had continued unchanged, such that a path equivalent to *A B* would lead from the latter position to the former. This acceleration may be considered as the sum of the accelerations represented by *A C* and *C B.*

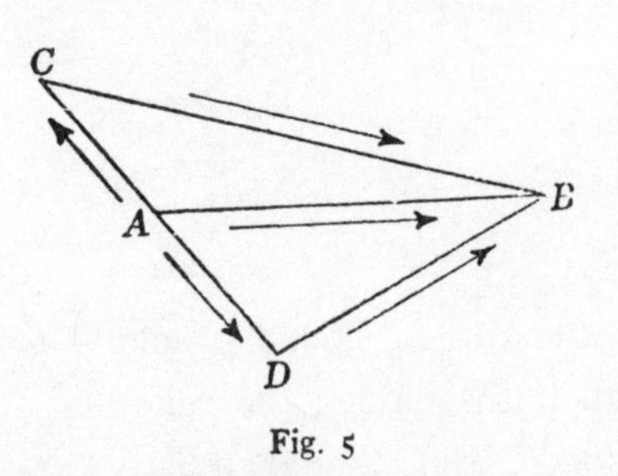

Fig. 5

It may also be considered as the sum of the very different accelerations represented by *A D* and *D B*, where *A D* is almost the opposite of *A C*. And it is clear that there is an immense variety of ways in which *A B* might be resolved into the sum of two accelerations.

After this tedious explanation, which I hope, in view of the extraordinary interest of the conception of force, may not have exhausted the reader's patience, we are prepared at last to state the grand fact which this conception embodies. This fact is that if the actual changes of motion which the different particles of bodies experience are each resolved in its appropriate way, each component acceleration is precisely such as is prescribed by a certain law of Nature, according to which bodies in the relative positions which the bodies in question actually have at the moment,[2] always receive certain accelerations, which, being compounded by geometrical addition, give the acceleration which the body actually experiences.

This is the only fact which the idea of force represents, and whoever will take the trouble clearly to apprehend what this fact is, perfectly comprehends what force is. Whether we ought to say that a force *is* an acceleration, or that it *causes* an acceleration, is a mere question of propriety of language, which has no more to do with our real meaning than the difference between the French idiom "*Il fait froid*" and its English equivalent "*It is cold.*" Yet it is surprising to see how this simple affair has muddled men's minds. In how many profound treatises is not force spoken of as a "mysterious entity," which seems to be

[2] Possibly the velocities also have to be taken into account.

only a way of confessing that the author despairs of ever getting a clear notion of what the word means! In a recent admired work on *Analytic Mechanics* it is stated that we understand precisely the effect of force, but what force itself is we do not understand! This is simply a self-contradiction. The idea which the word force excites in our minds has no other function than to affect our actions, and these actions can have no reference to force otherwise than through its effects. Consequently, if we know what the effects of force are, we are acquainted with every fact which is implied in saying that a force exists, and there is nothing more to know. The truth is, there is some vague notion afloat that a question may mean something which the mind cannot conceive; and when some hair-splitting philosophers have been confronted with the absurdity of such a view, they have invented an empty distinction between positive and negative conceptions, in the attempt to give their non-idea a form not obviously nonsensical. The nullity of it is sufficiently plain from the considerations given a few pages back; and, apart from those considerations, the quibbling character of the distinction must have struck every mind accustomed to real thinking.

IV

Let us now approach the subject of logic, and consider a conception which particularly concerns it, that of *reality*. Taking clearness in the sense of familiarity, no idea could be clearer than this. Every child uses it with perfect confidence, never dreaming that he does not understand it.

As for clearness in its second grade, however, it would probably puzzle most men, even among those of a reflective turn of mind, to give an abstract definition of the real. Yet such a definition may perhaps be reached by considering the points of difference between reality and its opposite, fiction. A figment is a product of somebody's imagination; it has such characters as his thought impresses upon it. That those characters are independent of how you or I think is an external reality. There are, however, phenomena within our own minds, dependent upon our thought, which are at the same time real in the sense that we really think them. But though their characters depend on how we think, they do not depend on what we think those characters to be. Thus, a dream has a real existence as a mental phenomenon, if somebody has really dreamt it; that he dreamt so and so, does not depend on what anybody thinks was dreamt, but is completely independent of all opinion on the subject. On the other hand, considering, not the fact of dreaming, but the thing dreamt, it retains its peculiarities by virtue of no other fact than that it was dreamt to possess them. Thus we may define the real as that whose characters are independent of what anybody may think them to be.

But, however satisfactory such a definition may be found, it would be a great mistake to suppose that it makes the idea of reality perfectly clear. Here, then, let us apply our rules. According to them, reality, like every other quality, consists in the peculiar sensible effects which things partaking of it produce. The only effect which real things have is to cause belief, for all the sensations which they excite emerge into consciousness in the form of beliefs. The question, therefore, is, how is true belief (or belief in the real) distinguished from false belief (or belief in fiction). Now, as we have seen in the former paper, the ideas of truth and falsehood, in their full development, appertain exclusively to the scientific method of settling opinion. A person who arbitrarily chooses the propositions which he will adopt can use the word truth only to emphasize the expression of his determination to hold on to his choice. Of course, the method of tenacity never prevailed exclusively; reason is too natural to men for that. But in the literature of the dark ages we find some fine examples of it. When Scotus Erigena is commenting upon a poetical passage in which hellebore is spoken of as having caused the death of Socrates, he does not hesitate to inform the inquiring reader that Helleborus and Socrates were two eminent Greek philosophers, and that the latter having been overcome in argument by the former took the matter to heart and died of it! What sort of an idea of truth could a man have who could adopt and teach, without the qualification of a perhaps, an opinion taken so entirely at random? The real spirit of Socrates, who I hope would have been delighted to have been "overcome in argument," because he would have learned something by it, is in curious contrast with the naïve idea of the glossist, for whom discussion would seem to have been simply a struggle. When philosophy began to awake from its long slumber, and before theology completely dominated it, the practice seems to have been for each professor to seize upon any philosophical position he found unoccupied and which seemed a strong one, to intrench himself in it, and to sally forth from time to time to give battle to the others. Thus, even the scanty records we possess of those disputes enable us to make out a dozen or more opinions held by different teachers at one time concerning the question of nominalism and realism. Read the opening part of the *Historia Calamitatum* of Abelard, who was certainly as philosophical as any of his contemporaries, and see the spirit of combat which it breathes. For him, the truth is simply his particular stronghold. When the method of authority prevailed, the truth meant little more than the Catholic faith. All the efforts of the scholastic doctors are directed toward harmonizing their faith in Aristotle and their faith in the Church, and one may search their ponderous folios through without finding an argument which goes any further. It is noticeable that where different faiths flourish side by side, renegades are looked upon with contempt even by the party whose belief they adopt; so completely has the idea of loyalty replaced that of truth-seeking. Since the time of Descartes, the defect in the conception of truth has been less apparent. Still, it will sometimes strike a scientific man that the philosophers have been less intent on finding out what the facts are, than on inquiring what belief is most in harmony with their system. It is hard to convince a follower of the *a priori* method by adducing facts; but show him that an opinion he is defending is inconsistent with what he has laid down elsewhere, and he will be very apt to retract it. These minds do not seem to believe that disputation is ever to cease; they seem to think that the opinion which is natural for one man is not so for another, and that belief will, consequently, never be settled. In contenting themselves with fixing their own opinions by a method which would lead another man to a different result, they betray their feeble hold of the conception of what truth is.

On the other hand, all the followers of science are fully persuaded that the processes of investigation, if only pushed far enough, will give one certain solution to every question to which they can be applied. One man may investigate the velocity of light by studying the transits of Venus and the aberration of the stars; another by the oppositions of Mars and the eclipses of Jupiter's satellites; a third by the method of Fizeau; a fourth by that of Foucault; a fifth by the motions of the curves of Lissajoux; a sixth, a seventh, an eighth, and a ninth, may follow the different methods of comparing the measures of statical and dynamical electricity. They may at first obtain different results, but, as each perfects his method and his processes, the results will move steadily together toward a destined center. So with all scientific research. Different minds may set out with the most antagonistic views, but the progress of investigation carries them by a force outside of themselves to one and the same conclusion. This activity of thought by which we are carried, not where we wish, but to a foreordained goal, is like the operation of destiny. No modification of the point of view taken, no selection of other facts for study, no natural bent of mind even, can enable a man to escape the predestinate opinion. This great law is embodied in the conception of truth and reality. The opinion which is fated[3] to be ultimately agreed to by all who investigate, is what we mean by the truth, and the object represented in this opinion is the real. That is the way I would explain reality.

But it may be said that this view is directly opposed to the abstract definition which we have given of reality, inasmuch as it makes the characters of the real depend on what is ultimately thought about them. But the answer to this is that, on the one hand, reality is independent, not necessarily of thought in general, but only of what you or I or any finite number of men may think about it; and that, on the other hand, though the object of the final opinion depends on what that opinion is, yet what that opinion is does not depend on what you or I or any man thinks. Our perversity and that of others may indefinitely postpone the settlement of opinion; it might even conceivably cause an arbitrary proposition to be universally accepted as long as the human race should last. Yet even that would not change the nature of the belief, which alone could be the result of investigation carried sufficiently far; and if, after the extinction of our race, another should arise with faculties and disposition for investigation, that true opinion must be the one which they would ultimately come to. "Truth crushed to earth shall rise again," and the opinion which would finally result from investigation does not depend on how anybody may actually think. But the reality of that which is real does depend on the real fact that investigation is

[3] Fate means merely that which is sure to come true, and can nohow be avoided. It is a superstition to suppose that a certain sort of events are ever fated, and it is another to suppose that the word fate can never be freed from its superstitious taint. We are all fated to die.

destined to lead, at last, if continued long enough, to a belief in it.

But I may be asked what I have to say to all the minute facts of history, forgotten never to be recovered, to the lost books of the ancients, to the buried secrets.

> "Full many a gem of purest ray serene
> The dark, unfathomed caves of ocean bear;
> Full many a flower is born to blush unseen,
> And waste its sweetness on the desert air."

Do these things not really exist because they are hopelessly beyond the reach of our knowledge? And then, after the universe is dead (according to the prediction of some scientists), and all life has ceased forever, will not the shock of atoms continue though there will be no mind to know it? To this I reply that, though in no possible state of knowledge can any number be great enough to express the relation between the amount of what rests unknown to the amount of the known, yet it is unphilosophical to suppose that, with regard to any given question (which has any clear meaning), investigation would not bring forth a solution of it, if it were carried far enough. Who would have said, a few years ago, that we could ever know of what substances stars are made whose light may have been longer in reaching us than the human race has existed? Who can be sure of what we shall not know in a few hundred years? Who can guess what would be the result of continuing the pursuit of science for ten thousand years, with the activity of the last hundred? And if it were to go on for a million, or a billion, or any number of years you please, how is it possible to say that there is any question which might not ultimately be solved?

But it may be objected, "Why make so much of these remote considerations, especially when it is your principle that only practical distinctions have a meaning?" Well, I must confess that it makes very little difference whether we say that a stone on the bottom of the ocean, in complete darkness, is brilliant or not — that is to say, that it *probably* makes no difference, remembering always that that stone *may* be fished up to-morrow. But that there are gems at the bottom of the sea, flowers in the untraveled desert, etc., are propositions which, like that about a diamond being hard when it is not pressed, concern much more the arrangement of our language than they do the meaning of our ideas.

It seems to me, however, that we have, by the application of our rule, reached so clear an apprehension of what we mean by reality, and of the fact which the idea rests on, that we should not, perhaps, be making a pretension so presumptuous as it would be singular, if we were to offer a metaphysical theory of existence for universal acceptance among those who employ the scientific method of fixing belief. However, as metaphysics is a subject much more curious than useful, the knowledge of which, like that of a sunken reef, serves chiefly to enable us to keep clear of it, I will not trouble the reader with any more Ontology at this moment. I have already been led much further into that path than I should have desired; and I have given the reader such a dose of mathematics, psychology, and all that is most abstruse, that I fear he may already have left me, and that what I am now writing is for the compositor and proofreader exclusively. I trusted to the importance of the subject. There is no royal road to logic, and really valuable ideas can only be had at the price of close attention. But I know that in the matter of ideas the public prefer the cheap and nasty; and in my next paper I am going to return to the easily intelligible, and not wander from it again. The reader who has been at the pains of wading through this paper, shall be rewarded in the next one by seeing how beautifully what has been developed in this tedious way can be applied to the ascertainment of the rules of scientific reasoning.

We have, hitherto, not crossed the threshold of scientific logic. It is certainly important to know how to make our ideas clear, but they may be ever so clear without being true. How to make them so, we have next to study. How to give birth to those vital and procreative ideas which multiply into a thousand forms and diffuse themselves everywhere, advancing civilization and making the dignity of man, is an art not yet reduced to rules, but of the secret of which the history of science affords some hints.

THIRD PAPER

THE DOCTRINE OF CHANCES[1]

I

It is a common observation that a science first begins to be exact when it is quantitatively treated. What are called the exact sciences are no others than the mathematical ones. Chemists reasoned vaguely until Lavoisier showed them how to apply the balance to the verification of their theories, when chemistry leaped suddenly into the position of the most perfect of the classificatory sciences. It has thus become so precise and certain that we usually think of it along with optics, thermotics, and electrics. But these are studies of general laws, while chemistry considers merely the relations and classification of certain objects; and belongs, in reality, in the same category as systematic botany and zoölogy. Compare it with these last, however, and the advantage that it derives from its quantitative treatment is very evident.

The rudest numerical scales, such as that by which the mineralogists distinguish the different degrees of hardness, are found useful. The mere counting of pistils and stamens sufficed to bring botany out of total chaos into some kind of form. It is not, however, so much from *counting* as from *measuring*, not so much from the conception of

[1] *Popular Science Monthly*, March, 1878.

number as from that of continuous quantity, that the advantage of mathematical treatment comes. Number, after all, only serves to pin us down to a precision in our thoughts which, however beneficial, can seldom lead to lofty conceptions, and frequently descends to pettiness. Of those two faculties of which Bacon speaks, that which marks differences and that which notes resemblances, the employment of number can only aid the lesser one; and the excessive use of it must tend to narrow the powers of the mind. But the conception of continuous quantity has a great office to fulfill, independently of any attempt at precision. Far from tending to the exaggeration of differences, it is the direct instrument of the finest generalizations. When a naturalist wishes to study a species, he collects a considerable number of specimens more or less similar. In contemplating them, he observes certain ones which are more or less alike in some particular respect. They all have, for instance, a certain S-shaped marking. He observes that they are not *precisely* alike, in this respect; the S has not precisely the same shape, but the differences are such as to lead him to believe that forms could be found intermediate between any two of those he possesses. He, now, finds other forms apparently quite dissimilar — say a marking in the form of a C — and the question is, whether he can find intermediate ones which will connect these latter with the others. This he often succeeds in doing in cases where it would at first be thought impossible; whereas, he sometimes finds those which differ, at first glance, much less, to be separated in Nature by the non-occurrence of intermediaries. In this way, he builds up from the study of Nature a new general conception of the character in question. He obtains, for example, an idea of a leaf which includes every part of the flower, and an idea of a vertebra which includes the skull. I surely need not say much to show what a logical engine there is here. It is the essence of the method of the naturalist.[2] How he applies it first to one character, and then to another, and finally obtains a notion of a species of animals, the differences between whose members, however great, are confined within limits, is a matter which does not here concern us. The whole method of classification must be considered later; but, at present, I only desire to point out that it is by taking advantage of the idea of continuity, or the passage from one form to another by insensible degrees, that the naturalist builds his conceptions. Now, the naturalists are the great builders of conceptions; there is no other branch of science where so much of this work is done as in theirs; and we must, in great measure, take them for our teachers in this important part of logic. And it will be found everywhere that the idea of continuity is a powerful aid to the formation of true and fruitful conceptions. By means of it, the greatest differences are broken down and resolved into differences of degree, and the incessant application of it is of the greatest value in broadening our conceptions. I propose to make a great use of this idea in the present series of papers; and the particular series of important fallacies, which, arising from a neglect of it, have desolated philosophy, must further on be closely studied.

[2] [Later, pp. 170 ff. and 215 ff., it is shown that continuity is also at the basis of mathematical generalization. See also article on Synechism in *Baldwin's Dictionary of Philosophy*.]

At present, I simply call the reader's attention to the utility of this conception.

In studies of numbers, the idea of continuity is so indispensable, that it is perpetually introduced even where there is no continuity in fact, as where we say that there are in the United States 10.7 inhabitants per square mile, or that in New York 14.72 persons live in the average house.[3] Another example is that law of the distribution of errors which Quetelet, Galton, and others, have applied with so much success to the study of biological and social matters. This application of continuity to cases where it does not really exist illustrates, also, another point which will hereafter demand a separate study, namely, the great utility which fictions sometimes have in science.

II

The theory of probabilities is simply the science of logic quantitatively treated. There are two conceivable certainties with reference to any hypothesis, the certainty of its truth and the certainty of its falsity. The numbers *one* and *zero* are appropriated, in this calculus, to marking these extremes of knowledge; while fractions having values intermediate between them indicate, as we may vaguely say, the degrees in which the evidence leans toward one or the other. The general problem of probabilities is, from a given state

[3] This mode of thought is so familiarly associated with all exact numerical consideration, that the phrase appropriate to it is imitated by shallow writers in order to produce the appearance of exactitude where none exists. Certain newspapers which affect a learned tone talk of "the average man," when they simply mean *most men*, and have no idea of striking an average.

of facts, to determine the numerical probability of a possible fact. This is the same as to inquire how much the given facts are worth, considered as evidence to prove the possible fact. Thus the problem of probabilities is simply the general problem of logic.

Probability is a continuous quantity, so that great advantages may be expected from this mode of studying logic. Some writers have gone so far as to maintain that, by means of the calculus of chances, every solid inference may be represented by legitimate arithmetical operations upon the numbers given in the premises. If this be, indeed, true, the great problem of logic, how it is that the observation of one fact can give us knowledge of another independent fact, is reduced to a mere question of arithmetic. It seems proper to examine this pretension before undertaking any more recondite solution of the paradox.

But, unfortunately, writers on probabilities are not agreed in regard to this result. This branch of mathematics is the only one, I believe, in which good writers frequently get results entirely erroneous. In elementary geometry the reasoning is frequently fallacious, but erroneous conclusions are avoided; but it may be doubted if there is a single extensive treatise on probabilities in existence which does not contain solutions absolutely indefensible. This is partly owing to the want of any regular method of procedure; for the subject involves too many subtilties to make it easy to put its problems into equations without such an aid. But, beyond this, the fundamental principles of its calculus are more or less in dispute. In regard to that class of questions to which it is chiefly applied for practical purposes, there is comparatively little doubt; but in regard to others to which it has been sought to extend it, opinion is somewhat unsettled.

This last class of difficulties can only be entirely overcome by making the idea of probability perfectly clear in our minds in the way set forth in our last paper.

III

To get a clear idea of what we mean by probability, we have to consider what real and sensible difference there is between one degree of probability and another.

The character of probability belongs primarily, without doubt, to certain inferences. Locke explains it as follows: After remarking that the mathematician positively knows that the sum of the three angles of a triangle is equal to two right angles because he apprehends the geometrical proof, he thus continues: "But another man who never took the pains to observe the demonstration, hearing a mathematician, a man of credit, affirm the three angles of a triangle to be equal to two right ones, *assents* to it; i.e., receives it for true. In which case the foundation of his assent is the probability of the thing, the proof being such as, for the most part, carries truth with it; the man on whose testimony he receives it not being wont to affirm anything contrary to, or besides his knowledge, especially in matters of this kind." The celebrated *Essay concerning Human Understanding* contains many passages which, like this one, make the first steps in profound analyses which are not further developed. It was shown in the first of these papers that the validity of an inference does not depend on any tendency of the mind to accept it, however strong such tendency may be; but consists in the real fact that, when premises like those of the argument in question are true, conclusions related to them like that of this argument are also true. It was remarked that in a logical mind an argument is always conceived as a member of a *genus* of arguments all constructed in the same way, and such that, when their premises are real facts, their conclusions are so also. If the argument is demonstrative, then this is always so; if it is only probable, then it is for the most part so. As Locke says, the probable argument is "*such as* for the most part carries truth with it."

According to this, that real and sensible difference between one degree of probability and another, in which the meaning of the distinction lies, is that in the frequent employment of two different modes of inference, one will carry truth with it oftener than the other. It is evident that this is the only difference there is in the existing fact. Having certain premises, a man draws a certain conclusion, and as far as this inference alone is concerned the only possible practical question is whether that conclusion is true or not, and between existence and non-existence there is no middle term. "Being only is and nothing is altogether not," said Parmenides; and this is in strict accordance with the analysis of the conception of reality given in the last paper. For we found that the distinction of reality and fiction depends on the supposition that sufficient investigation would cause one opinion to be universally received and all others to be rejected. That presupposition, involved in the very conceptions of reality and figment, involves a complete sundering of the two. It is the heaven-and-hell idea in the domain of thought. But, in the long run, there is a real fact which corresponds to the idea of probability, and it is that a given mode of inference sometimes proves successful and sometimes not, and that in a ratio ultimately fixed. As we go on drawing inference after inference of the given kind, during the first ten or hundred cases the ratio of successes may be expected to show considerable fluctuations; but when we come into the thousands and millions, these fluctuations become less and less; and if we continue long enough, the ratio will approximate toward a fixed limit. We may, therefore, define the probability of a mode of argument as the proportion of cases in which it carries truth with it.

The inference from the premise, A, to the conclusion, B, depends, as we have seen, on the guiding principle, that if a fact of the class A is true, a fact of the class B is true. The probability consists of the fraction whose numerator is the number of times in which both A and B are true, and whose denominator is the total number of times in which A is true, whether B is so or not. Instead of speaking of this as the probability of the inference, there is not the slightest objection to calling it the probability that, if A happens, B happens. But to speak of the probability of the event B, without naming the condition, really has no meaning at all. It is true that when it is perfectly obvious what condition is meant, the ellipsis may be permitted. But we should avoid contracting the habit of using language in this way (universal as the habit is), because it gives rise to a vague way of thinking, as if the action of causation might either determine an event to happen or determine it not to happen, or leave it more or less free to happen or not, so as to give rise to an *inherent* chance in regard to its occurrence.[4] It is quite clear to me that some of the worst and most persistent errors in the use of the doctrine of chances have arisen from this vicious mode of expression.[5]

IV

But there remains an important point to be cleared up. According to what has been said, the idea of probability essentially belongs to a kind of inference which is repeated indefinitely. An individual inference must be either true or false, and can show no effect of probability; and, therefore, in reference to a single case considered in itself, probability can have no meaning. Yet if a man had to choose between drawing a card from a pack containing twenty-five red cards and a black one, or from a pack containing twenty-five black cards and a red one, and if the drawing of a red card were destined to transport him to eternal felicity, and that of a black one to consign him to everlasting woe, it would be folly to deny that he ought to prefer the pack containing the larger portion of red cards, although, from the nature of the risk, it could not be repeated. It is not easy to reconcile this with our analysis of the conception

[4] *Cf.* pp. 179 ff. below.

[5] The conception of probability here set forth is substantially that first developed by Mr. Venn, in his *Logic of Chance.* Of course, a vague apprehension of the idea had always existed, but the problem was to make it perfectly clear, and to him belongs the credit of first doing this.

of chance. But suppose he should choose the red pack, and should draw the wrong card, what consolation would he have? He might say that he had acted in accordance with reason, but that would only show that his reason was absolutely worthless. And if he should choose the right card, how could he regard it as anything but a happy accident? He could not say that if he had drawn from the other pack, he might have drawn the wrong one, because an hypothetical proposition such as, "if A, then B," means nothing with reference to a single case. Truth consists in the existence of a real fact corresponding to the true proposition. Corresponding to the proposition, "if A, then B," there may be the fact that *whenever* such an event as A happens such an event as B happens. But in the case supposed, which has no parallel as far as this man is concerned, there would be no real fact whose existence could give any truth to the statement that, if he had drawn from the other pack, he might have drawn a black card. Indeed, since the validity of an inference consists in the truth of the hypothetical proposition that *if* the premises be true the conclusion will also be true, and since the only real fact which can correspond to such a proposition is that whenever the antecedent is true the consequent is so also, it follows that there can be no sense in reasoning in an isolated case, at all.

These considerations appear, at first sight, to dispose of the difficulty mentioned. Yet the case of the other side is not yet exhausted. Although probability will probably manifest its effect in, say, a thousand risks, by a certain proportion between the numbers of successes and failures, yet this, as we have seen, is only to say that it certainly will, at length, do so. Now the number of risks, the number of probable inferences, which a man draws in his whole life, is a finite one, and he cannot be absolutely *certain* that the mean result will accord with the probabilities at all. Taking all his risks collectively, then, it cannot be certain that they will not fail, and his case does not differ, except in degree, from the one last supposed. It is an indubitable result of the theory of probabilities that every gambler, if he continues long enough, must ultimately be ruined. Suppose he tries the martingale, which some believe infallible, and which is, as I am informed, disallowed in the gambling-houses. In this method of playing, he first bets say $1; if he loses it he bets $2; if he loses that he bets $4; if he loses that he bets $8; if he then gains he has lost $1 + 2 + 4 = 7$, and he has gained $1 more; and no matter how many bets he loses, the first one he gains will make him $1 richer than he was in the beginning. In that way, he will probably gain at first; but, at last, the time will come when the run of luck is so against him that he will not have money enough to double, and must, therefore, let his bet go. This will *probably* happen before he has won as much as he had in the first place, so that this run against him will leave him poorer than he began; some time or other it will be sure to happen. It is true that there is always a possibility of his winning any sum the bank can pay, and we thus come upon a celebrated paradox that, though he is certain to be ruined, the value of his expectation calculated according to the usual rules (which omit this consideration) is large. But, whether a gambler plays in this way or any other, the same thing is true, namely, that if he plays long enough he will be sure some time to have such a run against him as to exhaust his entire fortune. The same thing is true of an insurance company. Let the directors take the utmost pains to be independent of great conflagrations and pestilences, their actuaries can tell them that, according to the doctrine of chances, the time must come, at last, when their losses will bring them to a stop. They may tide over such a crisis by extraordinary means, but then they will start again in a weakened state, and the same thing will happen again all the sooner. An actuary might be inclined to deny this, because he knows that the expectation of his company is large, or perhaps (neglecting the interest upon money) is infinite. But calculations of expectations leave out of account the circumstance now under consideration, which reverses the whole thing. However, I must not be understood as saying that insurance is on this account unsound, more than other kinds of business. All human affairs rest upon probabilities, and the same thing is true everywhere. If man were immortal he could be perfectly sure of seeing the day when everything in which he had trusted should betray his trust, and, in short, of coming eventually to hopeless misery. He would break down, at last, as every good fortune, as every dynasty, as every civilization does. In place of this we have death.

But what, without death, would happen to every man, with death must happen to some man. At the same time, death makes the number of our risks, of our inferences, finite, and so makes their mean result uncertain. The very idea of probability and of reasoning rests on the assumption that this number is indefinitely great. We are thus landed in the same difficulty as before, and I can see but one solution of it. It seems to me that we are driven to this, that logicality inexorably requires that our interests shall *not* be limited. They must not stop at our own fate, but must embrace the whole community. This community, again, must not be limited, but must extend to all races of beings with whom we can come into immediate or mediate intellectual relation. It must reach, however vaguely, beyond this geological epoch, beyond all bounds. He who would not sacrifice his own soul to save the whole world, is, as it seems to me, illogical in all his inferences, collectively. Logic is rooted in the social principle.

To be logical men should not be selfish; and, in point of fact, they are not so selfish as they are thought. The willful prosecution of one's desires is a different thing from selfishness. The miser is not selfish; his money does him no good, and he cares for what shall become of it after his death. We are constantly speaking of *our* possessions on the Pacific, and of *our* destiny as a republic, where no personal interests are involved, in a way which shows that we have wider ones. We discuss with anxiety the possible exhaustion of coal in some hundreds of years, or the cooling-off of the sun in some millions, and show in the most popular of all religious tenets that we can conceive the possibility of a man's descending into hell for the salvation of his fellows.

Now, it is not necessary for logicality that a man should himself be capable of the heroism of self-sacrifice. It is sufficient that he should recognize the possibility of it, should perceive that only that man's inferences who has it are really logical, and should consequently regard his own as being only so far valid as they would be accepted by the hero. So far as he thus refers his inferences to that standard, he becomes identified with such a mind.

This makes logicality attainable enough. Sometimes we can personally attain to heroism. The soldier who runs to scale a wall knows that he will probably be shot, but that is not all he cares for. He also knows that if all the regiment, with whom in feeling he identifies himself, rush forward at once, the fort will be taken. In other cases we can only imitate the virtue. The man whom we have supposed as having to draw from the two packs, who if he is not a logician will draw from the red pack from mere habit, will see, if he is logician enough, that he cannot be logical so long as he is concerned only with his own fate, but that that man who should care equally for what was to happen in all possible cases of the sort could act logically, and would draw from the pack with the most red cards, and thus, though incapable himself of such sublimity, our logician would imitate the effect of that man's courage in order to share his logicality.

But all this requires a conceived identification of one's interests with those of an unlimited community. Now, there exist no reasons, and a later discussion will show that there can be no reasons, for thinking that the human race, or any intellectual race, will exist forever. On the other hand, there can be no reason against it; [6] and, fortunately, as the whole requirement is that we should have certain

[6] I do not here admit an absolutely unknowable. Evidence could show us what would probably be the case after any given lapse of time; and though a subsequent time might be assigned which that evidence might not cover, yet further evidence would cover it.

sentiments, there is nothing in the facts to forbid our having a *hope*, or calm and cheerful wish, that the community may last beyond any assignable date.

It may seem strange that I should put forward three sentiments, namely, interest in an indefinite community, recognition of the possibility of this interest being made supreme, and hope in the unlimited continuance of intellectual activity, as indispensable requirements of logic. Yet, when we consider that logic depends on a mere struggle to escape doubt, which, as it terminates in action, must begin in emotion, and that, furthermore, the only cause of our planting ourselves on reason is that other methods of escaping doubt fail on account of the social impulse, why should we wonder to find social sentiment presupposed in reasoning? As for the other two sentiments which I find necessary, they are so only as supports and accessories of that. It interests me to notice that these three sentiments seem to be pretty much the same as that famous trio of Charity, Faith, and Hope, which, in the estimation of St. Paul, are the finest and greatest of spiritual gifts. Neither Old nor New Testament is a textbook of the logic of science, but the latter is certainly the highest existing authority in regard to the dispositions of heart which a man ought to have.

V

Such average statistical numbers as the number of inhabitants per square mile, the average number of deaths per week, the number of convictions per indictment, or, generally speaking, the numbers of x's per y, where the x's are a class of things some or all of which are connected with another class of things, their y's, I term *relative numbers*. Of the two classes of things to which a relative number refers, that one of which it is a number may be called its *relate*, and that one *per* which the numeration is made may be called its *correlate*.

Probability is a kind of relative number; namely, it is the ratio of the number of arguments of a certain genus which carry truth with them to the total number of arguments of that genus, and the rules for the calculation of probabilities are very easily derived from this consideration. They may all be given here, since they are extremely simple, and it is sometimes convenient to know something of the elementary rules of calculation of chances.

RULE I. *Direct Calculation.*—To calculate, directly, any relative number, say for instance the number of passengers in the average trip of a street-car, we must proceed as follows:

Count the number of passengers for each trip; add all these numbers, and divide by the number of trips. There are cases in which this rule may be simplified. Suppose we wish to know the number of inhabitants to a dwelling in New York. The same person cannot inhabit two dwellings. If he divide his time between two dwellings he ought to be counted a half-inhabitant of each. In this case we have only to divide the total number of the inhabitants of New York by the number of their dwellings, without the necessity of counting separately those which inhabit each one. A similar proceeding will apply wherever each individual relate belongs to one individual correlate exclusively. If we want the number of x's per y, and no x belongs to more than one y, we have only to divide the whole number of x's of y's by the number of y's. Such a method would, of course, fail if applied to finding the average number of street-car passengers per trip. We could not divide the total number of travelers by the number of trips, since many of them would have made many passages.

To find the probability that from a given class of premises, A, a given class of conclusions, B, follow, it is simply necessary to ascertain what proportion of the times in which premises of that class are true, the appropriate conclusions are also true. In other words, it is the number of cases of the occurrence of both the events A and B, divided by the total number of cases of the occurrence of the event A.

RULE II. *Addition of Relative Numbers.* — Given two relative numbers having the same correlate, say the number of x's per y, and the number of z's per y; it is required to find the number of x's and z's together per y. If there is nothing which is at once an x and a z to the same y, the sum of the two given numbers would give the required number. Suppose, for example, that we had given the average number of friends that men have, and the average number of enemies, the sum of these two is the average number of persons interested in a man. On the other hand, it plainly would not do to add the average number of persons having constitutional diseases and over military age, to the average number exempted by each special cause from military service, in order to get the average number exempt in any way, since many are exempt in two or more ways at once.

This rule applies directly to probabilities, given the probability that two different and mutually exclusive events will happen under the same supposed set of circumstances. Given, for instance, the probability that if A then B, and also the probability that if A then C, then the sum of these two probabilities is the probability that if A then either B or C, so long as there is no event which belongs at once to the two classes B and C.

RULE III. *Multiplication of Relative Numbers.* — Suppose that we have given the relative number of x's per y; also the relative number of z's per x of y; or, to take a concrete example, suppose that we have given, first, the average number of children in families living in New York; and, second, the average number of teeth in the head of a New York child — then the product of these two numbers would give the average number of children's teeth in a New York family. But this mode of reckoning will only apply in general under two restrictions. In the first place, it would not be true if the same child could belong to different families, for in that case those children who belonged to several different families might have an exceptionally large or small number of teeth, which would affect the average number of children's teeth in a family more than it would affect the average number of teeth in a child's head. In the second place, the rule would not be true if different children could share the same teeth, the average number of children's teeth being in that case evidently something different from the average number of teeth belonging to a child.

In order to apply this rule to probabilities, we must proceed as follows: Suppose that we have given the probability that the conclusion B follows from the premise A, B and A representing as usual certain classes of propositions. Suppose that we also knew the probability of an inference in which B should be the premise, and a proposition of a third kind, C, the conclusion. Here, then, we have the materials for the application of this rule. We have, first, the relative number of B's per A. We next should have the relative number of C's per B following from A. But the classes of propositions being so selected that the probability of C following from any B in general is just the same as the probability of C's following from one of those B's which is deducible from an A, the two probabilities may be multiplied together, in order to give the probability of C following from A. The same restrictions exist as before. It might happen that the probability that B follows from A was affected by certain propositions of the class B following from several different propositions of the class A. But, practically speaking, all these restrictions are of very little consequence, and it is usually recognized as a principle universally true that the probability that, if A is true, B is, multiplied by the probability that, if B is true, C is, gives the probability that, if A is true, C is.

There is a rule supplementary to this, of which great use is made. It is not universally valid, and the greatest caution has to be exercised in making use of it — a double care, first, never to use it when it will involve serious error; and, second, never to fail to take advantage of it in cases in which it can be employed. This rule depends upon the fact that in very many cases the probability that C is true if B is, is substantially the same as the probability that C is true if A is. Suppose, for example, we have the average number of males among the children born in New York; suppose that we also have the average number of children born in the winter months among those born in New York. Now, we may assume without doubt, at least as a closely approximate proposition (and no very nice calculation would be in place in regard to probabilities), that the proportion of males among all the children born in New York is the same as the proportion of males born in summer in New York; and, therefore, if the names of all the children born during a year were put into an urn, we might multiply the probability that any name drawn would be the name of a male child by the probability that it would be the name of a child born in summer, in order to obtain the probability that it would be the name of a male child born in summer. The questions of probability, in the treatises upon the subject, have usually been such as relate to balls drawn from urns, and games of cards, and so on, in which the question of the *independence* of events, as it is called — that is to say, the question of whether the probability of C, under the hypothesis B, is the same as its probability under the hypothesis A, has been very simple; but, in the application of probabilities to the ordinary questions of life, it is often an exceedingly nice question whether two events may be considered as independent with sufficient accuracy or not. In all calculations about cards it is assumed that the cards are thoroughly shuffled, which makes one deal quite independent of another. In point of fact the cards seldom are, in practice, shuffled sufficiently to make this true; thus, in a game of whist, in which the cards have fallen in suits of four of the same suit, and are so gathered up, they will lie more or less in sets of four of the same suit, and this will be true even after they are shuffled. At least some traces of this arrangement will remain, in consequence of which the number of "short suits," as they are called — that is to say, the number of hands in which the cards are very unequally divided in regard to suits — is smaller than the calculation would make it to be; so that, when there is a misdeal, where the cards, being thrown about the table, get very thoroughly shuffled, it is a common saying that in the hands next dealt out there are generally short suits. A few years ago a friend of mine, who plays whist a great deal, was so good as to count the number of spades dealt to him in 165 hands, in which the cards had been, if anything, shuffled better than usual. According to calculation, there should have been 85 of these hands in which my friend held either three or four spades, but in point of fact there were 94, showing the influence of imperfect shuffling.

According to the view here taken, these are the only fundamental rules for the calculation of chances. An additional one, derived from a different conception of probability, is given in some treatises, which if it be sound might be made the basis of a theory of reasoning. Being, as I believe it is, absolutely absurd, the consideration of it serves to bring us to the true theory; and it is for the sake of this discussion, which must be postponed to the next number, that I have brought the doctrine of chances to the reader's attention at this early stage of our studies of the logic of science.

FOURTH PAPER

THE PROBABILITY OF INDUCTION[1]

I

We have found that every argument derives its force from the general truth of the class of inferences to which it belongs; and that probability is the proportion of arguments carrying truth with them among those of any *genus*. This is most conveniently expressed in the nomenclature of the medieval logicians. They called the fact expressed by a premise an *antecedent*, and that which follows from it its *consequent;* while the leading principle, that every (or almost every) such antecedent is followed by such a consequent, they termed the *consequence*. Using this language, we may say that probability belongs exclusively to *consequences*, and the probability of any consequence is the number of times in which antecedent and consequent both occur divided by the number of all the times in which the antecedent occurs. From this definition are deduced the following rules for the addition and multiplication of probabilities:

Rule for the Addition of Probabilities. — Given the separate probabilities of two consequences having the same antecedent and incompatible consequents. Then the sum of these two numbers is the probability of the consequence,

[1] *Popular Science Monthly*, April, 1878.

that from the same antecedent one or other of those consequents follows.

Rule for the Multiplication of Probabilities. — Given the separate probabilities of the two consequences, "If A then B," and "If both A and B, then C." Then the product of the these two numbers is the probability of the consequence, "If A, then both B and C."

Special Rule for the Multiplication of Independent Probabilities. — Given the separate probabilities of two consequences having the same antecedents, "If A, then B," and "If A, then C." Suppose that these consequences are such that the probability of the second is equal to the probability of the consequence, "If both A and B, then C." Then the product of the two given numbers is equal to the probability of the consequence, "If A, then both B and C."

To show the working of these rules we may examine the probabilities in regard to throwing dice. What is the probability of throwing a six with one die? The antecedent here is the event of throwing a die; the consequent, its turning up a six. As the die has six sides, all of which are turned up with equal frequency, the probability of turning up any one is $\frac{1}{6}$. Suppose two dice are thrown, what is the probability of throwing sixes? The probability of either coming up six is obviously the same when both are thrown as when one is thrown — namely, $\frac{1}{6}$. The probability that either will come up six when the other does is also the same as that of its coming up six whether the other does or not. The probabilities are, therefore, independent; and, by our rule, the probability that both events will happen together is the product of their several probabilities, or $\frac{1}{6} \times \frac{1}{6}$. What is the probability of throwing deuce-ace? The probability that the first die will turn up ace and the second deuce is the same as the probability that both will turn up sixes — namely, $\frac{1}{36}$; the probability that the *second* will turn up ace and the *first* deuce is likewise $\frac{1}{36}$; these two events — first, ace; second, deuce; and, second, ace; first, deuce — are incompatible. Hence the rule for addition holds, and the probability that either will come up ace and the other deuce is $\frac{1}{36} + \frac{1}{36}$, or $\frac{1}{18}$.

In this way all problems about dice, etc., may be solved. When the number of dice thrown is supposed very large, mathematics (which may be defined as the art of making groups to facilitate numeration) comes to our aid with certain devices to reduce the difficulties.

II

The conception of probability as a matter of *fact*, i.e., as the proportion of times in which an occurrence of one kind is accompanied by an occurrence of another kind, is termed by Mr. Venn the materialistic view of the subject. But probability has often been regarded as being simply the degree of belief which ought to attach to a proposition, and this mode of explaining the idea is termed by Venn the conceptualistic view. Most writers have mixed the two conceptions together. They, first, define the probability of an event as the reason we have to believe that it has taken place, which is conceptualistic; but shortly after they state that it is the ratio of the number of cases favorable to the event to the total number of cases favorable or contrary, and all equally possible. Except that this introduces the thoroughly unclear idea of cases equally possible in place of cases equally frequent, this is a tolerable statement of the materialistic view. The pure conceptualistic theory has been best expounded by Mr. De Morgan in his *Formal Logic: or, the Calculus of Inference, Necessary and Probable.*

The great difference between the two analyses is, that the conceptualists refer probability to an event, while the materialists make it the ratio of frequency of events of a *species* to those of a *genus* over that *species*, thus *giving it two terms instead of one.* The opposition may be made to appear as follows:

Suppose that we have two rules of inference, such that, of all the questions to the solution of which both can be applied, the first yields correct answers to $\frac{81}{100}$, and incorrect answers to the remaining $\frac{19}{100}$; while the second yields correct answers to $\frac{93}{100}$, and incorrect answers to the remaining $\frac{7}{100}$. Suppose, further, that the two rules are entirely independent as to their truth, so that the second answers correctly $\frac{93}{100}$ of the questions which the first answers correctly, and also $\frac{93}{100}$ of the questions which the first answers incorrectly, and answers incorrectly the remaining $\frac{7}{100}$ of the questions which the first answers correctly, and also the remaining $\frac{7}{100}$ of the questions which the first answers incorrectly. Then, of all the questions to the solution of which both rules can be applied —

both answer correctly.............................. $\frac{93}{100}$ of $\frac{81}{100}$ or $\frac{93 \times 81}{100 \times 100}$;

the second answers correctly and the first incorrectly $\frac{93}{100}$ of $\frac{19}{100}$ or $\frac{93 \times 19}{100 \times 100}$;

the second answers incorrectly and the first correctly $\frac{7}{100}$ of $\frac{81}{100}$ or $\frac{7 \times 81}{100 \times 100}$;

and both answer incorrectly .... $\frac{7}{100}$ of $\frac{19}{100}$ or $\frac{7 \times 19}{100 \times 100}$;

Suppose, now, that, in reference to any question, both give the same answer. Then (the questions being always such as are to be answered by *yes* or *no*), those in reference to which their answers agree are the same as those which both answer correctly together with those which both answer falsely, or $\frac{93 \times 81}{100 \times 100} + \frac{7 \times 19}{100 \times 100}$ of all. The proportion of those which both answer correctly out of those their answers to which agree is, therefore —

$$\frac{\frac{93 \times 81}{100 \times 100}}{\frac{93 \times 81}{100 \times 100} + \frac{7 \times 19}{100 \times 100}} \text{ or } \frac{93 \times 81}{(93 \times 81) + (7 \times 19)}.$$

This is, therefore, the probability that, if both modes of inference yield the same result, that result is correct. We may here conveniently make use of another mode of expression. *Probability* is the ratio of the favorable cases to all the cases. Instead of expressing our result in terms of this ratio, we may make use of another — the ratio of favorable to unfavorable cases. This last ratio may be called the *chance* of an event. Then the chance of a true answer by the first mode of inference is $\frac{81}{19}$ and by the second is $\frac{93}{7}$; and the chance of a correct answer from both, when they agree, is —

$$\frac{81 \times 93}{19 \times 7} \text{ or } \frac{81}{19} \times \frac{93}{7},$$

or the product of the chances of each singly yielding a true answer.

It will be seen that a chance is a quantity which may have any magnitude, however great. An event in whose favor there is an even chance, or $\frac{1}{1}$, has a probability of $\frac{1}{2}$. An argument having an even chance can do nothing toward re-enforcing others, since according to the rule its combination with another would only multiply the chance of the latter by 1.

Probability and chance undoubtedly belong primarily to consequences, and are relative to premises; but we may, nevertheless, speak of the chance of an event absolutely, meaning by that the chance of the combination of all arguments in reference to it which exist for us in the given state of our knowledge. Taken in this sense it is incontestable that the chance of an event has an intimate connection with the degree of our belief in it. Belief is certainly something more than a mere feeling; yet there is a feeling of believing, and this feeling does and ought to vary with the chance of the thing believed, as deduced from all the arguments. Any quantity which varies with the chance might, therefore, it would seem, serve as a thermometer for the proper intensity of belief. Among all such quantities there is one which is peculiarly appropriate. When there is a very great chance, the feeling of belief ought to be very intense. Absolute certainty, or an infinite chance, can never be attained by mortals, and this may be represented appropriately by an infinite belief. As the chance diminishes the feeling of believing should diminish, until an even chance is reached, where it should completely vanish and not incline either toward or away from the proposition. When the chance becomes less, then a contrary belief should spring up and should increase in intensity as the chance diminishes, and as the chance almost vanishes (which it can never quite do) the contrary belief should tend toward an infinite intensity. Now, there is one quantity which, more simply than any other, fulfills these conditions; it is the *logarithm* of the chance. But there is another consideration which must, if admitted, fix us to this choice for our thermometer. It is that our belief ought to be proportional to the weight of evidence, in this sense, that two arguments which are entirely independent, neither weakening nor strengthening each other, ought, when they concur, to produce a belief equal to the sum of the intensities of belief which either would produce separately. Now, we have seen that the chances of independent concurrent arguments are to be multiplied together to get the chance of their combination, and, therefore, the quantities which best express the intensities of belief should be such that they are to be *added* when the *chances* are multiplied in order to produce the quantity which corresponds to the combined chance. Now, the logarithm is the only quantity which fulfills this condition. There is a general law of sensibility, called Fechner's psychophysical law. It is that the intensity of any sensation is proportional to the logarithm of the external force which produces it. It is entirely in harmony with this law that the feeling of belief should be as the logarithm of the chance, this latter being the expression of the state of facts which produces the belief.

The rule for the combination of independent concurrent arguments takes a very simple form when expressed in terms of the intensity of belief, measured in the proposed way. It is this: Take the sum of all the feelings of belief which would be produced separately by all the arguments *pro*, subtract from that the similar sum for arguments *con*, and the remainder is the feeling of belief which we ought to have on the whole. This is a proceeding which men often resort to, under the name of *balancing reasons*.

These considerations constitute an argument in favor of the conceptualistic view. The kernel of it is that the conjoint probability of all the arguments in our possession, with reference to any fact, must be intimately connected with the just degree of our belief in that fact; and this point is supplemented by various others showing the consistency of the theory with itself and with the rest of our knowledge.

But probability, to have any value at all, must express a fact. It is, therefore, a thing to be inferred upon evidence. Let us, then, consider for a moment the formation of a belief of probability. Suppose we have a large bag of beans from which one has been secretly taken at random and hidden under a thimble. We are now to form a probable judgment of the color of that bean, by drawing others singly from the bag and looking at them, each one to be thrown back, and the whole well mixed up after each drawing. Suppose the first drawing is white and the next black. We conclude that there is not an immense preponderance of either color, and that there is something like an even chance that the bean under the thimble is black. But this judgment may be altered by the next few drawings. When we have drawn ten times, if 4, 5, or 6, are white, we have more confidence that the chance is even. When we have drawn a thousand times, if about half have been white, we have great confidence in this result. We now feel pretty sure that, if we were to make a large number of bets upon the color of single beans drawn from the bag, we could approximately insure ourselves in the long run by betting each time upon the white, a confidence which would be entirely wanting if, instead of sampling the bag by 1,000 drawings, we had done so by only two. Now, as the whole utility of probability is to insure us in the long run, and as that assurance depends, not merely on the value of the chance, but also on the accuracy of the evaluation, it follows that we ought not to have the same feeling of belief in reference to all events of which the chance is even. In short, to express the proper state of our belief, not *one* number but *two* are requisite, the first depending on the inferred probability, the second on the amount of knowledge on which that probability is based.[2] It is true that when our knowledge is very precise, when we have made many drawings from the bag, or, as in most of the examples in the books, when the total contents of the bag are absolutely known, the number which expresses the uncertainty of the assumed probability and its liability to be changed by further experience may become insignificant, or utterly vanish. But, when our knowledge is very slight, this number may be even more important than the probability itself; and when we have no knowledge at all this completely overwhelms the

[2] Strictly we should need an infinite series of numbers each depending on the probable error of the last.

other, so that there is no sense in saying that the chance of the totally unknown event is even (for what expresses absolutely no fact has absolutely no meaning), and what ought to be said is that the chance is entirely indefinite. We thus perceive that the conceptualistic view, though answering well enough in some cases, is quite inadequate.

Suppose that the first bean which we drew from our bag were black. That would constitute an argument, no matter how slender, that the bean under the thimble was also black. If the second bean were also to turn out black, that would be a second independent argument reënforcing the first. If the whole of the first twenty beans drawn should prove black, our confidence that the hidden bean was black would justly attain considerable strength. But suppose the twenty-first bean were to be white and that we were to go on drawing until we found that we had drawn 1,010 black beans and 990 white ones. We should conclude that our first twenty beans being black was simply an extraordinary accident, and that in fact the proportion of white beans to black was sensibly equal, and that it was an even chance that the hidden bean was black. Yet according to the rule of *balancing reasons,* since all the drawings of black beans are so many independent arguments in favor of the one under the thimble being black, and all the white drawings so many against it, an excess of twenty black beans ought to produce the same degree of belief that the hidden bean was black, whatever the total number drawn.

In the conceptualistic view of probability, complete ignorance, where the judgment ought not to swerve either toward or away from the hypothesis, is represented by the probability $\frac{1}{2}$.[3]

[3] "Perfect indecision, belief inclining neither way, an even chance."—De Morgan, p. 182.

But let us suppose that we are totally ignorant what colored hair the inhabitants of Saturn have. Let us, then, take a color-chart in which all possible colors are shown shading into one another by imperceptible degrees. In such a chart the relative areas occupied by different classes of colors are perfectly arbitrary. Let us inclose such an area with a closed line, and ask what is the chance on conceptualistic principles that the color of the hair of the inhabitants of Saturn falls within that area? The answer cannot be indeterminate because we must be in some state of belief; and, indeed, conceptualistic writers do not admit indeterminate probabilities. As there is no certainty in the matter, the answer lies between *zero* and *unity*. As no numerical value is afforded by the data, the number must be determined by the nature of the scale of probability itself, and not by calculation from the data. The answer can, therefore, only be one-half, since the judgment should neither favor nor oppose the hypothesis. What is true of this area is true of any other one; and it will equally be true of a third area which embraces the other two. But the probability for each of the smaller areas being one-half, that for the larger should be at least unity, which is absurd.

III

All our reasonings are of two kinds: 1. *Explicative, analytic,* or *deductive;* 2. *Amplifiative, synthetic,* or (loosely speaking) *inductive.* In explicative reasoning, certain facts are first laid down in the premises. These facts are, in every case, an inexhaustible multitude, but they may often be summed up in one simple proposition by means of some regularity which runs through them all. Thus, take the proposition that Socrates was a man; this implies (to go no further) that during every fraction of a second of his whole life (or, if you please, during the greater part of them) he was a man. He did not at one instant appear as a tree and at another as a dog; he did not flow into water, or appear in two places at once; you could not put your finger through him as if he were an optical image, etc. Now, the facts being thus laid down, some order among some of them, not particularly made use of for the purpose of stating them, may perhaps be discovered; and this will enable us to throw part or all of them into a new statement, the possibility of which might have escaped attention. Such a statement will be the conclusion of an analytic inference. Of this sort are all mathematical demonstrations. But synthetic reasoning is of another kind. In this case the facts summed up in the conclusion are not among those stated in the premises. They are different facts, as when one sees that the tide rises m times and concludes that it will rise the next time. These are the only inferences which increase our real knowledge, however useful the others may be.

In any problem in probabilities, we have given the relative frequency of certain events, and we perceive that in these facts the relative frequency of another event is given in a hidden way. This being stated makes the solution. This is, therefore, mere explicative reasoning, and is evidently entirely inadequate to the representation of synthetic reasoning, which goes out beyond the facts given in the premises. There is, therefore, a manifest impossibility in so tracing out any probability for a synthetic conclusion.

Most treatises on probability contain a very different doctrine. They state, for example, that if one of the ancient denizens of the shores of the Mediterranean, who had never heard of tides, had gone to the bay of Biscay, and had there seen the tide rise, say m times, he could know that there was a probability equal to

$$\frac{m+1}{m+2}$$

that it would rise the next time. In a well-known work by Quetelet, much stress is laid on this, and it is made the foundation of a theory of inductive reasoning.

But this solution betrays its origin if we apply it to the case in which the man has never seen the tide rise at all; that is, if we put $m = 0$. In this case, the probability that it will rise the next time comes out $\frac{1}{2}$, or, in other words, the solution involves the conceptualistic principle that there is an even chance of a totally unknown event. The manner in which it has been reached has been by considering a number of urns all containing the same number of balls, part white and part black. One urn contains all white balls, another one black and the rest white, a third two black and the rest white, and so on, one urn for each proportion, until an urn is reached containing only black balls. But the only possible reason for drawing any analogy between such an arrangement and that of Nature is the principle that alternatives of which we know nothing must be considered as equally probable. But this principle is absurd. There is an indefinite variety of ways of enumerating the different possibilities, which, on the application of this principle, would give different results. If there be any way of enumerating the possibilities so as to make them all equal, it is not that from which this solution is derived, but is the following: Suppose we had an immense granary filled with black and white balls well mixed up; and suppose each urn were filled by taking a fixed number of balls from this granary quite at random. The relative number of white balls in the granary might be anything, say one in three. Then in one-third of the urns the first ball would be white, and in two-thirds black. In one-third of those urns of which the first ball was white, and also in one-third of those in which the first ball was black, the second ball would be white. In this way, we should have a distribution like that shown in the following table, where *w* stands for a white ball and *b* for a black one. The reader can, if he chooses, verify the table for himself.

wwww.

wwwb. wwbw. wbww. bwww.
wwwb. wwbw. wbww. bwww.

wwbb. wbwb. bwwb. wbbw. bwbw. bbww.
wwbb. wbwb. bwwb. wbbw. bwbw. bbww.
wwbb. wbwb. bwwb. wbbw. bwbw. bbww.
wwbb. wbwb. bwwb. wbbw. bwbw. bbww.

wbbb. bwbb. bbwb. bbbw.
wbbb. bwbb. bbwb. bbbw.
wbbb. bwbb. bbwb. bbbw.
wbbb. bwbb. bbwb. bbbw.

wbbb. bwbb. bbwb. bbbw.
wbbb. bwbb. bbwb. bbbw.
wbbb. bwbb. bbwb. bbbw.
wbbb. bwbb. bbwb. bbbw.

bbbb.
bbbb.
bbbb.
bbbb.
bbbb.
bbbb.
bbbb.
bbbb.
bbbb.
bbbb.
bbbb.
bbbb.
bbbb.
bbbb.
bbbb.
bbbb.

In the second group, where there is one b, there are two sets just alike; in the third there are 4, in the fourth 8, and in the fifth 16, doubling every time. This is because we have supposed twice as many black balls in the granary as white ones; had we supposed 10 times as many, instead of

1, 2, 4, 8, 16

sets we should have had

1, 10, 100, 1000, 10000

sets; on the other hand, had the numbers of black and white balls in the granary been even, there would have been but one set in each group. Now suppose two balls were drawn from one of these urns and were found to be both white, what would be the probability of the next one being white? If the two drawn out were the first two put into the urns, and the next to be drawn out were the third put in, then the probability of this third being white would be the same whatever the colors of the first two, for it has been supposed that just the same proportion of urns has the third ball white among those which have the first two *white-white*, *white-black*, *black-white*, and *black-black*. Thus, in this case, the chance of the third ball being white would be the same whatever the first two were. But, by inspecting the table, the reader can see that in each group all orders of the balls occur with equal frequency, so that it makes no difference whether they are drawn out in the order they were put in or not. Hence the colors of the balls already drawn have no influence on the probability of any other being white or black.

Now, if there be any way of enumerating the possibilities of Nature so as to make them equally probable, it is clearly one which should make one arrangement or combination of the elements of Nature as probable as another, that is, a distribution like that we have supposed, and it, therefore, appears that the assumption that any such thing can be done, leads simply to the conclusion that reasoning from past to future experience is absolutely worthless. In fact, the moment that you assume that the chances in favor of that of which we are totally ignorant are even, the problem about the tides does not differ, in any arithmetical particular, from the case in which a penny (known to be equally likely to come up heads and tails) should turn up heads m times successively. In short, it would be to assume that Nature is a pure chaos, or chance combination of independent elements, in which reasoning from one fact to another would be impossible; and since, as we shall hereafter see, there is no judgment of pure observation without reasoning, it would be to suppose all human cognition illusory and no real knowledge possible. It would be to suppose that if we have found the order of Nature more or less regular in the past, this has been by a pure run of luck which we may expect is now at an end. Now, it may be we have no scintilla of proof to the contrary, but reason is unnecessary in reference to that belief which is of all the most settled, which nobody doubts or can doubt, and which he who should deny would stultify himself in so doing.

The relative probability of this or that arrangement of Nature is something which we should have a right to talk about if universes were as plenty as blackberries, if we could put a quantity of them in a bag, shake them well up, draw out a sample, and examine them to see what proportion of them had one arrangement and what proportion another. But, even in that case, a higher universe would contain us, in regard to whose arrangements the conception of probability could have no applicability.

IV

We have examined the problem proposed by the conceptualists, which, translated into clear language, is this: Given a synthetic conclusion; required to know out of all possible states of things how many will accord, to any assigned extent, with this conclusion; and we have found that it is only an absurd attempt to reduce synthetic to analytic reason, and that no definite solution is possible.

But there is another problem in connection with this subject. It is this: Given a certain state of things, required to know what proportion of all synthetic inferences relating to it will be true within a given degree of approximation. Now, there is no difficulty about this problem (except for its mathematical complication); it has been much studied, and the answer is perfectly well known. And is not this, after all, what we want to know much rather than the other? Why should we want to know the probability that the fact will accord with our conclusion? That implies that we are interested in all possible worlds, and not merely the one in which we find ourselves placed. Why is it not much more to the purpose to know the probability that our conclusion will accord with the fact? One of these questions is the first above stated and the other the second, and I ask the reader whether, if people, instead of using the word probability without any clear apprehension of their own meaning, had always spoken of relative frequency, they could have failed to see that what they wanted was not to follow along the synthetic procedure with an analytic one, in order to find the probability of the conclusion; but, on the contrary, to begin with the fact at which the synthetic inference aims, and follow back to the facts it uses for premises in order to see the probability of their being such as will yield the truth.

As we cannot have an urn with an infinite number of balls to represent the inexhaustibleness of Nature, let us suppose one with a finite number, each ball being thrown back into the urn after being drawn out, so that there is no exhaustion of them. Suppose one ball out of three is white and the rest black, and that four balls are drawn. Then the table on pages 95-96 represents the relative frequency of the different ways in which these balls might be drawn. It will be seen that if we should judge by these four balls of the proportion in the urn, 32 times out of 81 we should find it $\frac{1}{4}$, and 24 times out of 81 we should find it

$\frac{1}{2}$, the truth being $\frac{1}{3}$. To extend this table to high numbers would be great labor, but the mathematicians have found some ingenious ways of reckoning what the numbers would be. It is found that, if the true proportion of white balls is p, and s balls are drawn, then the error of the proportion obtained by the induction will be —

half the time within	$0.477\sqrt{\frac{2p(1-p)}{s}}$
9 times out of 10 within	$1.163\sqrt{\frac{2p(1-p)}{s}}$
99 times out of 100 within	$1.821\sqrt{\frac{2p(1-p)}{s}}$
999 times out of 1,000 within	$2.328\sqrt{\frac{2p(1-p)}{s}}$
9,999 times out of 10,000 within	$2.751\sqrt{\frac{2p(1-p)}{s}}$
9,999,999,999 times out of 10,000,000,000 within	$4.77\sqrt{\frac{2p(1-p)}{s}}$

The use of this may be illustrated by an example. By the census of 1870, it appears that the proportion of males among native white children under one year old was 0.5082, while among colored children of the same age the proportion was only 0.4977. The difference between these is 0.0105, or about one in a 100. Can this be attributed to chance, or would the difference always exist among a great number of white and colored children under like circumstances? Here p may be taken at $\frac{1}{2}$; hence $2p\ (1-p)$ is also $\frac{1}{2}$. The number of white children counted was near 1,000,000; hence the fraction whose square-root is to be taken is about $\frac{1}{2000000}$. The root is about $\frac{1}{1400}$, and this multiplied by 0.477 gives about 0.0003 as the probable error in the ratio of males among the whites as obtained from the induction. The number of black children was about 150,000, which gives 0.0008 for the probable error. We see that the actual discrepancy is ten times the sum of these, and such a result would happen, according to our table, only once out of 10,000,000,000 censuses, in the long run.

It may be remarked that when the real value of the probability sought inductively is either very large or very small, the reasoning is more secure. Thus, suppose there were in reality one white ball in 100 in a certain urn, and we were to judge of the number by 100 drawings. The probability of drawing no white ball would be $\frac{366}{1000}$; that of drawing one white ball would be $\frac{370}{1000}$; that of drawing two would be $\frac{185}{1000}$; that of drawing three would be $\frac{61}{1000}$; that of drawing four would be $\frac{15}{1000}$; that of drawing five would be only $\frac{3}{1000}$, etc. Thus we should be tolerably certain of not being in error by more than one ball in 100.

It appears, then, that in one sense we can, and in another we cannot, determine the probability of synthetic inference. When I reason in this way:

Ninety-nine Cretans in a hundred are liars;

But Epimenides is a Cretan;

Therefore, Epimenides is a liar: —

I know that reasoning similar to that would carry truth 99 times in 100. But when I reason in the opposite direction:

Minos, Sarpedon, Rhadamanthus, Deucalion, and Epimenides, are all the Cretans I can think of;

But these were all atrocious liars,

Therefore, pretty much all Cretans must have been liars;

I do not in the least know how often such reasoning would

carry me right. On the other hand, what I do know is that some definite proportion of Cretans must have been liars, and that this proportion can be probably approximated to by an induction from five or six instances. Even in the worst case for the probability of such an inference, that in which about half the Cretans are liars, the ratio so obtained would probably not be in error by more than $\frac{1}{6}$. So much I know; but, then, in the present case the inference is that pretty much all Cretans are liars, and whether there may not be a special improbability in that I do not know.

V

Late in the last century, Immanuel Kant asked the question, "How are synthetical judgments *a priori* possible?" By synthetical judgments he meant such as assert positive fact and are not mere affairs of arrangement; in short, judgments of the kind which synthetical reasoning produces, and which analytic reasoning cannot yield. By *a priori* judgments he meant such as that all outward objects are in space, every event has a cause, etc., propositions which according to him can never be inferred from experience. Not so much by his answer to this question as by the mere asking of it, the current philosophy of that time was shattered and destroyed, and a new epoch in its history was begun. But before asking *that* question he ought to have asked the more general one, "How are any synthetical judgments at all possible?" How is it that a man can observe one fact and straightway pronounce judgment concerning another different fact not involved in the first?

Such reasoning, as we have seen, has, at least in the usual sense of the phrase, no definite probability; how, then, can it add to our knowledge? This is a strange paradox; the Abbé Gratry says it is a miracle, and that every true induction is an immediate inspiration from on high.[4] I respect this explanation far more than many a pedantic attempt to solve the question by some juggle with probabilities, with the forms of syllogism, or what not. I respect it because it shows an appreciation of the depth of the problem, because it assigns an adequate cause, and because it is intimately connected — as the true account should be — with a general philosophy of the universe. At the same time, I do not accept this explanation, because an explanation should tell *how* a thing is done, and to assert a perpetual miracle seems to be an abandonment of all hope of doing that, without sufficient justification.

It will be interesting to see how the answer which Kant gave to his question about synthetical judgments *a priori* will appear if extended to the question of synthetical judgments in general. That answer is, that synthetical judgments *a priori* are possible because whatever is universally true is involved in the conditions of experience. Let us apply this to a general synthetical reasoning. I take from a bag a handful of beans; they are all purple, and I infer that all the beans in the bag are purple. How can I do that? Why, upon the principle that whatever is universally true of my experience (which is here the appearance

[4] *Logique.* The same is true, according to him, of every performance of a differentiation, but not of integration. He does not tell us whether it is the supernatural assistance which makes the former process so much the easier.

of these different beans) is involved in the condition of experience. The condition of this special experience is that all these beans were taken from that bag. According to Kant's principle, then, whatever is found true of all the beans drawn from the bag must find its explanation in some peculiarity of the contents of the bag. This is a satisfactory statement of the principle of induction.

When we draw a deductive or analytic conclusion, our rule of inference is that facts of a certain general character are either invariably or in a certain proportion of cases accompanied by facts of another general character. Then our premise being a fact of the former class, we infer with certainty or with the appropriate degree of probability the existence of a fact of the second class. But the rule for synthetic inference is of a different kind. When we sample a bag of beans we do not in the least assume that the fact of some beans being purple involves the necessity or even the probability of other beans being so. On the contrary, the conceptualistic method of treating probabilities, which really amounts simply to the deductive treatment of them, when rightly carried out leads to the result that a synthetic inference has just an even chance in its favor, or in other words is absolutely worthless. The color of one bean is entirely independent of that of another. But synthetic inference is founded upon a classification of facts, not according to their characters, but according to the manner of obtaining them. Its rule is, that a number of facts obtained in a given way will in general more or less resemble other facts obtained in the same way; or, *experiences whose conditions are the same will have the same general characters.*

In the former case, we know that premises precisely similar in form to those of the given ones will yield true conclusions, just once in a calculable number of times. In the latter case, we only know that premises obtained under circumstances similar to the given ones (though perhaps themselves very different) will yield true conclusions, at least once in a calculable number of times. We may express this by saying that in the case of analytic inference we know the probability of our conclusion (if the premises are true), but in the case of synthetic inferences we only know the degree of trustworthiness of our proceeding. As all knowledge comes from synthetic inference, we must equally infer that all human certainty consists merely in our knowing that the processes by which our knowledge has been derived are such as must generally have led to true conclusions.

Though a synthetic inference cannot by any means be reduced to deduction, yet that the rule of induction will hold good in the long run may be deduced from the principle that reality is only the object of the final opinion to which sufficient investigation would lead. That belief gradually tends to fix itself under the influence of inquiry is, indeed, one of the facts with which logic sets out.

FIFTH PAPER

THE ORDER OF NATURE[1]

I

Any proposition whatever concerning the order of Nature must touch more or less upon religion. In our day, belief, even in these matters, depends more and more upon the observation of facts. If a remarkable and universal orderliness be found in the universe, there must be some cause for this regularity, and science has to consider what hypotheses might account for the phenomenon. One way of accounting for it, certainly, would be to suppose that the world is ordered by a superior power. But if there is nothing in the universal subjection of phenomena to laws, nor in the character of those laws themselves (as being benevolent, beautiful, economical, etc.), which goes to prove the existence of a governor of the universe, it is hardly to be anticipated that any other sort of evidence will be found to weigh very much with minds emancipated from the tyranny of tradition.

Nevertheless, it cannot truly be said that even an absolutely negative decision of that question could altogether destroy religion, inasmuch as there are faiths in which, however much they differ from our own, we recognize those essential characters which make them worthy to be called religions, and which, nevertheless, do not postulate an

[1] *Popular Science Monthly*, June, 1878.

actually existing Deity. That one, for instance, which has had the most numerous and by no means the least intelligent following of any on earth, teaches that the Divinity in his highest perfection is wrapped away from the world in a state of profound and eternal sleep, which really does not differ from non-existence, whether it be called by that name or not. No candid mind who has followed the writings of M. Vacherot can well deny that his religion is as earnest as can be. He worships the Perfect, the Supreme Ideal; but he conceives that the very notion of the Ideal is repugnant to its real existence.[2] In fact, M. Vacherot finds it agreeable to his reason to assert that non-existence is an essential character of the perfect, just as St. Anselm and Descartes found it agreeable to theirs to assert the extreme opposite. I confess that there is one respect in which either of these positions seems to me more congruous with the religious attitude than that of a theology which stands upon evidences; for as soon as the Deity presents himself to either Anselm or Vacherot, and manifests his glorious attributes, whether it be in a vision of the night or day, either of them recognizes his adorable God, and sinks upon his knees at once; whereas the theologian of evidences will first demand that the divine apparition shall identify himself, and only after having scrutinized his credentials and weighed the probabilities of his being found among the totality of existences, will he finally render his circumspect homage, thinking that no characters can be adorable but those which belong to a real thing.

If we could find out any general characteristic of the

[2] [See Santayana, *Reason in Religion.*]

universe, any mannerism in the ways of Nature, any law everywhere applicable and universally valid, such a discovery would be of such singular assistance to us in all our future reasoning, that it would deserve a place almost at the head of the principles of logic. On the other hand, if it can be shown that there is nothing of the sort to find out, but that every discoverable regularity is of limited range, this again will be of logical importance. What sort of a conception we ought to have of the universe, how to think of the *ensemble* of things, is a fundamental problem in the theory of reasoning.

II

It is the legitimate endeavor of scientific men now, as it was twenty-three hundred years ago, to account for the formation of the solar system and of the cluster of stars which forms the galaxy, by the fortuitous concourse of atoms. The greatest expounder of this theory, when asked how he could write an immense book on the system of the world without one mention of its author, replied, very logically, "Je n'avais pas besoin de cette hypothèse-là." But, in truth, there is nothing atheistical in the theory, any more than there was in this answer. Matter is supposed to be composed of molecules which obey the laws of mechanics and exert certain attractions upon one another; and it is to these regularities (which there is no attempt to account for) that general arrangement of the solar system would be due, and not to hazard.

If any one has ever maintained that the universe is a pure throw of the dice, the theologians have abundantly refuted him. "How often," says Archbishop Tillotson, "might a man, after he had jumbled a set of letters in a bag, fling them out upon the ground before they would fall into an exact poem, yea, or so much as make a good discourse in prose! And may not a little book be as easily made by chance as this great volume of the world?" The chance world here shown to be so different from that in which we live would be one in which there were no laws, the characters of different things being entirely independent; so that, should a sample of any kind of objects ever show a prevalent character, it could only be by accident, and no general proposition could ever be established. Whatever further conclusions we may come to in regard to the order of the universe, thus much may be regarded as solidly established, that the world is not a mere chance-medley.

But whether the world makes an exact poem or not, is another question. When we look up at the heavens at night, we readily perceive that the stars are not simply splashed on to the celestial vault; but there does not seem to be any precise system in their arrangement either. It will be worth our while, then, to inquire into the degree of orderliness in the universe; and, to begin, let us ask whether the world we live in is any more orderly than a purely chance-world would be.

Any uniformity, or law of Nature, may be stated in the form, "Every A is B"; as, every ray of light is a non-curved line, every body is accelerated toward the earth's center, etc. This is the same as to say, "There does not exist any A which is not B"; there is no curved ray; there is no body not accelerated toward the earth; so that the uniformity consists in the non-occurrence in Nature of a certain combination of characters (in this case, the combination of being A with being non-B).[3] And, conversely, every case of the non-occurrence of a combination of characters would constitute a uniformity in Nature. Thus, suppose the quality A is never found in combination with the quality C: for example, suppose the quality of idiocy is never found in combination with that of having a well-developed brain. Then nothing of the sort A is of the sort C, or everything of the sort A is of the sort non-C (or say, every idiot has an ill-developed brain), which, being something universally true of the A's, is a uniformity in the world. Thus we see that, in a world where there were no uniformities, no logically possible combination of characters would be excluded, but every combination would exist in some object. But two objects not identical must differ in some of their characters, though it be only in the character of being in such-and-such a place. Hence, precisely the same combination of characters could not be found in two different objects; and, consequently, in a chance-world every combination involving either the positive or negative of every character would belong to just one thing. Thus, if there were but five simple characters in such a world,[4] we might denote them by A, B, C, D, E, and their negatives

[3] For the present purpose, the negative of a character is to be considered as much a character as the positive, for a uniformity may either be affirmative or negative. I do not say that no distinction can be drawn between positive and negative uniformities.

[4] There being 5 simple characters, with their negatives, they could be compounded in various ways so as to make 241 characters in all, without counting the characters *existence* and *non-existence*, which make up 243 or 3^5.

by a, b, c, d, e; and then, as there would be 2^5 or 32 different combinations of these characters, completely determinate in reference to each of them, that world would have just 32 objects in it, their characters being as in the following table:

TABLE I.

ABCDE	AbCDE	aBCDE	abCDE
ABCDe	AbCDe	aBCDe	abCDe
ABCdE	AbCdE	aBCdE	abCdE
ABCde	AbCde	aBCde	abCde
ABcDE	AbcDE	aBcDE	abcDE
ABcDe	AbcDe	aBcDe	abcDe
ABcdE	AbcdE	aBcdE	abcdE
ABcde	Abcde	aBcde	abcde

For example, if the five primary characters were *hard, sweet, fragrant, green, bright,* there would be one object which reunited all these qualities, one which was hard, sweet, fragrant, and green, but not bright; one which was hard, sweet, fragrant, and bright, but not green; one which was hard, sweet, and fragrant, but neither green nor bright; and so on through all the combinations.

This is what a thoroughly chance-world would be like, and certainly nothing could be imagined more systematic. When a quantity of letters are poured out of a bag, the appearance of disorder is due to the circumstance that the phenomena are only partly fortuitous. The laws of space are supposed, in that case, to be rigidly preserved, and there is also a certain amount of regularity in the formation of the letters. The result is that some elements are orderly and some are disorderly, which is precisely what we observe in the actual world. Tillotson, in the passage of which a part has been quoted, goes on to ask, " How long might 20,000 blind men which should be sent out from the several remote parts of England, wander up and down before they would all meet upon Salisbury Plains, and fall into rank and file in the exact order of an army? And yet this is much more easy to be imagined than how the innumerable blind parts of matter should rendezvous themselves into a world." This is very true, but in the actual world the *blind men* are, as far as we can see, *not* drawn up in any particular order at all. And, in short, while a certain amount of order exists in the world, it would seem that the world is not so orderly as it might be, and, for instance, not so much so as a world of pure chance would be.

But we can never get to the bottom of this question until we take account of a highly-important logical principle [5] which I now proceed to enounce. This principle is that any plurality or lot of objects whatever have some character in common (no matter how insignificant) which is peculiar to them and not shared by anything else. The word " character " here is taken in such a sense as to include negative characters, such as incivility, inequality, etc., as well as their positives, civility, equality, etc. To prove the theorem, I will show what character any two things, A and B, have in common, not shared by anything else. The things, A and B, are each distinguished from all other things by the possession of certain characters which may be named A-ness and B-ness. Corresponding to these posi-

[5] This principle was, I believe, first stated by Mr. De Morgan.

tive characters, are the negative characters un-A-ness, which is possessed by everything except A, and un-B-ness, which is possessed by everything except B. These two characters are united in everything except A and B; and this union of the characters un-A-ness and un-B-ness makes a compound character which may be termed A-B-lessness. This is not possessed by either A or B, but it is possessed by everything else. This character, like every other, has its corresponding negative un-A-B-lessness, and this last is the character possessed by both A and B, and by nothing else. It is obvious that what has thus been shown true of two things is *mutatis mutandis*, true of any number of things. Q. E. D.

In any world whatever, then, there must be a character peculiar to each possible group of objects. If, as a matter of nomenclature, characters peculiar to the same group be regarded as only different aspects of the same character, then we may say that there will be precisely one character for each possible group of objects. Thus, suppose a world to contain five things, α, β, γ, δ, ϵ. Then it will have a separate character for each of the 31 groups (with *non-existence* making up 32 or 2^5) shown in the following table:

TABLE II.

	$\alpha\beta$	$\alpha\beta\gamma$	$\alpha\beta\gamma\delta$	$\alpha\beta\gamma\delta\epsilon$
α	$\alpha\gamma$	$\alpha\beta\delta$	$\alpha\beta\gamma\epsilon$	
β	$\alpha\delta$	$\alpha\beta\epsilon$	$\alpha\beta\delta\epsilon$	
γ	$\alpha\epsilon$	$\alpha\gamma\delta$	$\alpha\gamma\delta\epsilon$	
δ	$\beta\gamma$	$\alpha\gamma\epsilon$	$\beta\gamma\delta\epsilon$	
ϵ	$\beta\delta$	$\alpha\delta\epsilon$		
	$\beta\epsilon$	$\beta\gamma\delta$		
	$\gamma\delta$	$\beta\gamma\epsilon$		
	$\gamma\epsilon$	$\beta\delta\epsilon$		
	$\delta\epsilon$	$\gamma\delta\epsilon$		

This shows that a contradiction is involved in the very idea [6] of a chance-world, for in a world of 32 things, instead of there being only 3^5 or 243 characters, as we have seen that the notion of a chance-world requires, there would, in fact, be no less than 2^{32}, or 4,294,967,296 characters, which would not be all independent, but would have all possible relations with one another.

We further see that so long as we regard characters abstractly, without regard to their relative importance, etc., there is no possibility of a more or less degree of orderliness in the world, the whole system of relationship between the different characters being given by mere logic; that is, being implied in those facts which are tacitly admitted as soon as we admit that there is any such thing as reasoning.

In order to descend from this abstract point of view, it is requisite to consider the characters of things as relative to the perceptions and active powers of living beings. Instead, then, of attempting to imagine a world in which there should be no uniformities, let us suppose one in which none of the uniformities should have reference to characters interesting or important to us. In the first place, there would be nothing to puzzle us in such a world. The small number of qualities which would directly meet the senses would be the ones which would afford the key to everything which could possibly interest us. The whole universe would have such an air of system and perfect regularity that there would be nothing to ask. In the next place, no action of ours, and no event of Nature, would have important consequences in such a world. We should be

[6] Not in every idea but only in the one so formulated.

perfectly free from all responsibility, and there would be nothing to do but to enjoy or suffer whatever happened to come along. Thus there would be nothing to stimulate or develop either the mind or the will, and we consequently should neither act nor think. We should have no memory, because that depends on a law of our organization. Even if we had any senses, we should be situated toward such a world precisely as inanimate objects are toward the present one, provided we suppose that these objects have an absolutely transitory and instantaneous consciousness without memory — a supposition which is a mere mode of speech, for that would be no consciousness at all. We may, therefore, say that a world of chance is simply our actual world viewed from the standpoint of an animal at the very vanishing-point of intelligence. The actual world is almost a chance-medley to the mind of a polyp. The interest which the uniformities of Nature have for an animal measures his place in the scale of intelligence.

Thus, nothing can be made out from the orderliness of Nature in regard to the existence of a God, unless it be maintained that the existence of a finite mind proves the existence of an infinite one.

III

In the last of these papers we examined the nature of inductive or synthetic reasoning. We found it to be a process of sampling. A number of specimens of a class are taken, not by selection within that class, but at random. These specimens will agree in a great number of respects. If, now, it were likely that a second lot would agree with the first in the majority of these respects, we might base on this consideration an inference in regard to any one of these characters. But such an inference would neither be of the nature of induction, nor would it (except in special cases) be valid, because the vast majority of points of agreement in the first sample drawn would generally be entirely accidental, as well as insignificant. To illustrate this, I take the ages at death of the first five poets given in Wheeler's *Biographical Dictionary*. They are:

Aagard, 48.
Abeille, 70.
Abulola, 84.
Abunowas, 48.
Accords, 45.

These five ages have the following characters in common:

1. The difference of the two digits composing the number, divided by three, leaves a remainder of *one*.

2. The first digit raised to the power indicated by the second, and divided by three, leaves a remainder of *one*.

3. The sum of the prime factors of each age, including one, is divisible by three.

It is easy to see that the number of accidental agreements of this sort would be quite endless. But suppose that, instead of considering a character because of its prevalence in the sample, we designate a character before taking the sample, selecting it for its importance, obviousness, or other point of interest. Then two considerable samples drawn at random are extremely likely to agree approximately in regard to the proportion of occurrences of a character so chosen. *The inference that a previously designated character has nearly the same frequency of occurrence in the whole of a class that it has in a sample drawn at random out of that class is induction.* If the character be not previously designated, then a sample in which it is found to be prevalent can only serve to suggest that it *may be* prevalent in the whole class. We may consider this surmise as an inference if we please — an inference of possibility; but a second sample must be drawn to test the question of whether the character actually is prevalent. Instead of designating beforehand a single character in reference to which we will examine a sample, we may designate two, and use the same sample to determine the relative frequencies of both. This will be making two inductive inferences at once; and, of course, we are less certain that both will yield correct conclusions than we should be that either separately would do so. What is true of two characters is true of any limited number. Now, the number of characters which have any considerable interest for us in reference to any class of objects is more moderate than might be supposed. As we shall be sure to examine any sample with reference to these characters, they may be regarded not exactly as predesignated, but as predetermined (which amounts to the same thing); and we may infer that the sample represents the class in all these respects if we please, remembering only that this is not so secure an inference as if the particular quality to be looked for had been fixed upon beforehand.

The demonstration of this theory of induction rests upon

principles and follows methods which are accepted by all those who display in other matters the particular knowledge and force of mind which qualify them to judge of this. The theory itself, however, quite unaccountably seems never to have occurred to any of the writers who have undertaken to explain synthetic reasoning. The most widely-spread opinion in the matter is one which was much promoted by Mr. John Stuart Mill — namely, that induction depends for its validity upon the uniformity of Nature — that is, on the principle that what happens once will, under a sufficient degree of similarity of circumstances, happen again as often as the same circumstances recur. The application is this: The fact that different things belong to the same class constitutes the similarity of circumstances, and the induction is good, provided this similarity is "sufficient." What happens once is, that a number of these things are found to have a certain character; what may be expected, then, to happen again as often as the circumstances recur consists in this, that all things belonging to the same class should have the same character.

This analysis of induction has, I venture to think, various imperfections, to some of which it may be useful to call attention. In the first place, when I put my hand in a bag and draw out a handful of beans, and, finding three-quarters of them black, infer that about three-quarters of all in the bag are black, my inference is obviously of the same kind as if I had found any larger proportion, or the whole, of the sample black, and had assumed that it represented in that respect the rest of the contents of the bag. But the analysis in question hardly seems adapted to the explanation of this *proportionate* induction, where the conclusion, instead of being that a certain event uniformly happens under certain circumstances, is precisely that it does not uniformly occur, but only happens in a certain proportion of cases. It is true that the whole sample may be regarded as a single object, and the inference may be brought under the formula proposed by considering the conclusion to be that any similar sample will show a similar proportion among its constituents. But this is to treat the induction as if it rested on a single instance, which gives a very false idea of its probability.

In the second place, if the uniformity of Nature were the sole warrant of induction, we should have no right to draw one in regard to a character whose constancy we knew nothing about. Accordingly, Mr. Mill says that, though none but white swans were known to Europeans for thousands of years, yet the inference that all swans were white was "not a good induction," because it was not known that color was a usual generic character (it, in fact, not being so by any means). But it is mathematically demonstrable that an inductive inference may have as high a degree of probability as you please independent of any antecedent knowledge of the constancy of the character inferred. Before it was known that color is not usually a character of *genera,* there was certainly a considerable probability that all swans were white. But the further study of the *genera* of animals led to the induction of their non-uniformity in regard to color. A deductive application of this general proposition would have gone far to overcome the probability of the universal whiteness of swans before the black species was discovered. When we do know anything in regard to the general constancy or inconstancy of a character, the application of that general knowledge to the particular class to which any induction relates, though it serves to increase or diminish the force of the induction, is, like every application of general knowledge to particular cases, deductive in its nature and not inductive.

In the third place, to say that inductions are true because similar events happen in similar circumstances — or, what is the same thing, because objects similar in some respects are likely to be similar in others — is to overlook those conditions which really are essential to the validity of inductions. When we take all the characters into account, any pair of objects resemble one another in just as many particulars as any other pair. If we limit ourselves to such characters as have for us any importance, interest, or obviousness, then a synthetic conclusion may be drawn, but only on condition that the specimens by which we judge have been taken at random from the class in regard to which we are to form a judgment, and not selected as belonging to any sub-class. The induction only has its full force when the character concerned has been designated before examining the sample. These are the essentials of induction, and they are not recognized in attributing the validity of induction to the uniformity of Nature. The explanation of induction by the doctrine of probabilities, given in the last of these papers, is not a mere metaphysical formula, but is one from which all the rules of synthetic reasoning can be deduced systematically and with mathematical cogency. But the account of the matter by a principle of Nature, even if it were in other respects satisfactory, presents the fatal disadvantage of leaving us quite as much afloat as before in regard to the proper method of induction. It does not surprise me, therefore, that those who adopt this theory have given erroneous rules for the conduct of reasoning, nor that the greater number of examples put forward by Mr. Mill in his first edition, as models of what inductions should be, proved in the light of further scientific progress so particularly unfortunate that they had to be replaced by others in later editions. One would have supposed that Mr. Mill might have based an induction on *this* circumstance, especially as it is his avowed principle that, if the conclusion of an induction turns out false, it cannot have been a good induction. Nevertheless, neither he nor any of his scholars seem to have been led to suspect, in the least, the perfect solidity of the framework which he devised for securely supporting the mind in its passage from the known to the unknown, although at its first trial it did not answer quite so well as had been expected.

IV

When we have drawn any statistical induction — such, for instance, as that one-half of all births are of male children — it is always possible to discover, by investigation sufficiently prolonged, a class of which the same predicate may be affirmed universally; to find out, for instance, *what sort of* births are of male children. The truth of this principle follows immediately from the theorem that there is a character peculiar to every possible group of objects. The form in which the principle is usually stated is, that *every event must have a cause.*

But, though there exists a cause for every event, and that of a kind which is capable of being discovered, yet if there be nothing to guide us to the discovery; if we have to hunt among all the events in the world without any scent; if, for instance, the sex of a child might equally be supposed to depend on the configuration of the planets, on what was going on at the antipodes, or on anything else — then the discovery would have no chance of ever getting made.

That we ever do discover the precise causes of things, that any induction whatever is absolutely without exception, is what we have no right to assume. On the contrary, it is an easy corollary, from the theorem just referred to, that every empirical rule has an exception.[7] But there are certain of our inductions which present an approach to universality so extraordinary that, even if we are to suppose that they are not strictly universal truths, we cannot possibly think that they have been reached merely by accident. The most remarkable laws of this kind are those of *time* and *space.* With reference to space, Bishop Berkeley first showed, in a very conclusive manner, that it was not a thing *seen,* but a thing *inferred.* Berkeley chiefly insists on the impossibility of directly seeing the third dimension of space, since the retina of the eye is a surface. But, in point of fact, the retina is not even a surface; it is a conglomeration of nerve-needles directed

[7] [Note that this corollary is itself a theoretical inference and not an empirical rule.]

toward the light and having only their extreme points sensitive, these points lying at considerable distances from one another compared with their areas. Now, of these points, certainly the excitation of no one singly can produce the perception of a surface, and consequently not the aggregate of all the sensations can amount to this. But certain relations subsist between the excitations of different nerve-points, and these constitute the premises upon which the hypothesis of space is founded, and from which it is inferred. That space is not immediately perceived is now universally admitted; and a mediate cognition is what is called an inference, and is subject to the criticism of logic. But what are we to say to the fact of every chicken as soon as it is hatched solving a problem whose data are of a complexity sufficient to try the greatest mathematical powers? It would be insane to deny that the tendency to light upon the conception of space is inborn in the mind of the chicken and of every animal. The same thing is equally true of time. That time is not directly perceived is evident, since no lapse of time is present, and we only perceive what is present. That, not having the idea of time, we should never be able to perceive the flow in our sensations without some particular aptitude for it, will probably also be admitted. The idea of force — at least, in its rudiments — is another conception so early arrived at, and found in animals so low in the scale of intelligence, that it must be supposed innate. But the innateness of an idea admits of degree, for it consists in the tendency of that idea to present itself to the mind. Some ideas, like that of space, do so present themselves irresistibly at the very dawn of intelligence, and take possession of the mind on small provocation, while of other conceptions we are prepossessed, indeed, but not so strongly, down a scale which is greatly extended. The tendency to personify every thing, and to attribute human characters to it, may be said to be innate; but it is a tendency which is very soon overcome by civilized man in regard to the greater part of the objects about him. Take such a conception as that of gravitation varying inversely as the square of the distance. It is a very simple law. But to say that it is simple is merely to say that it is one which the mind is particularly adapted to apprehend with facility. Suppose the idea of a quantity multiplied into another had been no more easy to the mind than that of a quantity raised to the power indicated by itself — should we ever have discovered the law of the solar system?

It seems incontestable, therefore, that the mind of man is strongly adapted to the comprehension of the world; at least, so far as this goes, that certain conceptions, highly important for such a comprehension, naturally arise in his mind; and, without such a tendency, the mind could never have had any development at all.

How are we to explain this adaptation? The great utility and indispensableness of the conceptions of time, space, and force, even to the lowest intelligence, are such as to suggest that they are the results of natural selection. Without something like geometrical, kinetical, and mechanical conceptions, no animal could seize his food or do anything which might be necessary for the preservation of the species. He might, it is true, be provided with an instinct which would generally have the same effect; that is to say, he might have conceptions different from those of time, space, and force, but which coincided with them in regard to the ordinary cases of the animal's experience. But, as that animal would have an immense advantage in the struggle for life whose mechanical conceptions did not break down in a novel situation (such as development must bring about), there would be a constant selection in favor of more and more correct ideas of these matters. Thus would be attained the knowledge of that fundamental law upon which all science rolls; namely, that forces depend upon relations of time, space, and mass. When this idea was once sufficiently clear, it would require no more than a comprehensible degree of genius to discover the exact nature of these relations. Such an hypothesis naturally suggests itself, but it must be admitted that it does not seem sufficient to account for the extraordinary accuracy with which these conceptions apply to the phenomena of Nature, and it is probable that there is some secret here which remains to be discovered.

V

Some important questions of logic depend upon whether we are to consider the material universe as of limited extent and finite age, or quite boundless in space and in time. In the former case, it is conceivable that a general plan or design embracing the whole universe should be discovered, and it would be proper to be on the alert for some traces of such a unity. In the latter case, since the proportion of the world of which we can have any experience is less than the smallest assignable fraction, it follows that we never could discover any *pattern* in the universe except a repeating one; any design embracing the whole would be beyond our powers to discern, and beyond the united powers of all intellects during all time. Now, what is absolutely incapable of being known is, as we have seen in a former paper, not real at all. An absolutely incognizable existence is a nonsensical phrase. If, therefore, the universe is infinite, the attempt to find in it any design embracing it as a whole is futile, and involves a false way of looking at the subject. If the universe never had any beginning, and if in space world stretches beyond world without limit, there is no *whole* of material things, and consequently no general character to the universe, and no need or possibility of any governor for it. But if there was a time before which absolutely no matter existed, if there are certain absolute bounds to the region of things outside of which there is a mere void, then we naturally seek for an explanation of it, and, since we cannot look for it among material things, the hypothesis of a great disembodied animal, the creator and governor of the world, is natural enough.

The actual state of the evidence as to the limitation of the universe is as follows: As to time, we find on our earth a constant progress of development since the planet was a red-hot ball; the solar system seems to have resulted from the condensation of a nebula, and the process appears to be still going on. We sometimes see stars (presumably with systems of worlds) destroyed and apparently resolved back into the nebulous condition, but we have no evidence of any existence of the world previous to the nebulous stage from which it seems to have been evolved. All this rather favors the idea of a beginning than otherwise. As for limits in space, we cannot be sure that we see anything outside of the system of the Milky Way. Minds of theological predilections have therefore no need of distorting the facts to reconcile them with their views.

But the only scientific presumption is, that the unknown parts of space and time are like the known parts, occupied; that, as we see cycles of life and death in all development which we can trace out to the end, the same holds good in regard to solar systems; that as enormous distances lie between the different planets of our solar system, relatively to their diameters, and as still more enormous distances lie between our system relatively to its diameter and other systems, so it may be supposed that other galactic clusters exist so remote from ours as not to be recognized as such with certainty. I do not say that these are strong inductions; I only say that they are the presumptions which, in our ignorance of the facts, should be preferred to hypotheses which involve conceptions of things and occurrences totally different in their character from any of which we have had any experience, such as disembodied spirits, the creation of matter, infringements of the laws of mechanics, etc.

The universe ought to be presumed too vast to have any character. When it is claimed that the arrangements of Nature are benevolent, or just, or wise, or of any other peculiar kind, we ought to be prejudiced against such opinions, as being the offspring of an ill-founded notion of the finitude of the world. And examination has hitherto shown that such beneficences, justice, etc., are of a most limited kind — limited in degree and limited in range.

In like manner, if any one claims to have discovered a plan in the structure of organized beings, or a scheme in their classification, or a regular arrangement among natural objects, or a system of proportionality in the human form, or an order of development, or a correspondence between conjunctions of the planets and human events, or a significance in numbers, or a key to dreams, the first thing we have to ask is whether such relations are susceptible of explanation on mechanical principles, and if not they should be looked upon with disfavor as having already a strong presumption against them; and examination has generally exploded all such theories.

There are minds to whom every prejudice, every presumption, seems unfair. It is easy to say what minds these are. They are those who never have known what it is to draw a well-grounded induction, and who imagine that other people's knowledge is as nebulous as their own. That all science rolls upon presumption (not of a formal but of a real kind) is no argument with them, because they cannot imagine that there is anything solid in human knowledge. These are the people who waste their time and money upon perpetual motions and other such rubbish.

But there are better minds who take up mystical theories (by which I mean all those which have no possibility of being mechanically explained). These are persons who are strongly prejudiced in favor of such theories. We all have natural tendencies to believe in such things; our education often strengthens this tendency; and the result is, that to many minds nothing seems so antecedently probable as a theory of this kind. Such persons find evidence enough in favor of their views, and in the absence of any recognized logic of induction they cannot be driven from their belief.

But to the mind of a physicist there ought to be a strong presumption against every mystical theory; and, therefore, it seems to me that those scientific men who have sought to make out that science was not hostile to theology have not been so clear-sighted as their opponents.

It would be extravagant to say that science can at present disprove religion; but it does seem to me that the spirit of science is hostile to any religion except such a one as that of M. Vacherot. Our appointed teachers inform us that Buddhism is a miserable and atheistical faith, shorn of the most glorious and needful attributes of a religion; that its priests can be of no use to agriculture by praying for rain, nor to war by commanding the sun to stand still. We also hear the remonstances of those who warn us that to shake the general belief in the living God would be to shake the general morals, public and private. This, too, must be admitted; such a revolution of thought could no more be accomplished without waste and desolation than a plantation of trees could be transferred to new ground, however wholesome in itself, without all of them languishing for a time, and many of them dying. Nor is it, by-the-way, a thing to be presumed that a man would have taken part in a movement having a possible atheistical issue without having taken serious and adequate counsel in regard to that responsibility. But, let the consequences of such a belief be as dire as they may, one thing is certain: that the state of the facts, whatever it may be, will surely get found out, and no human prudence can long arrest the triumphal car of truth — no, not if the discovery were such as to drive every individual of our race to suicide!

But it would be folly to suppose that any metaphysical theory in regard to the mode of being of the perfect is to destroy that aspiration toward the perfect which constitutes the essence of religion. It is true that, if the priests of any particular form of religion succeed in making it generally believed that religion cannot exist without the acceptance of certain formulas, or if they succeed in so interweaving certain dogmas with the popular religion that the people can see no essential analogy between a religion which accepts these points of faith and one which rejects them, the result may very well be to render those who cannot believe these things irreligious. Nor can we ever hope that any body of priests should consider themselves more teachers of religion in general than of the particular system of theology advocated by their own party. But no man need be excluded from participation in the common feelings, nor from so much of the public expression of them as is open to all the laity, by the unphilosophical narrowness of those who guard the mysteries of worship. Am I to be prevented from joining in that common joy at the revelation of enlightened principles of religion, which we celebrate at Easter and Christmas, because I think that certain scientific, logical, and metaphysical ideas which have been mixed up with these principles are untenable? No; to do so would be to estimate those errors as of more consequence than the truth — an opinion which few would admit. People who do not believe what are really the fundamental principles of Christianity are rare to find, and all but these few ought to feel at home in the churches.

SIXTH PAPER

DEDUCTION, INDUCTION, AND HYPOTHESIS[1]

I

THE chief business of the logician is to classify arguments; for all testing clearly depends on classification. The classes of the logicians are defined by certain typical forms called syllogisms. For example, the syllogism called *Barbara* is as follows:

S is M; M is P:
Hence, S is P.

Or, to put words for letters —

Enoch and Elijah were men; all men die:
Hence, Enoch and Elijah must have died.

The "is P" of the logicians stands for any verb, active or neuter. It is capable of strict proof (with which, however, I will not trouble the reader) that all arguments whatever can be put into this form; but only under the condition that the *is* shall mean "*is* for the purposes of the argument" or "is represented by." Thus, an induction will appear in this form something like this:

These beans are two-thirds white;

But, the beans in this bag are (represented by) these beans;

[1] *Popular Science Monthly*, August, 1878.

∴ The beans in the bag are two-thirds white.

But, because all inference may be reduced in some way to *Barbara,* it does not follow that this is the most appropriate form in which to represent every kind of inference. On the contrary, to show the distinctive characters of different sorts of inference, they must clearly be exhibited in different forms peculiar to each. *Barbara* particularly typifies deductive reasoning; and so long as the *is* is taken literally, no inductive reasoning can be put into this form. *Barbara* is, in fact, nothing but the application of a rule. The so-called major premise lays down this rule; as, for example, *All men are mortal.* The other or minor premise states a case under the rule; as, *Enoch was a man.* The conclusion applies the rule to the case and states the result: *Enoch is mortal.* All deduction is of this character; it is merely the application of general rules to particular cases. Sometimes this is not very evident, as in the following:

All quadrangles are figures,
But no triangle is a quadrangle;
Therefore, some figures are not triangles.

But here the reasoning is really this:

Rule. — Every quadrangle is other than a triangle.
Case. — Some figures are quadrangles.
Result. — Some figures are not triangles.

Inductive or synthetic reasoning, being something more than the mere application of a general rule to a particular case, can never be reduced to this form.

If, from a bag of beans of which we know that $\frac{2}{3}$ are white, we take one at random, it is a deductive inference that this bean is probably white, the probability being $\frac{2}{3}$. We have, in effect, the following syllogism:

Rule. — The beans in this bag are $\frac{2}{3}$ white.

Case. — This bean has been drawn in such a way that in the long run the relative number of white beans so drawn would be equal to the relative number in the bag.

Result. — This bean has been drawn in such a way that in the long run it would turn out white $\frac{2}{3}$ of the time.

If instead of drawing one bean we draw a handful at random and conclude that about $\frac{2}{3}$ of the handful are probably white, the reasoning is of the same sort. If, however, not knowing what proportion of white beans there are in the bag, we draw a handful at random and, finding $\frac{2}{3}$ of the beans in the handful white, conclude that about $\frac{2}{3}$ of those in the bag are white, we are rowing up the current of deductive sequence, and are concluding a rule from the observation of a result in a certain case. This is particularly clear when all the handful turn out one color. The induction then is:

These beans were in this bag.

These beans are white.

∴ All the beans in the bag were white.

Which is but an inversion of the deductive syllogism.

Rule. — All the beans in the bag were white.

Case. — These beans were in the bag.

Result. — These beans are white.

So that induction is the inference of the *rule* from the *case* and *result*.

But this is not the only way of inverting a deductive syllogism so as to produce a synthetic inference. Suppose I enter a room and there find a number of bags, containing different kinds of beans. On the table there is a handful of white beans; and, after some searching, I find one of the bags contains white beans only. I at once infer as a probability, or as a fair guess, that this handful was taken out of that bag. This sort of inference is called *making an hypothesis.*[2] It is the inference of a *case* from a *rule* and *result.* We have, then —

DEDUCTION.

Rule. — All the beans from this bag are white.
Case. — These beans are from this bag.
∴ *Result.* — These beans are white.

INDUCTION.

Case. — These beans are from this bag.
Result. — These beans are white.
∴ *Rule.* — All the beans from this bag are white.

HYPOTHESIS.

Rule. — All the beans from this bag are white.
Result. — These beans are white.
∴ *Case.* — These beans are from this bag.

We, accordingly, classify all inference as follows:

Inference.

Deductive or Analytic. Synthetic.

Induction. Hypothesis.

[2] [Later Pierce called it *presumptive inference.* See Baldwin's *Dictionary* art. *Probable Inference.*]

Induction is where we generalize from a number of cases of which something is true, and infer that the same thing is true of a whole class. Or, where we find a certain thing to be true of a certain proportion of cases and infer that it is true of the same proportion of the whole class. Hypothesis is where we find some very curious circumstance, which would be explained by the supposition that it was a case of a certain general rule, and thereupon adopt that supposition. Or, where we find that in certain respects two objects have a strong resemblance, and infer that they resemble one another strongly in other respects.

I once landed at a seaport in a Turkish province; and, as I was walking up to the house which I was to visit, I met a man upon horseback, surrounded by four horsemen holding a canopy over his head. As the governor of the province was the only personage I could think of who would be so greatly honored, I inferred that this was he. This was an hypothesis.

Fossils are found; say, remains like those of fishes, but far in the interior of the country. To explain the phenomenon, we suppose the sea once washed over this land. This is another hypothesis.

Numberless documents and monuments refer to a conqueror called Napoleon Bonaparte. Though we have not seen the man, yet we cannot explain what we have seen, namely, all these documents and monuments, without supposing that he really existed. Hypothesis again.

As a general rule, hypothesis is a weak kind of argument. It often inclines our judgment so slightly toward its conclusion that we cannot say that we believe the latter to be true; we only surmise that it may be so. But there is no difference except one of degree between such an inference and that by which we are led to believe that we remember the occurrences of yesterday from our feeling as if we did so.

II

Besides the way just pointed out of inverting a deductive syllogism to produce an induction or hypothesis, there is another. If from the truth of a certain premise the truth of a certain conclusion would necessarily follow, then from the falsity of the conclusion the falsity of the premise would follow. Thus, take the following syllogism in *Barbara:*

Rule. — All men are mortal.
Case. — Enoch and Elijah were men.
∴ *Result.* — Enoch and Elijah were mortal.

Now, a person who denies this result may admit the rule, and, in that case, he must deny the case. Thus:

Denial of Result. — Enoch and Elijah were not mortal.
Rule. — All men are mortal.
∴ *Denial of Case.* — Enoch and Elijah were not men.

This kind of syllogism is called *Baroco,* which is the typical mood of the second figure. On the other hand, the person who denies the result may admit the case, and in that case he must deny the rule. Thus:

Denial of the Result. — Enoch and Elijah were not mortal.
Case. — Enoch and Elijah were men.
∴ *Denial of the Rule.* — Some men are not mortal.

This kind of syllogism is called *Bocardo,* which is the typical mood of the third figure.

Baroco and *Bocardo* are, of course, deductive syllogisms; but of a very peculiar kind. They are called by logicians indirect moods, because they need some transformation to appear as the application of a rule to a particular case. But if, instead of setting out as we have here done with a necessary deduction in *Barbara,* we take a probable deduction of similar form, the indirect moods which we shall obtain will be —

Corresponding to *Baroco,* an hypothesis;
and, Corresponding to *Bocardo,* an induction.

For example, let us begin with this probable deduction in *Barbara:*

Rule. — Most of the beans in this bag are white.
Case. — This handful of beans are from this bag.
∴ *Result.* — Probably, most of this handful of beans are white.

Now, deny the result, but accept the rule:

Denial of Result. — Few beans of this handful are white.
Rule. — Most beans in this bag are white.
∴ *Denial of Case.* — Probably, these beans were taken from another bag.

This is an hypothetical inference. Next, deny the result, but accept the case:

Denial of Result. — Few beans of this handful are white.
Case. — These beans came from this bag.

∴ *Denial of Rule.* — Probably, few beans in the bag are white.

This is an induction.

The relation thus exhibited between synthetic and deductive reasoning is not without its importance. When we adopt a certain hypothesis, it is not alone because it will explain the observed facts, but also because the contrary hypothesis would probably lead to results contrary to those observed. So, when we make an induction, it is drawn not only because it explains the distribution of characters in the sample, but also because a different rule would probably have led to the sample being other than it is.

But the advantage of this way of considering the subject might easily be overrated. An induction is really the inference of a rule, and to consider it as the denial of a rule is an artificial conception, only admissible because, when statistical or proportional propositions are considered as rules, the denial of a rule is itself a rule. So, an hypothesis is really a subsumption of a case under a class and not the denial of it, except for this, that to deny a subsumption under one class is to admit a subsumption under another.

Bocardo may be considered as an induction, so timid as to lose its amplificative character entirely. Enoch and Elijah are specimens of a certan kind of men. All that kind of men are shown by these instances to be immortal. But instead of boldly concluding that all very pious men, or all men favorites of the Almighty, etc., are immortal, we refrain from specifying the description of men, and rest in the merely explicative inference that *some* men are immortal. So *Baroco* might be considered as a very timid hypothesis. Enoch and Elijah are not mortal. Now, we might boldly suppose them to be gods or something of that sort, but instead of that we limit ourselves to the inference that they are of *some* nature different from that of man.

But, after all, there is an immense difference between the relation of *Baroco* and *Bocardo* to *Barbara* and that of Induction and Hypothesis to Deduction. *Baroco* and *Bocardo* are based upon the fact that if the truth of a conclusion necessarily follows from the truth of a premise, then the falsity of the premise follows from the falsity of the conclusion. This is always true. It is different when the inference is only probable. It by no means follows that, because the truth of a certain premise would render the truth of a conclusion probable, therefore the falsity of the conclusion renders the falsity of the premise probable. At least, this is only true, as we have seen in a former paper, when the word probable is used in one sense in the antecedent and in another in the consequent.

III

A certain anonymous writing is upon a torn piece of paper. It is suspected that the author is a certain person. His desk, to which only he has had access, is searched, and in it is found a piece of paper, the torn edge of which exactly fits, in all its irregularities, that of the paper in question. It is a fair hypothetic inference that the suspected man was actually the author. The ground of this inference evidently is that two torn pieces of paper are extremely unlikely to fit together by accident. Therefore, of a great number of inferences of this sort, but a very small proportion would be deceptive. The analogy of hypothesis with induction is so strong that some logicians have confounded them. Hypothesis has been called an induction of characters. A number of characters belonging to a certain class are found in a certain object; whence it is inferred that all the characters of that class belong to the object in question. This certainly involves the same principle as induction; yet in a modified form. In the first place, characters are not susceptible of simple enumeration like objects; in the next place, characters run in categories. When we make an hypothesis like that about the piece of paper, we only examine a single line of characters, or perhaps two or three, and we take no specimen at all of others. If the hypothesis were nothing but an induction, all that we should be justified in concluding, in the example above, would be that the two pieces of paper which matched in such irregularities as have been examined would be found to match in other, say slighter, irregularities. The inference from the shape of the paper to its ownership is precisely what distinguishes hypothesis from induction, and makes it a bolder and more perilous step.

The same warnings that have been given against imagining that induction rests upon the uniformity of Nature might be repeated in regard to hypothesis. Here, as there, such a theory not only utterly fails to account for the validity of the inference, but it also gives rise to methods of conducting it which are absolutely vicious. There are, no doubt, certain uniformities in Nature, the knowledge of which will fortify an hypothesis very much. For example, we suppose that iron, titanium, and other metals exist in the sun, because we find in the solar spectrum many lines coincident in position with those which these metals would produce; and this hypothesis is greatly strengthened by our knowledge of the remarkable distinctiveness of the particular line of characters observed. But such a fortification of hypothesis is of a deductive kind, and hypothesis may still be probable when such reënforcement is wanting.

There is no greater nor more frequent mistake in practical logic than to suppose that things which resemble one another strongly in some respects are any the more likely for that to be alike in others. That this is absolutely false, admits of rigid demonstration; but, inasmuch as the reasoning is somewhat severe and complicated (requiring, like all such reasoning, the use of A, B, C, etc., to set it forth), the reader would probably find it distasteful, and I omit it. An example, however, may illustrate the proposition: The comparative mythologists occupy themselves with finding points of resemblance between solar phenomena and the careers of the heroes of all sorts of traditional stories; and upon the basis of such resemblances they infer that these heroes are impersonations of the sun. If there be anything more in their reasonings, it has never been made clear to me. An ingenious logician, to show how futile all that is, wrote a little book, in which he pretended to prove, in the same manner, that Napoleon Bonaparte is only an impersonation of the sun. It was really wonderful to see how many points of resemblance he made out. The truth is, that any two things resemble one another just as strongly as any two others, if recondite resemblances are admitted. But, in order that the process of making an hypothesis should lead to a probable result, the following rules must be followed:

1. The hypothesis should be distinctly put as a question, before making the observations which are to test its truth. In other words, we must try to see what the result of predictions from the hypothesis will be.

2. The respect in regard to which the resemblances are noted must be taken at random. We must not take a particular kind of predictions for which the hypothesis is known to be good.

3. The failures as well as the successes of the predictions must be honestly noted. The whole proceeding must be fair and unbiased.

Some persons fancy that bias and counter-bias are favorable to the extraction of truth — that hot and partisan debate is the way to investigate. This is the theory of our atrocious legal procedure. But Logic puts its heel upon this suggestion. It irrefragably demonstrates that knowledge can only be furthered by the real desire for it, and that the methods of obstinacy, of authority, and every mode of trying to reach a foregone conclusion, are absolutely of no value. These things are proved. The reader is at liberty to think so or not as long as the proof is not set forth, or as long as he refrains from examining it. Just so, he can preserve, if he likes, his freedom of opinion in regard to the propositions of geometry; only, in that case, if he takes a fancy to read Euclid, he will do well to skip whatever he finds with A, B, C, etc., for, if he reads attentively that disagreeable matter, the freedom of his opinion about geometry may unhappily be lost forever.

How many people there are who are incapable of putting to their own consciences this question, " Do I want to know how the fact stands, or not? "

The rules which have thus far been laid down for induction and hypothesis are such as are absolutely essential. There are many other maxims expressing particular contrivances for making synthetic inferences strong, which are extremely valuable and should not be neglected. Such are, for example, Mr. Mill's four methods. Nevertheless, in the total neglect of these, inductions and hypotheses may and sometimes do attain the greatest force.

IV

Classifications in all cases perfectly satisfactory hardly exist. Even in regard to the great distinction between explicative and ampliative inferences, examples could be found which seem to lie upon the border between the two classes, and to partake in some respects of the characters of either. The same thing is true of the distinction between induction and hypothesis. In the main, it is broad and decided. By induction, we conclude that facts, similar to observed facts, are true in cases not examined. By hypothesis, we conclude the existence of a fact quite different from anything observed, from which, according to known laws, something observed would necessarily result. The former, is reasoning from particulars to the general law; the latter, from effect to cause. The former classifies, the latter explains.

It is only in some special cases that there can be more than a momentary doubt to which category a given inference belongs. One exception is where we observe, not facts similar under similar circumstances, but facts different under different circumstances — the difference of the former having, however, a definite relation to the difference of the latter. Such inferences, which are really inductions, sometimes present nevertheless some indubitable resemblances to hypotheses.

Knowing that water expands by heat, we make a number of observations of the volume of a constant mass of water at different temperatures. The scrutiny of a few of these suggests a form of algebraical formula which will approximately express the relation of the volume to the temperature. It may be, for instance, that v being the relative volume, and t the temperature, a few observations examined indicate a relation of the form —

$$v = 1 + at + bt^2 + ct^3.$$

Upon examining observations at other temperatures taken at random, this idea is confirmed; and we draw the inductive conclusion that all observations within the limits of temperature from which we have drawn our observations could equally be so satisfied. Having once ascertained that such a formula is possible, it is a mere affair of arithmetic to find the values of a, b, and c, which will make the formula satisfy the observations best. This is what physicists call an *empirical formula,* because it rests upon mere induction, and is not explained by any hypothesis.

Such formulæ, though very useful as means of describing

in general terms the results of observations, do not take any high rank among scientific discoveries. The induction which they embody, that expansion by heat (or whatever other phenomenon is referred to) takes place in a perfectly gradual manner without sudden leaps or inummerable fluctuations, although really important, attracts no attention, because it is what we naturally anticipate. But the defects of such expressions are very serious. In the first place, as long as the observations are subject to error, as all observations are, the formula cannot be expected to satisfy the observations exactly. But the discrepancies cannot be due solely to the errors of the observations, but must be partly owing to the error of the formula which has been deducted from erroneous observations. Moreover, we have no right to suppose that the real facts, if they could be had free from error, could be expressed by such a formula at all. They might, perhaps, be expressed by a similar formula with an infinite number of terms; but of what use would that be to us, since it would require an infinite number of coefficients to be written down? When one quantity varies with another, if the corresponding values are exactly known, it is a mere matter of mathematical ingenuity to find some way of expressing their relation in a simple manner. If one quantity is of one kind — say, a specific gravity — and the other of another kind — say, a temperature — we do not desire to find an expression for their relation which is wholly free from numerical constants, since if it were free from them when, say, specific gravity as compared with water, and temperature as expressed by the Centigrade thermometer, were in question, numbers would have to be introduced when the scales of measurement were changed. We may, however, and do desire to find formulas expressing the relations of physical phenomena which shall contain no more arbitrary numbers than changes in the scales of measurement might require.

When a formula of this kind is discovered, it is no longer called an empirical formula, but a law of Nature; and is sooner or later made the basis of an hypothesis which is to explain it. These simple formulæ are not usually, if ever, exactly true, but they are none the less important for that; and the great triumph of the hypothesis comes when it explains not only the formula, but also the deviations from the formula. In the current language of the physicists, an hypothesis of this importance is called a theory, while the term hypothesis is restricted to suggestions which have little evidence in their favor. There is some justice in the contempt which clings to the word hypothesis. To think that we can strike out of our own minds a true preconception of how Nature acts, in a vain fancy. As Lord Bacon well says: "The subtlety of Nature far exceeds the subtlety of sense and intellect: so that these fine meditations, and speculations, and reasonings of men are a sort of insanity, only there is no one at hand to remark it." The successful theories are not pure guesses, but are guided by reasons.

The kinetical theory of gases is a good example of this. This theory is intended to explain certain simple formulæ, the chief of which is called the law of Boyle. It is, that if air or any other gas be placed in a cylinder with a piston, and if its volume be measured under the pressure of the atmosphere, say fifteen pounds on the square inch, and if then another fifteen pounds per square inch be placed on the piston, the gas will be compressed to one-half its bulk, and in similar inverse ratio for other pressures. The hypothesis which has been adopted to account for this law is that the molecules of a gas are small, solid particles at great distances from each other (relatively to their dimensions), and moving with great velocity, without sensible attractions or repulsions, until they happen to approach one another very closely. Admit this, and it follows that when a gas is under pressure what prevents it from collapsing is not the incompressibility of the separate molecules, which are under no pressure at all, since they do not touch, but the pounding of the molecules against the piston. The more the piston falls, and the more the gas is compressed, the nearer together the molecules will be; the greater number there will be at any moment within a given distance of the piston, the shorter the distance which any one will go before its course is changed by the influence of another, the greater number of new courses of each in a given time, and the oftener each, within a given distance of the piston, will strike it. This explains Boyle's law. The law is not exact; but the hypothesis does not lead us to it exactly. For, in the first place, if the molecules are large, they will strike each other oftener when their mean distances are diminished, and will consequently strike the piston oftener, and will produce more pressure upon it. On the other hand, if the molecules have an attraction for one another, they will remain for a sensible time within one another's influence, and consequently they will not strike the wall so often as they otherwise would, and the pressure will be less increased by compression.

When the kinetical theory of gases was first proposed by Daniel Bernoulli, in 1738, it rested only on the law of Boyle, and was therefore pure hypothesis. It was accordingly quite naturally and deservedly neglected. But, at present, the theory presents quite another aspect; for, not to speak of the considerable number of observed facts of different kinds with which it has been brought into relation, it is supported by the mechanical theory of heat. That bringing together bodies which attract one another, or separating bodies which repel one another, when sensible motion is not produced nor destroyed, is always accompanied by the evolution of heat, is little more than an induction. Now, it has been shown by experiment that, when a gas is allowed to expand without doing work, a very small amount of heat disappears. This proves that the particles of the gas attract one another slightly, and but very slightly. It follows that, when a gas is under pressure, what prevents it from collapsing is not any repulsion between the particles, since there is none. Now, there are only two modes of force known to us, force of position or attractions and repulsions, and force of motion. Since, therefore, it is not the force of position which gives a gas its expansive force, it must be the force of motion. In this point of view, the kinetical theory of gases appears as a deduction from the mechanical theory of heat. It is to be observed, however, that it supposes the same law of mechanics (that there are only those two modes of force) which holds in regard to bodies such as we can see and examine, to hold also for what are very different, the molecules of bodies. Such a supposition has but a slender support from induction. Our belief in it is greatly strengthened by its connection with the law of Boyle, and it is, therefore, to be considered as an hypothetical inference. Yet it must be admitted that the kinetical theory of gases would deserve little credence if it had not been connected with the principles of mechanics.

The great difference between induction and hypothesis is, that the former infers the existence of phenomena such as we have observed in cases which are similar, while hypothesis supposes something of a different kind from what we have directly observed, and frequently something which it would be impossible for us to observe directly. Accordingly, when we stretch an induction quite beyond the limits of our observation, the inference partakes of the nature of hypothesis. It would be absurd to say that we have no inductive warrant for a generalization extending a little beyond the limits of experience, and there is no line to be drawn beyond which we cannot push our inference; only it becomes weaker the further it is pushed. Yet, if an induction be pushed very far, we cannot give it much credence unless we find that such an extension explains some fact which we can and do observe. Here, then, we have a kind of mixture of induction and hypothesis supporting one another; and of this kind are most of the theories of physics.

V

That synthetic inferences may be divided into induction and hypothesis in the manner here proposed,[3] admits of no question. The utility and value of the distinction are to be tested by their applications.

Induction is, plainly, a much stronger kind of inference than hypothesis; and this is the first reason for distinguishing between them. Hypotheses are sometimes regarded as provisional resorts, which in the progress of science are to be replaced by inductions. But this is a false view of the subject. Hypothetic reasoning infers very frequently a fact not capable of direct observation. It is an hypothesis that Napoleon Bonaparte once existed. How is that hypothesis ever to be replaced by an induction? It may be said that from the premise that such facts as we have observed are as they would be if Napoleon existed, we are to infer by induction that *all* facts that are hereafter to be observed will be of the same character. There is no doubt that every hypothetic inference may be distorted into the appearance of an induction in this way. But the essence of an induction is that it infers from one set of facts another set of similar facts, whereas hypothesis infers from facts of one kind to facts of another. Now, the facts which serve as grounds for our belief in the historic reality of Napoleon are not by any means necessarily the only kind of facts which are explained by his existence. It may be that, at

[3] This division was first made in a course of lectures by the author before the Lowell Institute, Boston, in 1866, and was printed in the *Proceedings of the American Academy of Arts and Sciences,* for April 9, 1867.

the time of his career, events were being recorded in some way not now dreamed of, that some ingenious creature on a neighboring planet was photographing the earth, and that these pictures on a sufficiently large scale may some time come into our possession, or that some mirror upon a distant star will, when the light reaches it, reflect the whole story back to earth. Never mind how improbable these suppositions are; everything which happens is infinitely improbable. I am not saying that *these* things are likely to occur, but that *some* effect of Napoleon's existence which now seems impossible is certain nevertheless to be brought about. The hypothesis asserts that such facts, when they do occur, will be of a nature to confirm, and not to refute, the existence of the man. We have, in the impossibility of inductively inferring hypothetical conclusions, a second reason for distinguishing between the two kinds of inference.

A third merit of the distinction is, that it is associated with an important psychological or rather physiological difference in the mode of apprehending facts. Induction infers a rule. Now, the belief of a rule is a habit. That a habit is a rule active in us, is evident. That every belief is of the nature of a habit, in so far as it is of a general character, has been shown in the earlier papers of this series. Induction, therefore, is the logical formula which expresses the physiological process of formation of a habit. Hypothesis substitutes, for a complicated tangle of predicates attached to one subject, a single conception. Now, there is a peculiar sensation belonging to the act of thinking that each of these predicates inheres in the subject. In hypothetic inference this complicated feeling so produced is replaced by a single feeling of greater intensity, that belonging to the act of thinking the hypothetic conclusion. Now, when our nervous system is excited in a complicated way, there being a relation between the elements of the excitation, the result is a single harmonious disturbance which I call an emotion. Thus, the various sounds made by the instruments of an orchestra strike upon the ear, and the result is a peculiar musical emotion, quite distinct from the sounds themselves. This emotion is essentially the same thing as an hypothetic inference, and every hypothetic inference involves the formation of such an emotion. We may say, therefore, that hypothesis produces the *sensuous* element of thought, and induction the *habitual* element. As for deduction, which adds nothing to the premises, but only out of the various facts represented in the premises selects one and brings the attention down to it, this may be considered as the logical formula for paying attention, which is the *volitional* element of thought, and corresponds to nervous discharge in the sphere of physiology.

Another merit of the distinction between induction and hypothesis is, that it leads to a very natural classification of the sciences and of the minds which prosecute them. What must separate different kinds of scientific men more than anything else are the differences of their *techniques*. We cannot expect men who work with books chiefly to have much in common with men whose lives are passed in laboratories. But, after differences of this kind, the next most important are differences in the modes of reasoning. Of the natural sciences, we have, first, the classificatory sciences, which are purely inductive — systematic botany and zoölogy, mineralogy, and chemistry. Then, we have the sciences of theory, as above explained — astronomy, pure physics, etc. Then, we have sciences of hypothesis — geology, biology, etc.

There are many other advantages of the distinction in question which I shall leave the reader to find out by experience. If he will only take the custom of considering whether a given inference belongs to one or other of the two forms of synthetic inference given on page 134, I can promise him that he will find his advantage in it, in various ways.

PART II

LOVE AND CHANCE

LOVE AND CHANCE

I. THE ARCHITECTURE OF THEORIES[1]

Of the fifty or hundred systems of philosophy that have been advanced at different times of the world's history, perhaps the larger number have been, not so much results of historical evolution, as happy thoughts which have accidently occurred to their authors. An idea which has been found interesting and fruitful has been adopted, developed, and forced to yield explanations of all sorts of phenomena. The English have been particularly given to this way of philosophizing; witness, Hobbes, Hartley, Berkeley, James Mill. Nor has it been by any means useless labor; it shows us what the true nature and value of the ideas developed are, and in that way affords serviceable materials for philosophy. Just as if a man, being seized with the conviction that paper was a good material to make things of, were to go to work to build a *papier mâché* house, with roof of roofing-paper, foundations of pasteboard, windows of paraffined paper, chimneys, bath tubs, locks, etc., all of different forms of paper, his experiment would probably afford valuable lessons to builders, while it would certainly make a detestable house, so those one-idea'd philosophies are exceedingly interesting and instructive, and yet are quite unsound.

The remaining systems of philosophy have been of the nature of reforms, sometimes amounting to radical revolutions, suggested by certain difficulties which have been found

[1] *The Monist,* January, 1891.

to beset systems previously in vogue; and such ought certainly to be in large part the motive of any new theory. This is like partially rebuilding a house. The faults that have been committed are, first, that the repairs of the dilapidations have generally not been sufficiently thoroughgoing, and second, that not sufficient pains had been taken to bring the additions into deep harmony with the really sound parts of the old structure.

When a man is about to build a house, what a power of thinking he has to do, before he can safely break ground! With what pains he has to excogitate the precise wants that are to be supplied! What a study to ascertain the most available and suitable materials, to determine the mode of construction to which those materials are best adapted, and to answer a hundred such questions! Now without riding the metaphor too far, I think we may safely say that the studies preliminary to the construction of a great theory should be at least as deliberate and thorough as those that are preliminary to the building of a dwelling-house.

That systems ought to be constructed architectonically has been preached since Kant, but I do not think the full import of the maxim has by any means been apprehended. What I would recommend is that every person who wishes to form an opinion concerning fundamental problems, should first of all make a complete survey of human knowledge, should take note of all the valuable ideas in each branch of science, should observe in just what respect each has been successful and where it has failed, in order that in the light of the thorough acquaintance so attained of the available materials for a philosophical theory and of the nature and strength of each, he may proceed to the study of what the problem of philosophy consists in, and of the proper way of solving it. I must not be understood as endeavoring to state fully all that these preparatory studies should embrace; on the contrary, I purposely slur over many points, in order to give emphasis to one special recommendation, namely, to make a systematic study of the conceptions out of which a philosophical theory may be built, in order to ascertain what place each conception may fitly occupy in such a theory, and to what uses it is adapted.

The adequate treatment of this single point would fill a volume, but I shall endeavor to illustrate my meaning by glancing at several sciences and indicating conceptions in them serviceable for philosophy. As to the results to which long studies thus commenced have led me, I shall just give a hint at their nature.

We may begin with dynamics, — field in our day of perhaps the grandest conquest human science has ever made, — I mean the law of the conservation of energy. But let us revert to the first step taken by modern scientific thought, — and a great stride it was, — the inauguration of dynamics by Galileo. A modern physicist on examining Galileo's works is surprised to find how little experiment had to do with the establishment of the foundations of mechanics. His principal appeal is to common sense and *il lume naturale*. He always assumes that the true theory will be found to be a simple and natural one. And we can see why it should indeed be so in dynamics. For instance, a body left to its own inertia, moves in a straight line, and a straight line appears to us the simplest of curves. In *itself*, no curve is simpler than another. A system of straight lines has intersections precisely corresponding to those of a system of like parabolas similarly placed, or to those of any one of an infinity of systems of curves. But the straight line appears to us simple, because, as Euclid says, it lies evenly between its extremities; that is, because viewed endwise it appears as a point. That is, again, because light moves in straight lines. Now, light moves in straight lines because of the part which the straight line plays in the laws of dynamics. Thus it is that our minds having been formed under the influence of phenomena governed by the laws of mechanics, certain conceptions entering into those laws become implanted in our minds, so that we readily guess at what the laws are. Without such a natural prompting, having to search blindfold for a law which would suit the phenomena, our chance of finding it would be as one to infinity. The further physical studies depart from phenomena which have directly influenced the growth of the mind, the less we can expect to find the laws which govern them "simple," that is, composed of a few conceptions natural to our minds.

The researches of Galileo, followed up by Huygens and others, led to those modern conceptions of *Force* and *Law*, which have revolutionized the intellectual world. The great attention given to mechanics in the seventeenth century soon so emphasized these conceptions as to give rise to the Mechanical Philosophy, or doctrine that all the phenomena of the physical universe are to be explained upon mechanical principles. Newton's great discovery imparted a new impetus to this tendency. The old notion that heat consists in an agitation of corpuscles was now applied to the explanation of the chief properties of gases. The first suggestion in this direction was that the pressure of gases is explained by the battering of the particles against the walls of the containing vessel, which explained Boyle's law of the compressibility of air. Later, the expansion of gases, Avogadro's chemical law, the diffusion and viscosity of gases, and the action of Crookes's radiometer were shown to be consequences of the same kinetical theory; but other phenomena, such as the ratio of the specific heat at constant volume to that at constant pressure, require additional hypotheses, which we have little reason to suppose are simple, so that we find ourselves quite afloat. In like manner with regard to light. That it consists of vibrations was almost proved by the phenomena of diffraction, while those of polarization showed the excursions of the particles to be perpendicular to the line of propagation; but the phenomena of dispersion, etc., require additional hypotheses which may be very complicated. Thus, the further progress of molecular speculation appears quite uncertain. If hypotheses are to be tried haphazard, or simply because they will suit certain phenomena, it will occupy the mathematical physicists of the world say half a century on the average to bring each theory to the test, and since the number of possible theories may go up into the trillions, only one of which can be true, we have little prospect of making further solid additions to the subject in our time. When we come to atoms, the presumption in favor of a simple law seems very slender. There is room for serious doubt whether the fundamental laws of mechanics hold good for single atoms, and it seems quite likely that they are capable of motion in more than three dimensions.

To find out much more about molecules and atoms, we must search out a natural history of laws of nature, which may fulfil that function which the presumption in favor of simple laws fulfilled in the early days of dynamics, by showing us what kind of laws we have to expect and by answering such questions as this: Can we with reasonable prospect of not wasting time, try the supposition that atoms attract one another inversely as the seventh power of their distances, or can we not? To suppose universal laws of nature capable of being apprehended by the mind and yet having no reason for their special forms, but standing inexplicable and irrational, is hardly a justifiable position. Uniformities are precisely the sort of facts that need to be accounted for. That a pitched coin should sometimes turn up heads and sometimes tails calls for no particular explanation; but if it shows heads every time, we wish to know how this result has been brought about. Law is *par excellence* the thing that wants a reason.

Now the only possible way of accounting for the laws of nature and for uniformity in general is to suppose them results of evolution. This supposes them not to be absolute, not to be obeyed precisely. It makes an element of indeterminacy, spontaneity, or absolute chance in nature. Just as, when we attempt to verify any physical law, we find our observations cannot be precisely satisfied by it, and rightly attribute the discrepancy to errors of observation, so we must suppose far more minute discrepancies to exist owing to the imperfect cogency of the law itself, to a certain swerving of the facts from any definite formula.

Mr. Herbert Spencer wishes to explain evolution upon mechanical principles. This is illogical, for four reasons. First, because the principle of evolution requires no extraneous cause; since the tendency to growth can be supposed itself to have grown from an infinitesimal germ accidentally started. Second, because law ought more than anything else to be supposed a result of evolution. Third, because exact law obviously never can produce heterogeneity out of homogeneity; and arbitrary heterogeneity is the feature of the universe the most manifest and characteristic. Fourth, because the law of the conservation of energy is equivalent to the proposition that all operations governed by mechanical laws are reversible; so that an immediate corollary from it is that growth is not explicable by those laws, even if they be not violated in the process of growth. In short, Spencer is not a philosophical evolutionist, but only a half-evolutionist, — or, if you will, only a semi-Spencerian. Now philosophy requires thoroughgoing evolutionism or none.

The theory of Darwin was that evolution had been brought about by the action of two factors: first, heredity, as a principle making offspring nearly resemble their parents, while yet giving room for "sporting," or accidental variations, — for very slight variations often, for wider ones rarely; and, second, the destruction of breeds or races that are unable to keep the birth rate up to the death rate. This Darwinian principle is plainly capable of great generalization. Wherever there are large numbers of objects, having a tendency to retain certain characters unaltered, this tendency, however, not being absolute but giving room for chance variations, then, if the amount of variation is absolutely limited in certain directions by the destruction of everything which reaches those limits, there will be a gradual tendency to change in directions of departure from them. Thus, if a million players sit down to bet at an even game, since one after another will get ruined, the average wealth of those who remain will perpetually increase. Here is indubitably a genuine formula of possible evolution, whether its operation accounts for much or little in the development of animal and vegetable species.

The Lamarckian theory also supposes that the development of species has taken place by a long series of insensible changes, but it supposes that those changes have taken place during the lives of the individuals, in consequence of effort and exercise, and that reproduction plays no part in the process except in preserving these modifications. Thus, the Lamarckian theory only explains the development of characters for which individuals strive, while the Darwinian theory only explains the production of characters really beneficial to the race, though these may be fatal to individuals.[2] But more broadly and philosophically conceived, Darwinian evolution is evolution by the operation of chance, and the destruction of bad results, while Lamarckian evolution is evolution by the effect of habit and effort.

A third theory of evolution is that of Mr. Clarence King.

[2] The neo-Darwinian, Weismann, has shown that mortality would almost necessarily result from the action of the Darwinian principle.

The testimony of monuments and of rocks is that species are unmodified or scarcely modified, under ordinary circumstances, but are rapidly altered after cataclysms or rapid geological changes. Under novel circumstances, we often see animals and plants sporting excessively in reproduction, and sometimes even undergoing transformations during individual life, phenomena no doubt due partly to the enfeeblement of vitality from the breaking up of habitual modes of life, partly to changed food, partly to direct specific influence of the element in which the organism is immersed. If evolution has been brought about in this way, not only have its single steps not been insensible, as both Darwinians and Lamarckians suppose, but they are furthermore neither haphazard on the one hand, nor yet determined by an inward striving on the other, but on the contrary are effects of the changed environment, and have a positive general tendency to adapt the organism to that environment, since variation will particularly affect organs at once enfeebled and stimulated. This mode of evolution, by external forces and the breaking up of habits, seems to be called for by some of the broadest and most important facts of biology and paleontology; while it certainly has been the chief factor in the historical evolution of institutions as in that of ideas; and cannot possibly be refused a very prominent place in the process of evolution of the universe in general.

Passing to psychology, we find the elementary phenomena of mind fall into three categories. First, we have Feelings, comprising all that is immediately present, such as pain, blue, cheerfulness, the feeling that arises when we contemplate a consistent theory, etc. A feeling is a state of mind having its own living quality, independent of any other state of mind. Or, a feeling is an element of consciousness which might conceivably override every other state until it monopolized the mind, although such a rudimentary state cannot actually be realized, and would not properly be consciousness. Still, it is conceivable, or supposable, that the quality of blue should usurp the whole mind, to the exclusion of the ideas of shape, extension, contrast, commencement and cessation, and all other ideas, whatsoever. A feeling is necessarily perfectly simple, *in itself*, for if it had parts these would also be in the mind, whenever the whole was present, and thus the whole could not monopolize the mind.[3]

Besides Feelings, we have Sensations of reaction; as when a person blindfold suddenly runs against a post, when we make a muscular effort, or when any feeling gives way to a new feeling. Suppose I had nothing in my mind but a feeling of blue, which were suddenly to give place to a feeling of red; then, at the instant of transition there would be a shock, a sense of reaction, my blue life being transmuted into red life. If I were further endowed with a memory, that sense would continue for some time, and there would also be a peculiar feeling or sentiment connected with it. This last feeling might endure (conceivably I mean) after the memory of the occurrence and the feelings of blue and red had passed away. But the *sensation* of reaction cannot exist except in the actual presence of the

[3] A feeling may certainly be compound, but only in virtue of a perception which is not that feeling nor any feeling at all.

two feelings blue and red to which it relates. Wherever we have two feelings and pay attention to a relation between them of whatever kind, there is the sensation of which I am speaking. But the sense of action and reaction has two types: it may either be a perception of relation between two ideas, or it may be a sense of action and reaction between feeling and something out of feeling. And this sense of external reaction again has two forms; for it is either a sense of something happening to us, by no act of ours, we being passive in the matter, or it is a sense of resistance, that is, of our expending feeling upon something without. The sense of reaction is thus a sense of connection or comparison between feelings, either, *A*, between one feeling and another, or *B*, between feeling and its absence or lower degree; and under *B* we have, First, the sense of the access of feeling, and Second, the sense of remission of feeling.

Very different both from feelings and from reaction-sensations or disturbances of feeling are general conceptions. When we think, we are conscious that a connection between feelings is determined by a general rule, we are aware of being governed by a habit. Intellectual power is nothing but facility in taking habits and in following them in cases essentially analogous to, but in non-essentials widely remote from, the normal cases of connections of feelings under which those habits were formed.

The one primary and fundamental law of mental action consists in a tendency to generalization. Feeling tends to spread; connections between feelings awaken feelings; neighboring feelings become assimilated; ideas are apt to reproduce themselves. These are so many formulations of the one law of the growth of mind. When a disturbance of feeling takes place, we have a consciousness of gain, the gain of experience; and a new disturbance will be apt to assimilate itself to the one that preceded it. Feelings, by being excited, become more easily excited, especially in the ways in which they have previously been excited. The consciousness of such a habit constitutes a general conception.

The cloudiness of psychological notions may be corrected by connecting them with physiological conceptions. Feeling may be supposed to exist, wherever a nerve-cell is in an excited condition. The disturbance of feeling, or sense of reaction, accompanies the transmission of disturbance between nerve-cells or from a nerve-cell to a muscle-cell or the external stimulation of a nerve-cell. General conceptions arise upon the formation of habits in the nerve-matter, which are molecular changes consequent upon its activity and probably connected with its nutrition.

The law of habit exhibits a striking contrast to all physical laws in the character of its commands. A physical law is absolute. What it requires is an exact relation. Thus, a physical force introduces into a motion a component motion to be combined with the rest by the parallelogram of forces; but the component motion must actually take place exactly as required by the law of force. On the other hand, no exact conformity is required by the mental law. Nay, exact conformity would be in downright conflict with the law; since it would instantly crystallize thought and prevent all further formation of habit. The law of mind only makes a given feeling *more likely* to arise. It thus resembles the "non-conservative" forces of physics, such as viscosity and the like, which are due to statistical uniformities in the chance encounters of trillions of molecules.

The old dualistic notion of mind and matter, so prominent in Cartesianism, as two radically different kinds of substance, will hardly find defenders to-day. Rejecting this, we are driven to some form of hylopathy, otherwise called monism. Then the question arises whether physical laws on the one hand, and the psychical law on the other are to be taken —

(*A*) as independent, a doctrine often called *monism*, but which I would name *neutralism;* or,

(*B*) the psychical law as derived and special, the physical law alone as primordial, which is *materialism;* or,

(*C*) the physical law as derived and special, the psychical law alone as primordial, which is *idealism*.

The materialistic doctrine seems to me quite as repugnant to scientific logic as to common sense; since it requires us to suppose that a certain kind of mechanism will feel, which would be a hypothesis absolutely irreducible to reason, — an ultimate, inexplicable regularity; while the only possible justification of any theory is that it should make things clear and reasonable.

Neutralism is sufficiently condemned by the logical maxim known as Ockham's razor, i.e., that not more independent elements are to be supposed than necessary. By placing the inward and outward aspects of substance on a par, it seems to render both primordial.

The one intelligible theory of the universe is that of objective idealism, that matter is effete mind, inveterate habits becoming physical laws. But before this can be accepted it must show itself capable of explaining the tridimensionality of space, the laws of motion, and the general characteristics of the universe, with mathematical clearness and precision; for no less should be demanded of every Philosophy.

Modern mathematics is replete with ideas which may be applied to philosophy. I can only notice one or two. The manner in which mathematicians generalize is very instructive. Thus, painters are accustomed to think of a picture

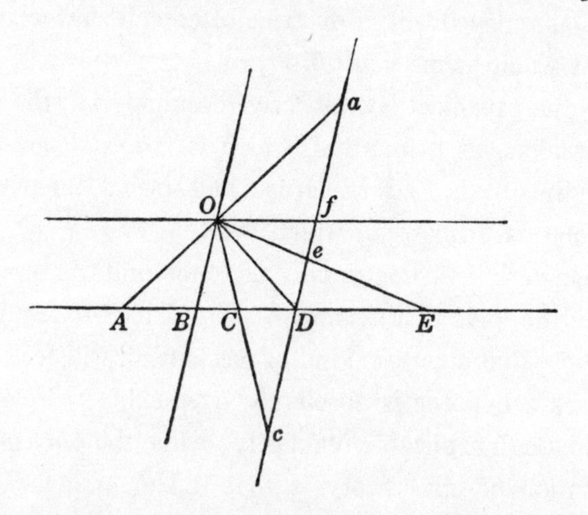

as consisting geometrically of the intersections of its plane by rays of light from the natural objects to the eye. But geometers use a generalized perspective.[4] For instance in the figure let *O* be the eye, let *A B C D E* be the edge-

[4] [The reader will find further light on the following illustration in any text-book of projective geometry, e.g., Reye, *Geometry of Position,* I, pp. 17–24, or *Encyc. Britannica,* XI, p. 689.]

wise view of any plane, and let *a f e D c* be the edgewise view of another plane. The geometers draw rays through *O* cutting both these planes, and treat the points of intersection of each ray with one plane as representing the point of intersection of the same ray with the other plane. Thus, *e* represents *E,* in the painter's way. *D* represents itself. *C* is represented by *c,* which is further from the eye; and *A* is represented by *a* which is on the other side of the eye. Such generalization is not bound down to sensuous images. Further, according to this mode of representation every point on one plane represents a point on the other, and every point on the latter is represented by a point on the former. But how about the point *f* which is in a direction from *O* parallel to the represented plane, and how about the point *B* which is in a direction parallel to the representing plane? Some will say that these are exceptions; but modern mathematics does not allow exceptions which can be annulled by generalization.[5] As a point moves from *C* to *D* and thence to *E* and off toward infinity, the corresponding point on the other plane moves from *c* to *D* and thence to *e* and toward *f.* But this second point can pass through *f* to *a;* and when it is there the first point has arrived at *A.* We therefore say that the first point has passed *through infinity,* and that every line joins in to itself somewhat like an oval. Geometers talk of

[5] [A more familiar example of this is the introduction of irrational or surd numbers like $\sqrt{2}$. After it was proved that no ratio of two integers could possibly equal $\sqrt{2}$ the idea of number was generalized to include the latter. Fractions and the so-called imaginary numbers illustrate the same process of generalization for the sake of making certain operations (i.e. division and finding the root) continuously applicable.

the parts of lines at an infinite distance as points. This is a kind of generalization very efficient in mathematics.

Modern views of measurement have a philosophical aspect. There is an indefinite number of systems of measuring along a line; thus, a perspective representation of a scale on one line may be taken to measure another, although of course such measurements will not agree with what we call the distances of points on the latter line. To establish a system of measurement on a line we must assign a distinct number to each point of it, and for this purpose we shall plainly have to suppose the numbers carried out into an infinite number of places of decimals. These numbers must be ranged along the line in unbroken sequence. Further, in order that such a scale of numbers should be of any use, it must be capable of being shifted into new positions, each number continuing to be attached to a single distinct point. Now it is found that if this is true for "imaginary" as well as for real points (an expression which I cannot stop to elucidate), any such shifting will necessarily leave two numbers attached to the same points as before. So that when the scale is moved over the line by any continuous series of shiftings of one kind, there are two points which no numbers on the scale can ever reach, except the numbers fixed there. This pair of points, thus unattainable in measurement, is called the Absolute. These two points may be distinct and real, or they may coincide, or they may be both imaginary. As an example of a linear quantity with a double absolute we may take probability, which ranges from an unattainable absolute certainty *against* a proposition to an equally unattainable absolute certainty *for* it. A line, according to ordinary notions, we have seen is a linear quantity where the two points at infinity coincide. A velocity is another example. A train going with infinite velocity from Chicago to New York would be at all the points on the line at the very same instant, and if the time of transit were reduced to less than nothing it would be moving in the other direction. An angle is a familiar example of a mode of magnitude with no real immeasurable values. One of the questions philosophy has to consider is whether the development of the universe is like the increase of an angle, so that it proceeds forever without tending toward anything unattained, which I take to be the Epicurean view, or whether the universe sprang from a chaos in the infinitely distant past to tend toward something different in the infinitely distant future, or whether the universe sprang from nothing in the past to go on indefinitely toward a point in the infinitely distant future, which, were it attained, would be the mere nothing from which it set out.

The doctrine of the absolute applied to space comes to this, that either —

First, space is, as Euclid teaches, both *unlimited* and *immeasurable,* so that the infinitely distant parts of any plane seen in perspective appear as a straight line, in which case the sum of the three angles of a triangle amounts to 180°; or,

Second, space is *immeasurable* but *limited,* so that the infinitely distant parts of any plane seen in perspective appear as a circle, beyond which all is blackness, and in this case the sum of the three angles of a triangle is less than 180° by an amount proportional to the area of the triangle; or,

Third, space is *unlimited* but *finite*, (like the surface of a sphere), so that it has no infinitely distant parts; but a finite journey along any straight line would bring one back to his original position, and looking off with an unobstructed view one would see the back of his own head enormously magnified, in which case the sum of the three angles of a triangle exceeds 180° by an amount proportional to the area.

Which of these three hypotheses is true we know not. The largest triangles we can measure are such as have the earth's orbit for base, and the distance of a fixed star for altitude. The angular magnitude resulting from subtracting the sum of the two angles at the base of such a triangle from 180° is called the star's *parallax*. The parallaxes of only about forty stars have been measured as yet. Two of them come out negative, that of Arided (*a* Cycni), a star of magnitude 1½, which is – 0.″082, according to C. A. F. Peters, and that of a star of magnitude 7¾, known as Piazzi III 422, which is – 0.″045, according to R. S. Ball. But these negative parallaxes are undoubtedly to be attributed to errors of observation; for the probable error of such a determination is about ± 0.″075, and it would be strange indeed if we were to be able to see, as it were, more than half way round space, without being able to see stars with larger negative parallaxes. Indeed, the very fact that of all the parallaxes measured only two come out negative would be a strong argument that the smallest parallaxes really amount to + 0.″1, were it not for the reflection that the publication of other negative parallaxes may have been suppressed. I think we may feel confident that the parallax of the furthest star lies somewhere between — 0.″05 and + 0.″15, and within another century our grandchildren will surely know whether the three angles of a triangle are greater or less than 180°, — that they are *exactly* that amount is what nobody ever can be justified in concluding. It is true that according to the axioms of geometry the sum of the three sides of a triangle are precisely 180°; but these axioms are now exploded, and geometers confess that they, as geometers, know not the slightest reason for supposing them to be precisely true. They are expressions of our inborn conception of space, and as such are entitled to credit, so far as their truth could have influenced the formation of the mind. But that affords not the slightest reason for supposing them exact.

Now, metaphysics has always been the ape of mathematics. Geometry suggested the idea of a demonstrative system of absolutely certain philosophical principles; and the ideas of the metaphysicians have at all times been in large part drawn from mathematics. The metaphysical axioms are imitations of the geometrical axioms; and now that the latter have been thrown overboard, without doubt the former will be sent after them. It is evident, for instance, that we can have no reason to think that every phenomenon in all its minutest details is precisely determined by law. That there is an arbitrary element in the universe we see, — namely, its variety. This variety must be attributed to spontaneity in some form.

Had I more space, I now ought to show how important

for philosophy is the mathematical conception of continuity. Most of what is true in Hegel is a darkling glimmer of a conception which the mathematicians had long before made pretty clear, and which recent researches have still further illustrated.

Among the many principles of Logic which find their application in Philosophy, I can here only mention one. Three conceptions are perpetually turning up at every point in every theory of logic, and in the most rounded systems they occur in connection with one another. They are conceptions so very broad and consequently indefinite that they are hard to seize and may be easily overlooked. I call them the conceptions of First, Second, Third. First is the conception of being or existing independent of anything else. Second is the conception of being relative to, the conception of reaction with, something else. Third is the conception of mediation, whereby a first and second are brought into relation. To illustrate these ideas, I will show how they enter into those we have been considering. The origin of things, considered not as leading to anything, but in itself, contains the idea of First, the end of things that of Second, the process mediating between them that of Third. A philosophy which emphasizes the idea of the One, is generally a dualistic philosophy in which the conception of Second receives exaggerated attention; for this One (though of course involving the idea of First) is always the other of a manifold which is not one. The idea of the Many, because variety is arbitrariness and arbitrariness is repudiation of any Secondness, has for its principal component the conception of First. In psychology Feeling is

First, Sense of reaction Second, General conception Third, or mediation. In biology, the idea of arbitrary sporting is First, heredity is Second, the process whereby the accidental characters become fixed is Third. Chance is First, Law is Second, the tendency to take habits is Third. Mind is First, Matter is Second, Evolution is Third.

Such are the materials out of which chiefly a philosophical theory ought to be built, in order to represent the state of knowledge to which the nineteenth century has brought us. Without going into other important questions of philosophical architectonic, we can readily foresee what sort of a metaphysics would appropriately be constructed from those conceptions. Like some of the most ancient and some of the most recent speculations it would be a Cosmogonic Philosophy. It would suppose that in the beginning, — infinitely remote, — there was a chaos of unpersonalized feeling, which being without connection or regularity would properly be without existence. This feeling, sporting here and there in pure arbitrariness, would have started the germ of a generalizing tendency. Its other sportings would be evanescent, but this would have a growing virtue. Thus, the tendency to habit would be started; and from this with the other principles of evolution all the regularities of the universe would be evolved. At any time, however, an element of pure chance survives and will remain until the world becomes an absolutely perfect, rational, and symmetrical system, in which mind is at last crystallized in the infinitely distant future.

That idea has been worked out by me with elaboration. It accounts for the main features of the universe as we know it, — the characters of time, space, matter, force, gravitation, electricity, etc. It predicts many more things which new observations can alone bring to the test. May some future student go over this ground again, and have the leisure to give his results to the world.

II. THE DOCTRINE OF NECESSITY EXAMINED[1]

IN *The Monist* for January, 1891, I endeavored to show what elementary ideas ought to enter into our view of the universe. I may mention that on those considerations I had already grounded a cosmical theory, and from it had deduced a considerable number of consequences capable of being compared with experience. This comparison is now in progress, but under existing circumstances must occupy many years.

I propose here to examine the common belief that every single fact in the universe is precisely determined by law. It must not be supposed that this is a doctrine accepted everywhere and at all times by all rational men. Its first advocate appears to have been Democritus, the atomist, who was led to it, as we are informed, by reflecting upon the "impenetrability, translation, and impact of matter (ἀντιτυπία καὶ φορὰ καὶ πληγὴ τῆς ὕλης)." That is to say, having restricted his attention to a field where no influence other than mechanical constraint could possibly come before his notice, he straightway jumped to the conclusion that throughout the universe that was the sole principle of action, — a style of reasoning so usual in our day with men not unreflecting as to be more than excusable in the infancy of thought. But Epicurus, in revising the atomic doctrine and repairing its defences, found himself obliged

[1] *The Monist*, April, 1892.

to suppose that atoms swerve from their courses by spontaneous chance; and thereby he conferred upon the theory life and entelechy. For we now see clearly that the peculiar function of the molecular hypothesis in physics is to open an entry for the calculus of probabilities. Already, the prince of philosophers had repeatedly and emphatically condemned the dictum of Democritus (especially in the "Physics," Book II, chapters iv, v, vi), holding that events come to pass in three ways, namely, (1) by external compulsion, or the action of efficient causes, (2) by virtue of an inward nature, or the influence of final causes, and (3) irregularly without definite cause, but just by absolute chance; and this doctrine is of the inmost essence of Aristotelianism. It affords, at any rate, a valuable enumeration of the possible ways in which anything can be supposed to have come about. The freedom of the will, too, was admitted both by Aristotle and by Epicurus. But the Stoa, which in every department seized upon the most tangible, hard, and lifeless element, and blindly denied the existence of every other, which, for example, impugned the validity of the inductive method and wished to fill its place with the *reductio ad absurdum*, very naturally became the one school of ancient philosophy to stand by a strict necessitarianism, thus returning to a single principle of Democritus that Epicurus had been unable to swallow. Necessitarianism and materialism with the Stoics went hand in hand, as by affinity they should. At the revival of learning, Stoicism met with considerable favor, partly because it departed just enough from Aristotle to give it the spice of novelty, and partly because its superficialities well adapted it for acceptance by students of literature and art who wanted their philosophy drawn mild. Afterwards, the great discoveries in mechanics inspired the hope that mechanical principles might suffice to explain the universe; and though without logical justification, this hope has since been continually stimulated by subsequent advances in physics. Nevertheless, the doctrine was in too evident conflict with the freedom of the will and with miracles to be generally acceptable, at first. But meantime there arose that most widely spread of philosophical blunders, the notion that associationalism belongs intrinsically to the materialistic family of doctrines; and thus was evolved the theory of motives; and libertarianism became weakened. At present, historical criticism has almost exploded the miracles, great and small; so that the doctrine of necessity has never been in so great vogue as now.

The proposition in question is that the state of things existing at any time, together with certain immutable laws, completely determine the state of things at every other time (for a limitation to *future* time is indefensible). Thus, given the state of the universe in the original nebula, and given the laws of mechanics, a sufficiently powerful mind could deduce from these data the precise form of every curlicue of every letter I am now writing.

Whoever holds that every act of the will as well as every idea of the mind is under the rigid governance of a necessity co-ordinated with that of the physical world, will logically be carried to the proposition that minds are part of the physical world in such a sense that the laws of mechanics determine everything that happens according to immutable attractions and repulsions. In that case, that instantaneous state of things from which every other state of things is calculable consists in the positions and velocities of all the particles at any instant. This, the usual and most logical form of necessitarianism, is called the mechanical philosophy.

When I have asked thinking men what reason they had to believe that every fact in the universe is precisely determined by law, the first answer has usually been that the proposition is a "presupposition" or postulate of scientific reasoning. Well, if that is the best that can be said for it, the belief is doomed. Suppose it be "postulated": that does not make it true, nor so much as afford the slightest rational motive for yielding it any credence. It is as if a man should come to borrow money, and when asked for his security, should reply he "postulated" the loan. To "postulate" a proposition is no more than to hope it is true. There are, indeed, practical emergencies in which we act upon assumptions of certain propositions as true, because if they are not so, it can make no difference how we act. But all such propositions I take to be hypotheses of individual facts. For it is manifest that no universal principle can in its universality be comprised in a special case or can be requisite for the validity of any ordinary inference. To say, for instance, that the demonstration by Archimedes of the property of the lever would fall to the ground if men were endowed with free-will, is extravagant; yet this is implied by those who make a proposition incompatible with the freedom of the will the postulate of all inference. Considering, too, that the conclusions of science make no pretence to being more than probable, and considering that a probable inference can at most only suppose something to be most frequently, or otherwise approximately, true, but never that anything is precisely true without exception throughout the universe, we see how far this proposition in truth is from being so postulated.

But the whole notion of a postulate being involved in reasoning appertains to a by-gone and false conception of logic. Non-deductive, or ampliative inference, is of three kinds: induction, hypothesis, and analogy. If there be any other modes, they must be extremely unusual and highly complicated, and may be assumed with little doubt to be of the same nature as those enumerated. For induction, hypothesis, and analogy, as far as their ampliative character goes, that is, so far as they conclude something not implied in the premises, depend upon one principle and involve the same procedure. All are essentially inferences from sampling. Suppose a ship arrives at Liverpool laden with wheat in bulk. Suppose that by some machinery the whole cargo be stirred up with great thoroughness. Suppose that twenty-seven thimblefuls be taken equally from the forward, midships, and aft parts, from the starboard, center, and larboard parts, and from the top, half depth, and lower parts of her hold, and that these being mixed and the grains counted, four-fifths of the latter are found to be of quality *A*. Then we infer, experientially and provisionally, that approximately four-fifths of all the grain in the cargo is of the same quality. I say we infer this *experientially* and *provisionally*. By saying that we infer it *experientially*, I mean that our conclusion makes no pretension to knowledge of wheat-in-itself, our ἀλήθεια, as the derivation of that word implies, has nothing to do with *latent* wheat. We are dealing only with the matter of possible experience, — experience in the full acceptation of the term as something not merely affecting the senses but also as the subject of thought. If there be any wheat hidden on the ship, so that it can neither turn up in the sample nor be heard of subsequently from purchasers, — or if it be half-hidden, so that it may, indeed, turn up, but is less likely to do so than the rest, — or if it can affect our senses and our pockets, but from some strange cause or causelessness cannot be reasoned about, — all such wheat is to be excluded (or have only its proportional weight) in calculating that true proportion of quality *A*, to which our inference seeks to approximate. By saying that we draw the inference *provisionally*, I mean that we do not hold that we have reached any assigned degree of approximation as yet, but only hold that if our experience be indefinitely extended, and if every fact of whatever nature, as fast as it presents itself, be duly applied, according to the inductive method, in correcting the inferred ratio, then our approximation will become indefinitely close in the long run; that is to say, close to the experience *to come* (not merely close by the exhaustion of a finite collection) so that if experience in general is to fluctuate irregularly to and fro, in a manner to deprive the ratio sought of all definite value, we shall be able to find out approximately within what limits it fluctuates, and if, after having one definite value, it changes and assumes another, we shall be able to find that out, and in short, whatever may be the variations of this ratio in experience, experience indefinitely extended will enable us to detect them, so as to predict rightly, at last, what its ultimate value may be, if it have any ultimate value, or what the ultimate law of succession of values may be, if there be any such ultimate law, or that it ultimately fluctuates irregularly within certain limits, if it do so ultimately fluctuate. Now our inference, claiming to be no more than thus experiential and provisional, manifestly involves no postulate whatever.

For what is a postulate? It is the formulation of a material fact which we are not entitled to assume as a premise, but the truth of which is requisite to the validity of an inference. Any fact, then, which might be supposed postulated, must either be such that it would ultimately present itself in experience, or not. If it will present itself, we need not postulate it now in our provisional inference, since we shall ultimately be entitled to use it as a premise. But if it never would present itself in experience, our conclusion is valid but for the possibility of this fact being otherwise than assumed, that is, it is valid as far as possible experience goes, and that is all that we claim. Thus, every postulate is cut off, either by the provisionality or by the experientiality of our inference. For instance, it has been said that induction postulates that, if an indefinite succession of samples be drawn, examined, and thrown back each before the next is drawn, then in the long run every grain will be drawn as often as any other, that is to say, postulates that the ratio of the numbers of times in which any two are drawn will indefinitely approximate to unity. But no such postulate is made; for if, on the one hand, we are to have no other experience of the wheat than from such drawings, it is the ratio that presents itself in those drawings and not the ratio which belongs to the wheat in its latent existence that we are endeavoring to determine; while if, on the other hand, there is some other mode by which the wheat is to come under our knowledge, equivalent to another kind of sampling, so that after all our care in stirring up the wheat, some experiential grains will present themselves in the first sampling operation more often than others in the long run, this very singular fact will be sure to get discovered by the inductive method, which must avail itself of every sort of experience; and our inference, which was only provisional, corrects itself at last. Again, it has been said, that induction postulates that under like circumstances like events will happen, and that this postulate is at bottom the same as the principle of universal causation. But this is a blunder, or *bevue*, due to thinking exclusively of inductions where the concluded ratio is either 1 or 0. If any such proposition were postulated, it would be that under like circumstances (the circumstances of drawing the different samples) different events occur in the same proportions in all the different sets, — a proposition which is false and even absurd. But in truth no such thing is postulated, the experiential character of the inference reducing the condition of validity to this, that if a certain result does not occur, the opposite result will be manifested, a condition assured by the provisionality of the inference. But it may be asked whether it is not conceivable that every instance of a certain class destined to be ever employed as a datum of induction should have one character, while every instance destined not to be so employed should have the opposite character. The answer is that in that case, the instances excluded from being subjects of reasoning would not be experienced in the full sense of the word, but would be among these *latent* individuals of which our conclusion does not pretend to speak.

To this account of the rationale of induction I know of but one objection worth mention: it is that I thus fail to deduce the full degree of force which this mode of inference in fact possesses; that according to my view, no matter how thorough and elaborate the stirring and mixing process had been, the examination of a single handful of grain would not give me any assurance, sufficient to risk money upon that the next handful would not greatly modify the concluded value of the ratio under inquiry, while, in fact, the assurance would be very high that this ratio was not greatly in error. If the true ratio of grains of quality *A* were 0.80 and the handful contained a thousand grains, nine such handfuls out of every ten would contain from 780 to 820 grains of quality *A*. The answer to this is that the calculation given is correct when we know that the units of this handful and the quality inquired into have the normal independence of one another, if for instance the stirring has been complete and the character sampled for has been settled upon in advance of the examination of the sample. But in so far as these conditions are not known to be complied with, the above figures cease to be applicable. Random sampling and predesignation of the character sampled for should always be striven after in inductive reasoning, but when they cannot be attained, so long as it is conducted honestly, the inference retains some value. When we cannot ascertain how the sampling has been done or the sample-character selected, induction still has the essential validity which my present account of it shows it to have.

I do not think a man who combines a willingness to be convinced with a power of appreciating an argument upon a difficult subject can resist the reasons which have been given to show that the principle of universal necessity cannot be defended as being a postulate of reasoning. But then the question immediately arises whether it is not proved to be true, or at least rendered highly probable, by observation of nature.

Still, this question ought not long to arrest a person accustomed to reflect upon the force of scientific reasoning. For the essence of the necessitarian position is that certain continuous quantities have certain exact values. Now, how can observation determine the value of such a quantity with a probable error absolutely *nil?* To one who is behind the scenes, and knows that the most refined comparisons of masses, lengths, and angles, far surpassing in precision all other measurements, yet fall behind the accuracy of bank-accounts, and that the ordinary determinations of physical constants, such as appear from month to month in the journals, are about on a par with an upholsterer's measurements of carpets and curtains, the idea of mathematical exactitude being demonstrated in the laboratory will appear simply ridiculous. There is a recognized method of estimating the probable magnitudes of errors in physics, — the method of least squares. It is universally admitted that this method makes the errors smaller than they really are;

yet even according to that theory an error indefinitely small is indefinitely improbable; so that any statement to the effect that a certain continuous quantity has a certain exact value, if well-founded at all, must be founded on something other than observation.

Still, I am obliged to admit that this rule is subject to a certain qualification. Namely, it only applies to continuous [2] quantity. Now, certain kinds of continuous quantity are discontinuous at one or at two limits, and for such limits the rule must be modified. Thus, the length of a line cannot be less than zero. Suppose, then, the question arises how long a line a certain person had drawn from a marked point on a piece of paper. If no line at all can be seen, the observed length is zero; and the only conclusion this observation warrants is that the length of the line is less than the smallest length visible with the optical power employed. But indirect observations, — for example, that the person supposed to have drawn the line was never within fifty feet of the paper, — may make it probable that no line at all was made, so that the concluded length will be strictly zero. In like manner, experience no doubt would warrant the conclusion that there is absolutely *no* indigo in a given ear of wheat, and absolutely *no* attar in a given lichen. But such inferences can only be rendered valid by positive experiential evidence, direct or remote, and cannot rest upon a mere inability to detect the quantity in question. We have reason to think there is no indigo in the wheat, because we have remarked that wherever indigo is pro-

[2] *Continuous* is not exactly the right word, but I let it go to avoid a long and irrelevant discussion.

duced it is produced in considerable quantities, to mention only one argument. We have reason to think there is no attar in the lichen, because essential oils seem to be in general peculiar to single species. If the question had been whether there was iron in the wheat or the lichen, though chemical analysis should fail to detect its presence, we should think some of it probably was there, since iron is almost everywhere. Without any such information, one way or the other, we could only abstain from any opinion as to the presence of the substance in question. It cannot, I conceive, be maintained that we are in any *better* position than this in regard to the presence of the element of chance or spontaneous departures from law in nature.

Those observations which are generally adduced in favor of mechanical causation simply prove that there is an element of regularity in nature, and have no bearing whatever upon the question of whether such regularity is exact and universal, or not. Nay, in regard to this *exactitude,* all observation is directly *opposed* to it; and the most that can be said is that a good deal of this observation can be explained away. Try to verify any law of nature, and you will find that the more precise your observations, the more certain they will be to show irregular departures from the law. We are accustomed to ascribe these, and I do not say wrongly, to errors of observation; yet we cannot usually account for such errors in any antecedently probable way. Trace their causes back far enough, and you will be forced to admit they are always due to arbitrary determination, or chance.

But it may be asked whether if there were an element

of real chance in the universe it must not occasionally be productive of signal effects such as could not pass unobserved. In answer to this question, without stopping to point out that there is an abundance of great events which one might be tempted to suppose were of that nature, it will be simplest to remark that physicists hold that the particles of gases are moving about irregularly, substantially as if by real chance, and that by the principles of probabilities there must occasionally happen to be concentrations of heat in the gases contrary to the second law of thermodynamics, and these concentrations, occurring in explosive mixtures, must sometimes have tremendous effects. Here, then, is in substance the very situation supposed; yet no phenomena ever have resulted which we are forced to attribute to such chance concentration of heat, or which anybody, wise or foolish, has ever dreamed of accounting for in that manner.

In view of all these considerations, I do not believe that anybody, not in a state of case-hardened ignorance respecting the logic of science, can maintain that the precise and universal conformity of facts to law is clearly proved, or even rendered particularly probable, by any observations hitherto made. In this way, the determined advocate of exact regularity will soon find himself driven to *a priori* reasons to support his thesis. These received such a socdolager from Stuart Mill in his Examination of Hamilton, that holding to them now seems to me to denote a high degree of imperviousness to reason; so that I shall pass them by with little notice.

To say that we cannot help believing a given proposition is no argument, but it is a conclusive fact if it be true; and with the substitution of "I" for "we," it is true in the mouths of several classes of minds, the blindly passionate, the unreflecting and ignorant, and the person who has overwhelming evidence before his eyes. But that which has been inconceivable to-day has often turned out indisputable on the morrow. Inability to conceive is only a stage through which every man must pass in regard to a number of beliefs, — unless endowed with extraordinary obstinacy and obtuseness. His understanding is enslaved to some blind compulsion which a vigorous mind is pretty sure soon to cast off.

Some seek to back up the *a priori* position with empirical arguments. They say that the exact regularity of the world is a natural belief, and that natural beliefs have generally been confirmed by experience. There is some reason in this. Natural beliefs, however, if they generally have a foundation of truth, also require correction and purification from natural illusions. The principles of mechanics are undoubtedly natural beliefs; but, for all that, the early formulations of them were exceedingly erroneous. The general approximation to truth in natural beliefs is, in fact, a case of the general adaptation of genetic products to recognizable utilities or ends. Now, the adaptations of nature, beautiful and often marvelous as they verily are, are never found to be quite perfect; so that the argument is quite *against* the absolute exactitude of any natural belief, including that of the principle of causation.

Another argument, or convenient commonplace, is that absolute chance is *inconceivable*. (This word has eight current significations. The *Century Dictionary* enumerates six.) Those who talk like this will hardly be persuaded to say in what sense they mean that chance is inconceivable. Should they do so, it would easily be shown either that they have no sufficient reason for the statement or that the inconceivability is of a kind which does not prove that chance is non-existent.

Another *a priori* argument is that chance is unintelligible; that is to say, while it may perhaps be conceivable, it does not disclose to the eye of reason the how or why of things; and since a hypothesis can only be justified so far as it renders some phenomenon intelligible, we never can have any right to suppose absolute chance to enter into the production of anything in nature. This argument may be considered in connection with two others. Namely, instead of going so far as to say that the supposition of chance can *never* properly be used to explain any observed fact, it may be alleged merely that no facts are known which such a supposition could in any way help in explaining. Or again, the allegation being still further weakened, it may be said that since departures from law are not unmistakably observed, chance is not a *vera causa,* and ought not unnecessarily to be introduced into a hypothesis.

These are no mean arguments, and require us to examine the matter a little more closely. Come, my superior opponent, let me learn from your wisdom. It seems to me that every throw of sixes with a pair of dice is a manifest instance of chance.

"While you would hold a throw of deuce-ace to be brought about by necessity?" (The opponent's supposed remarks are placed in quotation marks.)

Clearly one throw is as much chance as another.

"Do you think throws of dice are of a different nature from other events?"

I see that I must say that *all* the diversity and specificalness of events is attributable to chance.

"Would you, then, deny that there is any regularity in the world?"

That is clearly undeniable. I must acknowledge there is an approximate regularity, and that every event is influenced by it. But the diversification, specificalness, and irregularity of things I suppose is chance. A throw of sixes appears to me a case in which this element is particularly obtrusive.

"If you reflect more deeply, you will come to see that *chance* is only a name for a cause that is unknown to us."

Do you mean that we have no idea whatever what kind of causes could bring about a throw of sixes?

"On the contrary, each die moves under the influence of precise mechanical laws."

But it appears to me that it is not these *laws* which made the die turn up sixes; for these laws act just the same when other throws come up. The chance lies in the diversity of throws; and this diversity cannot be due to laws which are immutable.

"The diversity is due to the diverse circumstances under which the laws act. The dice lie differently in the box, and the motion given to the box is different. These are the unknown causes which produce the throws, and to which we give the name of chance; not the mechanical law which regulates the operation of these causes. You see you are already beginning to think more clearly about this subject."

Does the operation of mechanical law not increase the diversity?

"Properly not. You must know that the instantaneous state of a system of particles is defined by six times as many numbers as there are particles, three for the co-ordinates of each particle's position, and three more for the components of its velocity. This number of numbers, which expresses the amount of diversity in the system, remains the same at all times. There may be, to be sure, some kind of relation between the co-ordinates and component velocities of the different particles, by means of which the state of the system might be expressed by a smaller number of numbers. But, if this is the case, a precisely corresponding relationship must exist between the co-ordinates and component velocities at any other time, though it may doubtless be a relation less obvious to us. Thus, the intrinsic complexity of the system is the same at all times."

Very well, my obliging opponent, we have now reached an issue. You think all the arbitrary specifications of the universe were introduced in one dose, in the beginning, if there was a beginning, and that the variety and complication of nature has always been just as much as it is now. But I, for my part, think that the diversification, the specification, has been continually taking place. Should you condescend to ask me why I so think, I should give my reasons as follows:

(1) Question any science which deals with the course of time. Consider the life of an individual animal or plant, or of a mind. Glance at the history of states, of institutions, of language, of ideas. Examine the successions of

forms shown by paleontology, the history of the globe as set forth in geology, of what the astronomer is able to make out concerning the changes of stellar systems. Everywhere the main fact is growth and increasing complexity. Death and corruption are mere accidents or secondary phenomena. Among some of the lower organisms, it is a moot point with biologists whether there be anything which ought to be called death. Races, at any rate, do not die out except under unfavorable circumstances. From these broad and ubiquitous facts we may fairly infer, by the most unexceptionable logic, that there is probably in nature some agency by which the complexity and diversity of things can be increased; and that consequently the rule of mechanical necessity meets in some way with interference.

(2) By thus admitting pure spontaneity or life as a character of the universe, acting always and everywhere though restrained within narrow bounds by law, producing infinitesimal departures from law continually, and great ones with infinite infrequency, I account for all the variety and diversity of the universe, in the only sense in which the really *sui generis* and new can be said to be accounted for. The ordinary view has to admit the inexhaustible multitudinous variety of the world, has to admit that its mechanical law cannot account for this in the least, that variety can spring only from spontaneity, and yet denies without any evidence or reason the existence of this spontaneity, or else shoves it back to the beginning of time and supposes it dead ever since. The superior logic of my view appears to me not easily controverted.

(3) When I ask the necessitarian how he would explain the diversity and irregularity of the universe, he replies to me out of the treasury of his wisdom that irregularity is something which from the nature of things we must not seek to explain. Abashed at this, I seek to cover my confusion by asking how he would explain the uniformity and regularity of the universe, whereupon he tells me that the laws of nature are immutable and ultimate facts, and no account is to be given of them. But my hypothesis of spontaneity does explain irregularity, in a certain sense; that is, it explains the general fact of irregularity, though not, of course, what each lawless event is to be. At the same time, by thus loosening the bond of necessity, it gives room for the influence of another kind of causation, such as seems to be operative in the mind in the formation of associations, and enables us to understand how the uniformity of nature could have been brought about. That single events should be hard and unintelligible, logic will permit without difficulty: we do not expect to make the shock of a personally experienced earthquake appear natural and reasonable by any amount of cogitation. But logic does expect things *general* to be understandable. To say that there is a universal law, and that it is a hard, ultimate, unintelligible fact, the why and wherefore of which can never be inquired into, at this a sound logic will revolt; and will pass over at once to a method of philosophizing which does not thus barricade the road of discovery.

(4) Necessitarianism cannot logically stop short of making the whole action of the mind a part of the physical universe. Our notion that we decide what we are going to

do, if as the necessitarian says, it has been calculable since the earliest times, is reduced to illusion. Indeed, consciousness in general thus becomes a mere illusory aspect of a material system. What we call red, green, and violet are in reality only different rates of vibration. The sole reality is the distribution of qualities of matter in space and time. Brain-matter is protoplasm in a certain degree and kind of complication, — a certain arrangement of mechanical particles. Its feeling is but an inward aspect, a phantom. For, from the positions and velocities of the particles at any one instant, and the knowledge of the immutable forces, the positions at all other times are calculable; so that the universe of space, time, and matter is a rounded system uninterfered with from elsewhere. But from the state of feeling at any instant, there is no reason to suppose the states of feeling at all other instants are thus exactly calculable; so that feeling is, as I said, a mere fragmentary and illusive aspect of the universe. This is the way, then, that necessitarianism has to make up its accounts. It enters consciousness under the head of sundries, as a forgotten trifle; its scheme of the universe would be more satisfactory if this little fact could be dropped out of sight. On the other hand, by supposing the rigid exactitude of causation to yield, I care not how little, — be it but by a strictly infinitesimal amount, — we gain room to insert mind into our scheme, and to put it into the place where it is needed, into the position which, as the sole self-intelligible thing, it is entitled to occupy, that of the fountain of existence; and in so doing we resolve the problem of the connection of soul and body.

(5) But I must leave undeveloped the chief of my reasons, and can only adumbrate it. The hypothesis of chance-spontaneity is one whose inevitable consequences are capable of being traced out with mathematical precision into considerable detail. Much of this I have done and find the consequences to agree with observed facts to an extent which seems to me remarkable. But the matter and methods of reasoning are novel, and I have no right to promise that other mathematicians shall find my deductions as satisfactory as I myself do, so that the strongest reason for my belief must for the present remain a private reason of my own, and cannot influence others. I mention it to explain my own position; and partly to indicate to future mathematical speculators a veritable goldmine, should time and circumstances and the abridger of all joys prevent my opening it to the world.

If now I, in my turn, inquire of the necessitarian why he prefers to suppose that all specification goes back to the beginning of things, he will answer me with one of those last three arguments which I left unanswered.

First, he may say that chance is a thing absolutely unintelligible, and, therefore, that we never can be entitled to make such a supposition. But does not this objection smack of naïve impudence? It is not mine, it is his own conception of the universe which leads abruptly up to hard, ultimate, inexplicable, immutable law, on the one hand, and to inexplicable specification and diversification of circumstances on the other. My view, on the contrary, hypothetises nothing at all, unless it be hypothesis to say that all specification came about in some sense, and is not to be accepted as unaccountable. To undertake to account for anything by saying boldly that it is due to chance would, indeed, be futile. But this I do not do. I make use of chance chiefly to make room for a principle of generalization, or tendency to form habits, which I hold has produced all regularities. The mechanical philosopher leaves the whole specification of the world utterly unaccounted for, which is pretty nearly as bad as to boldly attribute it to chance. I attribute it altogether to chance, it is true, but to chance in the form of a spontaneity which is to some degree regular. It seems to me clear at any rate that one of these two positions must be taken, or else specification must be supposed due to a spontaneity which develops itself in a certain and not in a chance way, by an objective logic like that of Hegel. This last way I leave as an open possibility, for the present; for it is as much opposed to the necessitarian scheme of existence as my own theory is.

Secondly, the necessitarian may say there are, at any rate, no observed phenomena which the hypothesis of chance could aid in explaining. In reply, I point first to the phenomenon of growth and developing complexity, which appears to be universal, and which though it may possibly be an affair of mechanism perhaps, certainly presents all the appearance of increasing diversification. Then, there is variety itself, beyond comparison the most obtrusive character of the universe: no mechanism can account for this. Then, there is the very fact the necessitarian most insists upon, the regularity of the universe which for him serves only to block the road of inquiry. Then, there are the regular relationships between the laws of nature, — similarities and comparative characters, which appeal to our intelligence as its cousins, and call upon us for a reason. Finally, there is consciousness, feeling, a patent fact enough, but a very inconvenient one to the mechanical philosopher.

Thirdly, the necessitarian may say that chance is not a *vera causa,* that we cannot know positively there is any such element in the universe. But the doctrine of the *vera causa* has nothing to do with elementary conceptions. Pushed to that extreme, it at once cuts off belief in the existence of a material universe; and without that necessitarianism could hardly maintain its ground. Besides, variety is a fact which must be admitted; and the theory of chance merely consists in supposing this diversification does not antedate all time. Moreover, the avoidance of hypotheses involving causes nowhere positively known to act — is only a recommendation of logic, not a positive command. It cannot be formulated in any precise terms without at once betraying its untenable character, — I mean as rigid rule, for as a recommendation it is wholesome enough.

I believe I have thus subjected to fair examination all the important reasons for adhering to the theory of universal necessity, and have shown their nullity. I earnestly beg that whoever may detect any flaw in my reasoning will point it out to me, either privately or publicly; for if I am wrong, it much concerns me to be set right speedily. If my argument remains unrefuted, it will be time, I think, to doubt the absolute truth of the principle of universal law; and when once such a doubt has obtained a living root in any man's mind, my cause with him, I am persuaded, is gained.

III. THE LAW OF MIND[1]

IN an article published in *The Monist* for January, 1891, I endeavored to show what ideas ought to form the warp of a system of philosophy, and particularly emphasized that of absolute chance. In the number of April, 1892, I argued further in favor of that way of thinking, which it will be convenient to christen *tychism* (from τύχη, chance). A serious student of philosophy will be in no haste to accept or reject this doctrine; but he will see in it one of the chief attitudes which speculative thought may take, feeling that it is not for an individual, nor for an age, to pronounce upon a fundamental question of philosophy. That is a task for a whole era to work out. I have begun by showing that *tychism* must give birth to an evolutionary cosmology, in which all the regularities of nature and of mind are regarded as products of growth, and to a Schelling-fashioned idealism which holds matter to be mere specialized and partially deadened mind. I may mention, for the benefit of those who are curious in studying mental biographies, that I was born and reared in the neighborhood of Concord, — I mean in Cambridge, — at the time when Emerson, Hedge, and their friends were disseminating the ideas that they had caught from Schelling, and Schelling from Plotinus, from Boehm, or from God knows what minds stricken with the monstrous mysticism of the East. But the atmosphere

[1] *The Monist*, July, 1892.

of Cambridge held many an antiseptic against Concord transcendentalism; and I am not conscious of having contracted any of that virus. Nevertheless, it is probable that some cultured bacilli, some benignant form of the disease was implanted in my soul, unawares, and that now, after long incubation, it comes to the surface, modified by mathematical conceptions and by training in physical investigations.

The next step in the study of cosmology must be to examine the general law of mental action. In doing this, I shall for the time drop my tychism out of view, in order to allow a free and independent expansion to another conception signalized in my first *Monist* paper as one of the most indispensable to philosophy, though it was not there dwelt upon; I mean the idea of continuity. The tendency to regard continuity, in the sense in which I shall define it, as an idea of prime importance in philosophy may conveniently be termed *synechism*. The present paper is intended chiefly to show what synechism is, and what it leads to. I attempted, a good many years ago, to develop this doctrine in the *Journal of Speculative Philosophy* (Vol. II.); but I am able now to improve upon that exposition, in which I was a little blinded by nominalistic prepossessions. I refer to it, because students may possibly find that some points not sufficiently explained in the present paper are cleared up in those earlier ones.

WHAT THE LAW IS

Logical analysis applied to mental phenomena shows that there is but one law of mind, namely, that ideas tend to spread continuously and to affect certain others which stand to them in a peculiar relation of affectibility. In this spreading they lose intensity, and especially the power of affecting others, but gain generality and become welded with other ideas.

I set down this formula at the beginning, for convenience; and now proceed to comment upon it.

INDIVIDUALITY OF IDEAS

We are accustomed to speak of ideas as reproduced, as passed from mind to mind, as similar or dissimilar to one another, and, in short, as if they were substantial things; nor can any reasonable objection be raised to such expressions. But taking the word "idea" in the sense of an event in an individual consciousness, it is clear that an idea once past is gone forever, and any supposed recurrence of it is another idea. These two ideas are not present in the same state of consciousness, and therefore cannot possibly be compared. To say, therefore, that they are similar can only mean that an occult power from the depths of the soul forces us to connect them in our thoughts after they are both no more. We may note, here, in passing, that of the two generally recognized principles of association, contiguity and similarity, the former is a connection due to a power without, the latter a connection due to a power within.

But what can it mean to say that ideas wholly past are thought of at all, any longer? They are utterly unknowable. What distinct meaning can attach to saying that an idea in the past in any way affects an idea in the future, from which it is completely detached? A phrase between the assertion and the denial of which there can in no case be any sensible difference is mere gibberish.

I will not dwell further upon this point, because it is a commonplace of philosophy.

CONTINUITY OF IDEAS

We have here before us a question of difficulty, analogous to the question of nominalism and realism. But when once it has been clearly formulated, logic leaves room for one answer only. How can a past idea be present? Can it be present vicariously? To a certain extent, perhaps; but not merely so; for then the question would arise how the past idea can be related to its vicarious representation. The relation, being between ideas, can only exist in some consciousness: now that past idea was in no consciousness but that past consciousness that alone contained it; and that did not embrace the vicarious idea.

Some minds will here jump to the conclusion that a past idea cannot in any sense be present. But that is hasty and illogical. How extravagant, too, to pronounce our whole knowledge of the past to be mere delusion! Yet it would seem that the past is as completely beyond the bounds of possible experience as a Kantian thing-in-itself.

How can a past idea be present? Not vicariously. Then, only by direct perception. In other words, to be present, it must be *ipso facto* present. That is, it cannot be wholly past; it can only be going, infinitesimally past, less past than any assignable past date. We are thus brought to the conclusion that the present is connected with the past by a series of real infinitesimal steps.

It has already been suggested by psychologists that consciousness necessarily embraces an interval of time. But if a finite time be meant, the opinion is not tenable. If the sensation that precedes the present by half a second were still immediately before me, then, on the same principle the sensation preceding that would be immediately present, and so on *ad infinitum*. Now, since there is a time, say a year, at the end of which an idea is no longer *ipso facto* present, it follows that this is true of any finite interval, however short.

But yet consciousness must essentially cover an interval of time; for if it did not, we could gain no knowledge of time, and not merely no veracious cognition of it, but no conception whatever. We are, therefore, forced to say that we are immediately conscious through an infinitesimal interval of time.

This is all that is requisite. For, in this infinitesimal interval, not only is consciousness continuous in a subjective sense, that is, considered as a subject or substance having the attribute of duration; but also, because it is immediate consciousness, its object is *ipso facto* continuous. In fact, this infinitesimally spread-out consciousness is a direct feeling of its contents as spread out. This will be further elucidated below. In an infinitesimal interval we directly perceive the temporal sequence of its beginning, middle, and end, — not, of course, in the way of recognition, for recognition is only of the past, but in the way of immediate feeling. Now upon this interval follows another, whose beginning is the middle of the former, and whose middle is the end of the former. Here, we have an immediate perception of the temporal sequence of its beginning, middle, and end, or say of the second, third, and fourth instants. From these two immediate perceptions, we gain a mediate, or inferential, perception of the relation of all four instants. This mediate perception is objectively, or as to the object represented, spread over the four instants; but subjectively, or as itself the subject of duration, it is completely embraced in the second moment. (The reader will observe that I use the word *instant* to mean a point of time, and *moment* to mean an infinitesimal duration.) If it is objected that, upon the theory proposed, we must have more than a mediate perception of the succession of the four instants, I grant it; for the sum of the two infinitesimal intervals is itself infinitesimal, so that it is immediately perceived. It is immediately perceived in the whole interval, but only mediately perceived in the last two-thirds of the interval. Now, let there be an indefinite succession of these inferential acts of comparative perception; and it is plain that the last moment will contain objectively the whole series. Let there be, not merely an indefinite succession, but a continuous flow of inference through a finite time; and the result will be a mediate objective consciousness of the whole time in the last moment. In this last moment, the whole series will be recognized, or known as known before, except only the last moment, which of course will be absolutely unrecognizable to itself. Indeed, even this last moment will be recognized like the rest, or, at least, be just beginning to be so. There is a little *elenchus*, or appearance of contradiction, here, which the ordinary logic of reflection quite suffices to resolve.

INFINITY AND CONTINUITY, IN GENERAL

Most of the mathematicians who during the last two generations have treated the differential calculus have been of the opinion that an infinitesimal quantity is an absurdity; although, with their habitual caution, they have often added "or, at any rate, the conception of an infinitesimal is so difficult, that we practically cannot reason about it with confidence and security." Accordingly, the doctrine of limits has been invented to evade the difficulty, or, as some say, to explain the signification of the word "infinitesimal." This doctrine, in one form or another, is taught in all the text-books, though in some of them only as an alternative view of the matter; it answers well enough the purposes of calculation, though even in that application it has its difficulties.

The illumination of the subject by a strict notation for the logic of relatives had shown me clearly and evidently that the idea of an infinitesimal involves no contradiction, before I became acquainted with the writings of Dr. Georg Cantor (though many of these had already appeared in the *Mathematische Annalen* and in *Borchardt's Journal,* if not yet in the *Acta Mathematica,* all mathematical journals of the first distinction), in which the same view is defended with extraordinary genius and penetrating logic.

The prevalent opinion is that finite numbers are the only ones that we can reason about, at least, in any ordinary mode of reasoning, or, as some authors express it, they are the only numbers that can be reasoned about mathematically. But this is an irrational prejudice. I long ago showed that finite collections are distinguished from infinite ones only by one circumstance and its consequences, namely, that to them is applicable a peculiar and unusual mode of reasoning called by its discoverer, De Morgan, the "syllogism of transposed quantity."

Balzac, in the introduction of his *Physiologie du mariage,* remarks that every young Frenchman boasts of having seduced some Frenchwoman. Now, as a woman can only be seduced once, and there are no more Frenchwomen than Frenchmen, it follows, if these boasts are true, that no French women escape seduction. If their number be finite, the reasoning holds. But since the population is continually increasing, and the seduced are on the average younger than the seducers, the conclusion need not be true. In like manner, De Morgan, as an actuary, might have argued that if an insurance company pays to its insured on an average more than they have ever paid it, including interest, it must lose money. But every modern actuary would see a fallacy in that, since the business is continually on the increase. But should war, or other cataclysm, cause the class of insured to be a finite one, the conclusion would turn out painfully correct, after all. The above two reasonings are examples of the syllogism of transposed quantity.

The proposition that finite and infinite collections are distinguished by the applicability to the former of the syllogism of transposed quantity ought to be regarded as the basal one of scientific arithmetic.

If a person does not know how to reason logically, and I must say that a great many fairly good mathematicians, — yea, distinguished ones, — fall under this category, but simply uses a rule of thumb in blindly drawing inferences like other inferences that have turned out well, he will, of course, be continually falling into error about infinite numbers. The truth is such people do not reason, at all. But for the few who do reason, reasoning about infinite numbers is easier than about finite numbers, because the complicated syllogism of transposed quantity is not called for. For example, that the whole is greater than its part is not an axiom, as that eminently bad reasoner, Euclid, made it to be. It is a theorem readily proved by means of a syllogism of transposed quantity, but not otherwise. Of finite collections it is true, of infinite collections false. Thus, a part of the whole numbers are even numbers. Yet the even numbers are no fewer than all the numbers; an evident proposition since if every number in the whole series of whole numbers be doubled, the result will be the series of even numbers.

1, 2, 3, 4, 5, 6, etc.
2, 4, 6, 8, 10, 12, etc.

So for every number there is a distinct even number. In fact, there are as many distinct doubles of numbers as there are of distinct numbers. But the doubles of numbers are all even numbers.

In truth, of infinite collections there are but two grades of magnitude, the *endless* and the *innumerable*. Just as a finite collection is distinguished from an infinite one by the applicability to it of a special mode of reasoning, the syllogism of transposed quantity, so, as I showed in the paper last referred to, a numerable collection is distinguished from an innumerable one by the applicability to it of a certain mode of reasoning, the Fermatian inference, or, as it is sometimes improperly termed, "mathematical induction."

As an example of this reasoning, Euler's demonstration of the binomial theorem for integral powers may be given. The theorem is that $(x+y)^n$, where n is a whole number, may be expanded into the sum of a series of terms of which the first is $x^n y^0$ and each of the others is derived from the next preceding by diminishing the exponent of x by 1 and multiplying by that exponent and at the same time increasing the exponent of y by 1 and dividing by that increased exponent. Now, suppose this proposition to be true for a certain exponent, $n = M$, then it must also be true for $n = M + 1$. For let one of the terms in the expansion of $(x+y)^M$ be written $Ax^p y^q$. Then, this term with the two following will be

$$Ax^p y^q + A\frac{p}{q+1}x^{p-1}y^{q+1} + A\frac{p}{q+1}\frac{p-1}{q+2}x^{p-2}y^{q+2}$$

Now, when $(x+y)^M$ is multiplied by $x+y$ to give $(x+y)^{M+1}$, we multiply first by x and then by y instead of by x and add the two results. When we multiply by x, the second of the above three terms will be the only one giving a term involving $x^p y^{q+1}$ and the third will be the only one giving a term in $x^{p-1}y^{q+2}$; and when we multiply by y the first will be the only term giving a term in $x^p y^{q+1}$, and the second will be the only term giving a term in $x^{p-1}y^{q+2}$. Hence, adding like terms, we find that the coefficient of $x^p y^{q+1}$ in the expansion of $(x+y)^{M+1}$ will be the sum of the coefficients of the first two of the above three terms, and that the coefficient of $x^{p-1}y^{q+2}$ will be the sum of the coefficients of the last two terms. Hence, two successive terms in the expansion of $(x+y)^{M+1}$ will be

$$A\left[1+\frac{p}{q+1}\right]x^p y^{q+1} + A\frac{p}{q+1}\left[1+\frac{p-1}{q+2}\right]x^{p-1}y^{q+2}$$
$$= A\frac{p+q+1}{q+1}x^p y^{q+1} + A\frac{p+q+1}{q+1}\frac{p}{q+2}x^{p-1}y^{q+2}$$

It is, thus, seen that the succession of terms follows the rule. Thus if any integral power follows the rule, so also does the next higher power. But the first power obviously follows the rule. Hence, all powers do so.

Such reasoning holds good of any collection of objects capable of being ranged in a series which though it may be endless, can be numbered so that each member of it receives a definite integral number. For instance, all the whole numbers constitute such a numerable collection. Again, all numbers resulting from operating according to any definite rule with any finite number of whole numbers form such a collection. For they may be arranged in a series thus. Let F be the symbol of operation. First operate on 1, giving F (1). Then, operate on a second 1, giving F(1,1). Next, introduce 2, giving 3rd, F(2); 4th F(2,1); 5th, F(1,2); 6th, F(2,2). Next use a third variable giving 7th, F(1,1,1); 8th, F(2,1,1); 9th, F(1,2,1); 10th, F(2,2,1); 11th, F(1,1,2); 12th, F(2,1,2); 13th, F(1,2,2); 14th, F(2,2,2). Next introduce 3, and so on, alternately introducing new variables and new figures; and in this way it is plain that every arrangement of integral values of the variables will receive a numbered place in the series.[2]

The class of endless but numerable collections (so called because they can be so ranged that to each one corresponds

[2] This proposition is substantially the same as a theorem of Cantor, though it is enunciated in a much more general form.

a distinct whole number) is very large. But there are collections which are certainly innumerable. Such is the collection of all numbers to which endless series of decimals are capable of approximating. It has been recognized since the time of Euclid that certain numbers are surd or incommensurable, and are not exactly expressible by any finite series of decimals, nor by a circulating decimal. Such is the ratio of the circumference of a circle to its diameter, which we know is nearly 3.1415926. The calculation of this number has been carried to over 700 figures without the slightest appearance of regularity in their sequence. The demonstrations that this and many other numbers are incommensurable are perfect. That the entire collection of incommensurable numbers is innumerable has been clearly proved by Cantor. I omit the demonstration; but it is easy to see that to discriminate one from some other would, in general, require the use of an endless series of numbers. Now if they cannot be exactly expressed and discriminated, clearly they cannot be ranged in a linear series.

It is evident that there are as many points on a line or in an interval of time as there are of real numbers in all. These are, therefore, innumerable collections. Many mathematicians have incautiously assumed that the points on a surface or in a solid are more than those on a line. But this has been refuted by Cantor. Indeed, it is obvious that for every set of values of coördinates there is a single distinct number. Suppose, for instance, the values of the coördinates all lie between 0 and + 1. Then if we compose a number by putting in the first decimal place the first figure of the first coördinate, in the second the first figure of the second coördinate, and so on, and when the first figures are all dealt out go on to the second figures in like manner, it is plain that the values of the coördinates can be read off from the single resulting number, so that a triad or tetrad of numbers, each having innumerable values, has no more values than a single incommensurable number.

Were the number of dimensions infinite, this would fail; and the collection of infinite sets of numbers having each innumerable variations, might, therefore, be greater than the simple innumerable collection, and might be called *endlessly infinite.* The single individuals of such a collection could not, however, be designated, even approximately, so that this is indeed a magnitude concerning which it would be possible to reason only in the most general way, if at all.

Although there are but two grades of magnitudes of infinite collections, yet when certain conditions are imposed upon the order in which individuals are taken, distinctions of magnitude arise from that cause. Thus, if a simply endless series be doubled by separating each unit into two parts, the successive first parts and also the second parts being taken in the same order as the units from which they are derived, this double endless series will, so long as it is taken in that order, appear as twice as large as the original series. In like manner the product of two innumerable collections, that is, the collection of possible pairs composed of one individual of each, if the order of continuity is to be maintained, is, by virtue of that order, infinitely greater than either of the component collections.

We now come to the difficult question. What is continuity? Kant confounds it with infinite divisibility, saying that the essential character of a continuous series is that between any two members of it a third can always be found. This is an analysis beautifully clear and definite; but unfortunately, it breaks down under the first test. For according to this, the entire series of rational fractions arranged in the order of their magnitude, would be an infinite series, although the rational fractions are numerable, while the points of a line are innumerable. Nay, worse yet, if from that series of fractions any two with all that lie between them be excised, and any number of such finite gaps be made, Kant's definition is still true of the series, though it has lost all appearance of continuity.

Cantor defines a continuous series as one which is *concatenated* and *perfect*. By a concatenated series, he means such a one that if any two points are given in it, and any finite distance, however small, it is possible to proceed from the first point to the second through a succession of points of the series each at a distance from the preceding one less than the given distance. This is true of the series of rational fractions ranged in the order of their magnitude. By a perfect series, he means one which contains every point such that there is no distance so small that this point has not an infinity of points of the series within that distance of it. This is true of the series of numbers between 0 and 1 capable of being expressed by decimals in which only the digits 0 and 1 occur.

It must be granted that Cantor's definition includes every series that is continuous; nor can it be objected that it includes any important or indubitable case of a series not continuous. Nevertheless, it has some serious defects. In the first place, it turns upon metrical considerations; while the distinction between a continuous and a discontinuous series is manifestly non-metrical. In the next place, a perfect series is defined as one containing "every point" of a certain description. But no positive idea is conveyed of what all the points are: that is definition by negation, and cannot be admitted. If that sort of thing were allowed, it would be very easy to say, at once, that the continuous linear series of points is one which contains every point of the line between its extremities. Finally, Cantor's definition does not convey a distinct notion of what the components of the conception of continuity are. It ingeniously wraps up its properties in two separate parcels, but does not display them to our intelligence.

Kant's definition expresses one simple property of a continuum; but it allows of gaps in the series. To mend the definition, it is only necessary to notice how these gaps can occur. Let us suppose, then, a linear series of points extending from a point, *A*, to a point, *B*, having a gap from *B* to a third point, *C*, and thence extending to a final limit, *D;* and let us suppose this series conforms to Kant's definition. Then, of the two points, *B* and *C*, one or both must be excluded from the series; for otherwise, by the definition, there would be points between them. That is, if the series contains *C*, though it contains all the points up to *B*, it cannot contain *B*. What is required, therefore, is to state in non-metrical terms that if a series of points up to a limit is included in a continuum the limit is included. It may be remarked that this is the property of a continuum to which Aristotle's attention seems to have been directed when he defines a continuum as something whose parts have a common limit. The property may be exactly stated as follows: If a linear series of points is continuous between two points, *A* and *D*, and if an endless series of points be taken, the first of them between *A* and *D* and each of the others between the last preceding one and *D*, then there is a point of the continuous series between all that endless series of points and *D*, and such that every other point of which this is true lies between this point and *D*. For example, take any number between 0 and 1, as 0.1; then, any number between 0.1 and 1, as 0.11; then any number between 0.11 and 1, as 0.111; and so on, without end. Then, because the series of real numbers between 0 and 1 is continuous, there must be a *least* real number, greater than every number of that endless series. This property, which may be called the Aristotelicity of the series, together with Kant's property, or its Kanticity, completes the definition of a continuous series.

The property of Aristotelicity may be roughly stated thus: a continuum contains the end point belonging to every endless series of points which it contains. An obvious corollary is that every continuum contains its limits. But in using this principle it is necessary to observe that a series may be continuous except in this, that it omits one or both of the limits.

Our ideas will find expression more conveniently if, instead of points upon a line, we speak of real numbers. Every real number is, in one sense, the limit of a series, for it can be indefinitely approximated to. Whether every real number is a limit of a *regular* series may perhaps be open to doubt. But the series referred to in the definition of Aristotelicity must be understood as including all series whether regular or not. Consequently, it is implied that between any two points an innumerable series of points can be taken.

Every number whose expression in decimals requires but a finite number of places of decimals is commensurable. Therefore, incommensurable numbers suppose an infinitieth place of decimals. The word infinitesimal is simply the Latin form of infinitieth; that is, it is an ordinal formed from *infinitum,* as centesimal from *centum.* Thus, continuity supposes infinitesimal quantities. There is nothing contradictory about the idea of such quantities. In adding and multiplying them the continuity must not be broken up, and consequently they are precisely like any other quantities, except that neither the syllogism of transposed quantity, nor the Fermatian inference applies to them.

If A is a finite quantity and i an infinitesimal, then in a certain sense we may write $A + i = A$. That is to say, this is so for all purposes of measurement. But this principle must not be applied except to get rid of *all* the terms in the highest order of infinitesimals present. As a mathematician, I prefer the method of infinitesimals to that of limits, as far easier and less infested with snares. Indeed, the latter, as stated in some books, involves propositions that are false; but this is not the case with the forms of the method used by Cauchy, Duhamel, and others. As they understand the doctrine of limits, it involves the notion of continuity, and, therefore, contains in another shape the very same ideas as the doctrine of infinitesimals.

Let us now consider an aspect of the Aristotelical principle which is particularly important in philosophy. Suppose a surface to be part red and part blue; so that every point on it is either red or blue, and, of course, no part can be both red and blue. What, then, is the color of the boundary line between the red and the blue? The answer is that red or blue, to exist at all, must be spread over a surface; and the color of the surface is the color of the surface in the immediate neighborhood of the point. I purposely use a vague form of expression. Now, as the parts of the surface in the immediate neighborhood of any ordinary point upon a curved boundary are half of them red and half blue, it follows that the boundary is half red and half blue. In like manner, we find it necessary to hold that consciousness essentially occupies time; and what is present to the mind at any ordinary instant, is what is present during a moment in which that instant occurs.

Thus, the present is half past and half to come. Again, the color of the parts of a surface at any finite distance from a point, has nothing to do with its color just at that point; and, in the parallel, the feeling at any finite interval from the present has nothing to do with the present feeling, except vicariously. Take another case: the velocity of a particle at any instant of time is its mean velocity during an infinitesimal instant in which that time is contained. Just so my immediate feeling is my feeling through an infinitesimal duration containing the present instant.

ANALYSIS OF TIME

One of the most marked features about the law of mind is that it makes time to have a definite direction of flow from past to future. The relation of past to future is, in reference to the law of mind, different from the relation of future to past. This makes one of the great contrasts between the law of mind and the law of physical force, where there is no more distinction between the two opposite directions in time than between moving northward and moving southward.

In order, therefore, to analyze the law of mind, we must begin by asking what the flow of time consists in. Now, we find that in reference to any individual state of feeling, all others are of two classes, those which affect this one (or have a tendency to affect it, and what this means we shall inquire shortly), and those which do not. The present is affectible by the past but not by the future.

Moreover, if state A is affected by state B, and state B by state C, then A is affected by state C, though not so much so. It follows, that if A is affectible by B, B is not affectible by A.

If, of two states, each is absolutely unaffectible by the other, they are to be regarded as parts of the same state. They are contemporaneous.

To say that a state is *between* two states means that it affects one and is affected by the other. Between any two states in this sense lies an innumerable series of states affecting one another; and if a state lies between a given state and any other state which can be reached by inserting states between this state and any third state, these inserted states not immediately affecting or being affected by either, then the second rate mentioned, immediately affects or is affected by the first, in the sense that in the one the other is *ipso facto* present in a reduced degree.

These propositions involve a definition of time and of its flow. Over and above this definition they involve a doctrine, namely, that every state of feeling is affectible by every earlier state.

THAT FEELINGS HAVE INTENSIVE CONTINUITY

Time with its continuity logically involves some other kind of continuity than its own. Time, as the universal form of change, cannot exist unless there is something to undergo change, and to undergo a change continuous in time, there must be a continuity of changeable qualities. Of the continuity of intrinsic qualities of feeling we can now form but a feeble conception. The development of the human mind has practically extinguished all feelings, except a few sporadic kinds, sound, colors, smells, warmth, etc., which now appear to be disconnected and disparate. In the case of colors, there is a tridimensional spread of feelings. Originally, all feelings may have been connected in the same way, and the presumption is that the number of dimensions was endless. For development essentially involves a limitation of possibilities. But given a number of dimensions of feeling, all possible varieties are obtainable by varying the intensities of the different elements. Accordingly, time logically supposes a continuous range of intensity in feeling. It follows, then, from the definition of continuity, that when any particular kind of feeling is present, an infinitesimal continuum of all feelings differing infinitesimally from that is present.

THAT FEELINGS HAVE SPATIAL EXTENSION

Consider a gob of protoplasm, say an amœba or a slime-mould. It does not differ in any radical way from the contents of a nerve-cell, though its functions may be less specialized. There is no doubt that this slime-mould, or this amœba, or at any rate some similar mass of protoplasm feels. That is to say, it feels when it is in its excited condition. But note how it behaves. When the whole is quiescent and rigid, a place upon it is irritated. Just at this point, an active motion is set up, and this gradually spreads to other parts. In this action, no unity nor relation to a nucleus, or other unitary organ can be discerned. It is a mere amorphous continuum of protoplasm, with feeling passing from one part to another. Nor is there anything like a wave-motion. The activity does not advance to new parts, just as fast as it leaves old parts. Rather, in the beginning, it dies out at a slower rate than that at which it spreads. And while the process is going on, by exciting the mass at another point, a second quite independent state of excitation will be set up. In some places, neither excitation will exist, in others each separately, in still other places, both effects will be added together. Whatever there is in the whole phenomenon to make us think there is feeling in such a mass of protoplasm, — *feeling*, but plainly no *personality*, — goes logically to show that that feeling has a subjective, or substantial, spatial extension, as the excited state has. This is, no doubt, a difficult idea to seize, for the reason that it is a subjective, not an objective, extension. It is not that we have a feeling of bigness; though Professor James, perhaps rightly, teaches that we have. It is that the feeling, as a subject of inhesion, is big. Moreover, our own feelings are focused in attention to such a degree that we are not aware that ideas are not brought to an absolute unity; just as nobody not instructed by special experiment has any idea how very, very little of the field of vision is distinct. Still, we all know how the attention wanders about among our feelings; and this fact shows that those feelings that are not co-ordinated in attention have a reciprocal externality, although they are present at the same time. But we must not tax introspection to make a phenomenon manifest which essentially involves externality.

Since space is continuous, it follows that there must be an immediate community of feeling between parts of mind infinitesimally near together. Without this, I believe it would have been impossible for minds external to one another, ever to become co-ordinated, and equally impossible for any coördination to be established in the action of the nerve-matter of one brain.

AFFECTIONS OF IDEAS

But we are met by the question what is meant by saying that one idea affects another. The unravelment of this problem requires us to trace out phenomena a little further.

Three elements go to make up an idea. The first is its intrinsic quality as a feeling. The second is the energy with which it affects other ideas, an energy which is infinite in the here-and-nowness of immediate sensation, finite and relative in the recency of the past. The third element is the tendency of an idea to bring along other ideas with it.

As an idea spreads, its power of affecting other ideas gets rapidly reduced; but its intrinsic quality remains nearly unchanged. It is long years now since I last saw a cardinal in his robes; and my memory of their color has become much dimmed. The color itself, however, is not remembered as dim. I have no inclination to call it a dull red. Thus, the intrinsic quality remains little changed; yet more accurate observation will show a slight reduction of it. The third element, on the other hand, has increased. As well as I can recollect, it seems to me the cardinals I used to see wore robes more scarlet than vermillion is, and highly luminous. Still, I know the color commonly called cardinal is on the crimson side of vermillion and of quite moderate luminosity, and the original idea calls up so many other hues with it, and asserts itself so feebly, that I am unable any longer to isolate it.

A finite interval of time generally contains an innumerable series of feelings; and when these become welded together in association, the result is a general idea. For we have just seen how by continuous spreading an idea becomes generalised.

The first character of a general idea so resulting is that it is living feeling. A continuum of this feeling, infinitesimal in duration, but still embracing innumerable parts, and also, though infinitesimal, entirely unlimited, is immediately present. And in its absence of boundedness a vague possibility of more than is present is directly felt.

Second, in the presence of this continuity of feeling, nominalistic maxims appear futile. There is no doubt about one idea affecting another, when we can directly perceive the one gradually modified and shaping itself into the other. Nor can there any longer be any difficulty about one idea resembling another, when we can pass along the continuous field of quality from one to the other and back again to the point which we had marked.

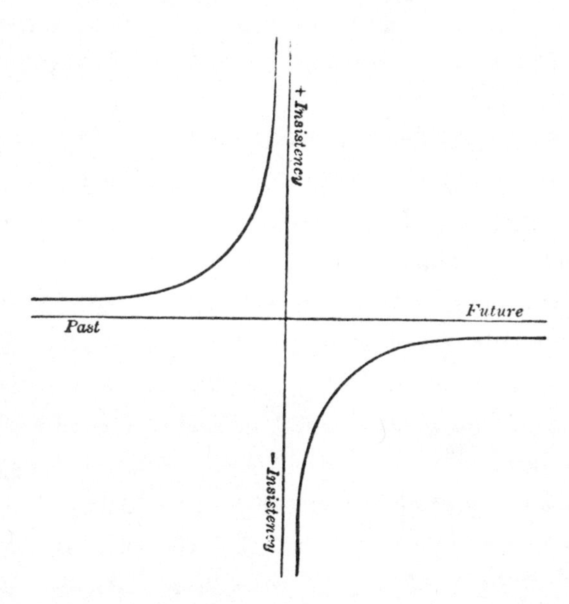

Third, consider the insistency of an idea. The insistency of a past idea with reference to the present is a quantity which is less the further back that past idea is, and rises to infinity as the past idea is brought up into coincidence with the present. Here we must make one of those inductive applications of the law of continuity which have produced such great results in all the positive sciences. We must extend the law of insistency into the future. Plainly, the insistency of a future idea with reference to the present is a quantity affected by the minus sign; for it is the present that affects the future, if there be any effect, not the future that affects the present. Accordingly, the curve of insistency is a sort of equilateral hyperbola. (See the figure.) Such a conception is none the less mathematical, that its quantification cannot now be exactly specified.

Now consider the induction which we have here been led into. This curve says that feeling which has not yet emerged into immediate consciousness is already affectible and already affected. In fact, this is habit, by virtue of which an idea is brought up into present consciousness by a bond that had already been established between it and another idea while it was still *in futuro*.

We can now see what the affection of one idea by another consists in. It is that the affected idea is attached as a logical predicate to the affecting idea as subject. So when a feeling emerges into immediate consciousness, it always appears as a modification of a more or less general object already in the mind. The word suggestion is well adapted to expressing this relation. The future is suggested by, or rather is influenced by the suggestions of, the past.

IDEAS CANNOT BE CONNECTED EXCEPT BY CONTINUITY

That ideas can nowise be connected without continuity is sufficiently evident to one who reflects upon the matter. But still the opinion may be entertained that after continuity has once made the connection of ideas possible, then they may get to be connected in other modes than through continuity. Certainly, I cannot see how anyone can deny that the infinite diversity of the universe, which we call chance, may bring ideas into proximity which are not associated in one general idea. It may do this many times. But then the law of continuous spreading will produce a mental association; and this I suppose is an abridged statement of the way the universe has been evolved. But if I am asked whether a blind ἀνάγκη cannot bring ideas together, first I point out that it would not remain blind. There being a continuous connection between the ideas, they would infallibly become associated in a living, feeling, and perceiving general idea. Next, I cannot see what the mustness or necessity of this ἀνάγκη would consist in. In the absolute uniformity of the phenomenon, says the nominalist. Absolute is well put in; for if it merely happened so three times in succession, or three million times in succession, in the absence of any reason, the coincidence could only be attributed to chance. But absolute uniformity must extend over the whole infinite future; and it is idle to talk of that except as an idea. No; I think we can only hold that wherever ideas come together they tend to weld into general ideas; and wherever they are generally connected, general ideas govern the connection; and these general ideas are living feelings spread out.

MENTAL LAW FOLLOWS THE FORMS OF LOGIC

The three main classes of logical inference are Deduction, Induction, and Hypothesis. These correspond to three chief modes of action of the human soul. In deduction the mind is under the dominion of a habit or association by virtue of which a general idea suggests in each case a corresponding reaction. But a certain sensation is seen to involve that idea. Consequently, that sensation is followed by that reaction. That is the way the hind legs of a frog, separated from the rest of the body, reason, when you pinch them. It is the lowest form of psychical manifestation.

By induction, a habit becomes established. Certain sensations, all involving one general idea, are followed each by the same reaction; and an association becomes established, whereby that general idea gets to be followed uniformly by that reaction.

Habit is that specialization of the law of mind whereby a general idea gains the power of exciting reactions. But in order that the general idea should attain all its functionality, it is necessary, also, that it should become suggestible by sensations. That is accomplished by a psychical process having the form of hypothetic inference. By hypothetic inference, I mean, as I have explained in other writings, an induction from qualities. For example, I know that the kind of man known and classed as a "mugwump" has certain characteristics. He has a high self-respect and places great value upon social distinction. He laments the great part that rowdyism and unrefined good-fellowship play in the dealings of American politicians with their constituency. He thinks that the reform which would follow from the abandonment of the system by which the distribution of offices is made to strengthen party organizations and a return to the original and essential conception of office-filling would be found an unmixed good. He holds that monetary considerations should usually be the decisive ones in questions of public policy. He respects the principle of individualism and of *laissez-faire* as the greatest agency of civilization. These views, among others, I know to be obtrusive marks of a "mugwump." Now, suppose I casually meet a man in a railway-train, and falling into conversation find that he holds opinions of this sort; I am naturally led to suppose that he is a "mugwump." That is hypothetic inference. That is to say, a number of readily verifiable marks of a mugwump being selected, I find this man has these, and infer that he has all the other characters which go to make a thinker of that stripe. Or let us suppose that I meet a man of a semi-clerical appearance and a sub-pharisaical sniff, who appears to look at things from the point of view of a rather wooden dualism. He cites several texts of scripture and always with particular attention to their logical implications; and he exhibits a sternness, almost amounting to vindictiveness, toward evil-doers, in general. I readily conclude that he is a minister of a certain denomination. Now the mind acts in a way similar to this, every time we acquire a power of co-ordinating reactions in a peculiar way, as in performing any act requiring skill. Thus, most persons have a difficulty in moving the two hands simultaneously and in opposite directions through two parallel circles nearly in the medial plane of the body. To learn to do this, it is necessary to attend, first, to the different actions in different parts of the motion, when suddenly a general conception of the action springs up and it becomes perfectly easy. We think the motion we are trying to do involves this action, and this, and this. Then, the general idea comes which unites all those actions, and thereupon the desire to perform the motion calls up the general idea. The same mental process is many times employed whenever we are learning to speak a language or are acquiring any sort of skill.

Thus, by induction, a number of sensations followed by one reaction become united under one general idea followed by the same reaction; while by the hypothetic process, a number of reactions called for by one occasion get united in a general idea which is called out by the same occasion. By deduction, the habit fulfils its function of calling out certain reactions on certain occasions.

UNCERTAINTY OF MENTAL ACTION

The inductive and hypothetic forms of inference are essentially probable inferences, not necessary; while deduction may be either necessary or probable.

But no mental action seems to be necessary or invariable in its character. In whatever manner the mind has reacted under a given sensation, in that manner it is the more likely to react again; were this, however, an absolute necessity, habits would become wooden and ineradicable, and no room being left for the formation of new habits, intellectual life would come to a speedy close. Thus, the uncertainty of the mental law is no mere defect of it, but is on the contrary of its essence. The truth is, the mind is not subject to "law," in the same rigid sense that matter is. It only experiences gentle forces which merely render it more likely to act in a given way than it otherwise would be. There always remains a certain amount of arbitrary spontaneity in its action, without which it would be dead.

Some psychologists think to reconcile the uncertainty of reactions with the principle of necessary causation by means of the law of fatigue. Truly for a *law,* this law of fatigue is a little lawless. I think it is merely a case of the general principle that an idea in spreading loses its insistency. Put me tarragon into my salad, when I have not tasted it for years, and I exclaim "What nectar is this!" But add it to every dish I taste for week after week, and a habit of expectation has been created; and in thus spreading into habit, the sensation makes hardly any more impression upon me; or, if it be noticed, it is on a new side from which it appears as rather a bore. The doctrine that fatigue is one of the primordial phenomena of mind I am much disposed to doubt. It seems a somewhat little thing to be allowed as an exception to the great principle of mental uniformization. For this reason, I prefer to explain it in the manner here indicated, as a special case of that great principle. To consider it as something distinct in its nature, certainly somewhat strengthens the necessitarian position; but even if it be distinct, the hypothesis that all the variety and apparent arbitrariness of mental action ought to be explained away in favor of absolute determinism does not seem to me to recommend itself to a sober and sound judgment, which seeks the guidance of observed facts and not that of prepossessions.

RESTATEMENT OF THE LAW

Let me now try to gather up all these odds and ends of commentary and restate the law of mind, in a unitary way.

First, then, we find that when we regard ideas from a nominalistic, individualistic, sensualistic way, the simplest facts of mind become utterly meaningless. That one idea should resemble another or influence another, or that one state of mind should so much as be thought of in another is, from that standpoint, sheer nonsense.

Second, by this and other means we are driven to perceive, what is quite evident of itself, that instantaneous feelings flow together into a continuum of feeling, which has in a modified degree the peculiar vivacity of feeling and has gained generality. And in reference to such general ideas, or continua of feeling, the difficulties about resemblance and suggestion and reference to the external, cease to have any force.

Third, these general ideas are not mere words, nor do they consist in this, that certain concrete facts will every time happen under certain descriptions of conditions; but they are just as much, or rather far more, living realities than the feelings themselves out of which they are concreted. And to say that mental phenomena are governed by law does not mean merely that they are describable by a general formula; but that there is a living idea, a conscious continuum of feeling, which pervades them, and to which they are docile.

Fourth, this supreme law, which is the celestial and living harmony, does not so much as demand that the special ideas shall surrender their peculiar arbitrariness and caprice entirely; for that would be self-destructive. It only requires that they shall influence and be influenced by one another.

Fifth, in what measure this unification acts, seems to be regulated only by special rules; or, at least, we cannot in our present knowledge say how far it goes. But it may be said that, judging by appearances, the amount of arbitrariness in the phenomena of human minds is neither altogether trifling nor very prominent.

PERSONALITY

Having thus endeavored to state the law of mind, in general, I descend to the consideration of a particular phenomenon which is remarkably prominent in our own consciousnesses, that of personality. A strong light is thrown upon this subject by recent observations of double and multiple personality. The theory which at one time seemed plausible that two persons in one body corresponded to the two halves of the brain will, I take it, now be universally acknowledged to be insufficient. But that which these cases make quite manifest is that personality is some kind of co-ordination or connection of ideas. Not much to say, this, perhaps. Yet when we consider that, according to the principle which we are tracing out, a connection between ideas is itself a general idea, and that a general idea is a living feeling, it is plain that we have at least taken an appreciable step toward the understanding of personality. This personality, like any general idea, is not a thing to be apprehended in an instant. It has to be lived in time;

nor can any finite time embrace it in all its fullness. Yet in each infinitesimal interval it is present and living, though specially colored by the immediate feelings of that moment. Personality, so far as it is apprehended in a moment, is immediate self-consciousness.

But the word co-ordination implies somewhat more than this; it implies a teleological harmony in ideas, and in the case of personality this teleology is more than a mere purposive pursuit of a predeterminate end; it is a developmental teleology. This is personal character. A general idea, living and conscious now, it is already determinative of acts in the future to an extent to which it is not now conscious.

This reference to the future is an essential element of personality. Were the ends of a person already explicit, there would be no room for development, for growth, for life; and consequently there would be no personality. The mere carrying out of predetermined purposes is mechanical. This remark has an application to the philosophy of religion. It is that a genuine evolutionary philosophy, that is, one that makes the principle of growth a primordial element of the universe, is so far from being antagonistic to the idea of a personal creator, that it is really inseparable from that idea; while a necessitarian religion is in an altogether false position and is destined to become disintegrated. But a pseudo-evolutionism which enthrones mechanical law above the principle of growth, is at once scientifically unsatisfactory, as giving no possible hint of how the universe has come about, and hostile to all hopes of personal relations to God.

COMMUNICATION

Consistently with tne doctrine laid down in the beginning of this paper, I am bound to maintain that an idea can only be affected by an idea in continuous connection with it. By anything but an idea, it cannot be affected at all. This obliges me to say, as I do say, on other grounds, that what we call matter is not completely dead, but is merely mind hide-bound with habits. It still retains the element of diversification; and in that diversification there is life. When an idea is conveyed from one mind to another, it is by forms of combination of the diverse elements of nature, say by some curious symmetry, or by some union of a tender color with a refined odor. To such forms the law of mechanical energy has no application. If they are eternal, it is in the spirit they embody; and their origin cannot be accounted for by any mechanical necessity. They are embodied ideas; and so only can they convey ideas. Precisely how primary sensations, as colors and tones, are excited, we cannot tell, in the present state of psychology. But in our ignorance, I think that we are at liberty to suppose that they arise in essentially the same manner as the other feelings, called secondary. As far as sight and hearing are in question, we know that they are only excited by vibrations of inconceivable complexity; and the chemical senses are probably not more simple. Even the least psychical of peripheral sensations, that of pressure, has in its excitation conditions which, though apparently simple, are seen to be complicated enough when we consider the molecules and their attractions. The principle with which I set out requires me to maintain that these feelings are communicated to the nerves by continuity, so that there must be something like them in the excitants themselves. If this seems extravagant, it is to be remembered that it is the sole possible way of reaching any explanation of sensation, which otherwise must be pronounced a general fact, absolutely inexplicable and ultimate. Now absolute inexplicability is a hypothesis which sound logic refuses under any circumstances to justify.

I may be asked whether my theory would be favorable or otherwise to telepathy. I have no decided answer to give to this. At first sight, it seems unfavorable. Yet there may be other modes of continuous connection between minds other than those of time and space.

The recognition by one person of another's personality takes place by means to some extent identical with the means by which he is conscious of his own personality. The idea of the second personality, which is as much as to say that second personality itself, enters within the field of direct consciousness of the first person, and is as immediately perceived as his ego, though less strongly. At the same time, the opposition between the two persons is perceived, so that the externality of the second is recognized.

The psychological phenomena of intercommunication between two minds have been unfortunately little studied. So that it is impossible to say, for certain, whether they are favorable to this theory or not. But the very extraordinary insight which some persons are able to gain of others from indications so slight that it is difficult to ascertain what they are, is certainly rendered more comprehensible by the view here taken.

A difficulty which confronts the synechistic philosophy is this. In considering personality, that philosophy is forced to accept the doctrine of a personal God; but in considering communication, it cannot but admit that if there is a personal God, we must have a direct perception of that person and indeed be in personal communication with him. Now, if that be the case, the question arises how it is possible that the existence of this being should ever have been doubted by anybody. The only answer that I can at present make is that facts that stand before our face and eyes and stare us in the face are far from being, in all cases, the ones most easily discerned. That has been remarked from time immemorial.

CONCLUSION

I have thus developed as well as I could in a little space the *synechistic* philosophy, as applied to mind. I think that I have succeeded in making it clear that this doctrine gives room for explanations of many facts which without it are absolutely and hopelessly inexplicable; and further that it carries along with it the following doctrines: 1st, a logical realism of the most pronounced type; 2nd, objective idealism; 3rd, tychism, with its consequent thoroughgoing evolutionism. We also notice that the doctrine presents no hindrances to spiritual influences, such as some philosophies are felt to do.

IV. MAN'S GLASSY ESSENCE[1]

In *The Monist* for January, 1891, I tried to show what conceptions ought to form the brick and mortar of a philosophical system. Chief among these was that of absolute chance for which I argued again in last April's number.[2] In July, I applied another fundamental idea, that of continuity, to the law of mind. Next in order, I have to elucidate, from the point of view chosen, the relation between the psychical and physical aspects of a substance.

The first step towards this ought, I think, to be the framing of a molecular theory of protoplasm. But before doing that, it seems indispensable to glance at the constitution of matter, in general. We shall, thus, unavoidably make a long detour; but, after all, our pains will not be wasted, for the problems of the papers that are to follow in the series will call for the consideration of the same question.

All physicists are rightly agreed the evidence is overwhelming which shows all sensible matter is composed of molecules in swift motion and exerting enormous mutual attractions, and perhaps repulsions, too. Even Sir William Thomson, Lord Kelvin, who wishes to explode action at a distance and return to the doctrine of a plenum, not only speaks of molecules, but undertakes to assign definite mag-

[1] *The Monist,* October, 1892.

[2] I am rejoiced to find, since my last paper was printed, that a philosopher as subtle and profound as Dr. Edmund Montgomery has long been arguing for the same element in the universe. Other world-renowned thinkers, as M. Renouvier and M. Delbœuf, appear to share this opinion.

nitudes to them. The brilliant Judge Stallo, a man who did not always rightly estimate his own qualities in accepting tasks for himself, declared war upon the atomic theory in a book well worth careful perusal. To the old arguments in favor of atoms which he found in Fechner's monograph, he was able to make replies of considerable force, though they were not sufficient to destroy those arguments. But against modern proofs he made no headway at all. These set out from the mechanical theory of heat. Rumford's experiments showed that heat is not a substance. Joule demonstrated that it was a form of energy. The heating of gases under constant volume, and other facts instanced by Rankine, proved that it could not be an energy of strain. This drove physicists to the conclusion that it was a mode of motion. Then it was remembered that John Bernoulli had shown that the pressure of gases could be accounted for by assuming their molecules to be moving uniformly in rectilinear paths. The same hypothesis was now seen to account for Avogadro's law, that in equal volumes of different kinds of gases exposed to the same pressure and temperature are contained equal numbers of molecules. Shortly after, it was found to account for the laws of diffusion and viscosity of gases, and for the numerical relation between these properties. Finally, Crookes's radiometer furnished the last link in the strongest chain of evidence which supports any physical hypothesis.

Such being the constitution of gases, liquids must clearly be bodies in which the molecules wander in curvilinear paths, while in solids they move in orbits or quasi-orbits. (See my definition *solid* II, 1, in the *Century Dictionary*.)

We see that the resistance to compression and to interpenetration between sensible bodies is, by one of the prime propositions of the molecular theory, due in large measure to the kinetical energy of the particles, which must be supposed to be quite remote from one another, on the average, even in solids. This resistance is no doubt influenced by finite attractions and repulsions between the molecules. All the impenetrability of bodies which we can observe is, therefore, a limited impenetrability due to kinetic and positional energy. This being the case, we have no logical right to suppose that absolute impenetrability, or the exclusive occupancy of space, belongs to molecules or to atoms. It is an unwarranted hypothesis, not a *vera causa*.[3] Unless we are to give up the theory of energy, finite positional attractions and repulsions between molecules must be admitted. Absolute impenetrability would amount to an infinite repulsion at a certain distance. No analogy of known phenomena exists to excuse such a wanton violation of the principle of continuity as such a hypothesis is. In short, we are logically bound to adopt the Boscovichian idea that an atom is simply a distribution of component potential energy throughout space (this distribution being absolutely rigid), combined with inertia. The potential energy belongs to two molecules, and is to be conceived as different between molecules *A* and *B* from what it is between molecules *A* and *C*. The distribution of energy is not necessarily spherical. Nay, a molecule may conceivably have more than one center; it may even have a central curve,

[3] By a *vera causa,* in the logic of science, is meant a state of things known to exist in some cases and supposed to exist in other cases, because it would account for observed phenomena.

returning into itself. But I do not think there are any observed facts pointing to such multiple or linear centers. On the other hand, many facts relating to crystals, especially those observed by Voigt,[4] go to show that the distribution of energy is harmonical but not concentric. We can easily calculate the forces which such atoms must exert upon one another by considering [5] that they are equivalent to aggregations of pairs of electrically positive and negative points infinitely near to one another. About such an atom there would be regions of positive and of negative potential, and the number and distribution of such regions would determine the valency of the atom, a number which it is easy to see would in many cases be somewhat indeterminate. I must not dwell further upon this hypothesis, at present. In another paper, its consequences will be further considered.

I cannot assume that the students of philosophy who read this magazine are thoroughly versed in modern molecular physics, and, therefore, it is proper to mention that the governing principle in this branch of science is Clausius's law of the virial. I will first state the law, and then explain the peculiar terms of the statement. This statement is that the total kinetic energy of the particles of a system in stationary motion is equal to the total virial. By a *system* is here meant a number of particles acting upon one another.[6] Stationary motion is a quasi-orbital motion among

[4] Wiedemann, *Annalen,* 1887–1889.

[5] See Maxwell on Spherical Harmonics, in his *Electricity and Magnetism.*

[6] The word *system* has three peculiar meanings in mathematics. (*A.*) It means an orderly exposition of the truths of astronomy, and hence

a system of particles so that none of them are removed to indefinitely great distances nor acquire indefinitely great velocities. The kinetic energy of a particle is the work which would be required to bring it to rest, independently of any forces which may be acting upon it. The virial of a pair of particles is half the work which the force which actually operates between them would do if, being independent of the distance, it were to bring them together. The equation of the virial is

$$\tfrac{1}{2}\Sigma mv^2 = \tfrac{1}{2}\Sigma\Sigma Rr.$$

Here m is the mass of a particle, v its velocity, R is the attraction between two particles, and r is the distance between them. The sign Σ on the left hand side signifies that the values of mv^2 are to be summed for all the particles, and $\Sigma\Sigma$ on the right hand side signifies that the values of Rr are to be summed for all the pairs of particles. If there is an external pressure P (as from the atmosphere) upon the system, and the volume of vacant space within the boundary of that pressure is V, then the virial must be understood as including $\tfrac{3}{2}PV$, so that the equation is

$$\tfrac{1}{2}\Sigma mv^2 = \tfrac{3}{2}PV + \tfrac{1}{2}\Sigma\Sigma Rr.$$

There is strong (if not demonstrative) reason for thinking that the temperature of any body above the absolute zero (−273° C.), is proportional to the average kinetic energy

a theory of the motions of the stars; as the Ptolemaic *system*, the Copernican *system*. This is much like the sense in which we speak of the Calvinistic *system* of theology, the Kantian *system* of philosophy, etc. (*B.*) It means the aggregate of the planets considered as all moving in somewhat the same way, as the solar *system;* and hence any aggregate of particles moving under mutual forces. (*C.*) It means a number of forces acting simultaneously upon a number of particles.

of its molecules, or say $a\theta$, where a is a constant and θ is the absolute temperature. Hence, we may write the equation

$$a\theta = \tfrac{1}{2}\overline{mv^2} = \tfrac{3}{2}P\overline{V} + \tfrac{1}{2}\Sigma\overline{Rr}$$

where the heavy lines above the different expressions signify that the average values for single molecules are to be taken. In 1872, a student in the University of Leyden, Van der Waals, propounded in his thesis for the doctorate a specialization of the equation of the virial which has since attracted great attention. Namely, he writes it

$$a\theta = \left(P + \frac{c}{V^2}\right)\left(V - b.\right)$$

The quantity b is the volume of a molecule, which he supposes to be an impenetrable body, and all the virtue of the equation lies in this term which makes the equation a cubic in V, which is required to account for the shape of certain isothermal curves.[7] But if the idea of an impenetrable atom is illogical, that of an impenetrable molecule is almost absurd. For the kinetical theory of matter teaches us that a molecule is like a solar system or star-cluster in miniature. Unless we suppose that in all heating of gases and vapors internal work is performed upon the molecules, implying that their atoms are at considerable distances, the whole kinetical theory of gases falls to the ground. As for the term added to P, there is no more than a partial and roughly approximative justification for it. Namely, let us imagine

[7] But, in fact, an inspection of these curves is sufficient to show that they are of a higher degree than the third. For they have the line $V = 0$, or some line V a constant for an asymptote, while for small values of P, the values of $d^2p/(dV)^2$ are positive.

two spheres described round a particle as their center, the radius of the larger being so great as to include all the particles whose action upon the center is sensible, while the radius of the smaller is so large that a good many molecules are included within it. The possibility of describing such a sphere as the outer one implies that the attraction of the particles varies at some distances inversely as some higher power of the distance than the cube, or, to speak more clearly, that the attraction multiplied by the cube of the distance diminishes as the distance increases; for the number of particles at a given distance from any one particle is proportionate to the square of that distance and each of these gives a term of the virial which is the product of the attraction into the distance. Consequently, unless the attraction multiplied by the cube of the distance diminished so rapidly with the distance as soon to become insensible, no such outer sphere as is supposed could be described. However, ordinary experience shows that such a sphere is possible; and consequently there must be distances at which the attraction does thus rapidly diminish as the distance increases. The two spheres, then, being so drawn, consider the virial of the central particle due to the particles between them. Let the density of the substance be increased, say, N times. Then, for every turn, Rr, of the virial before the condensation, there will be N terms of the same magnitude after the condensation. Hence, the virial of each particle will be proportional to the density, and the equation of the virial becomes

$$a\theta = P\overline{V} + \frac{c}{\overline{V}}.$$

This omits the virial within the inner sphere, the radius of which is so taken that within that distance the number of particles is not proportional to the number in a large sphere. For Van der Waals this radius is the diameter of his hard molecules, which assumption gives his equation. But it is plain that the attraction between the molecules must to a certain extent modify their distribution, unless some peculiar conditions are fulfilled. The equation of Van der Waals can be approximately true, therefore, only for a gas. In a solid or liquid condition, in which the removal of a small amount of pressure has little effect on the volume, and where consequently the virial must be much greater than $P\overline{V}$, the virial must increase with the volume. For suppose we had a substance in a critical condition in which an increase of the volume would diminish the virial more than it would increase $\frac{3}{2}P\overline{V}$. If we were forcibly to diminish the volume of such a substance, when the temperature became equalized, the pressure which it could withstand would be less than before, and it would be still further condensed, and this would go on indefinitely until a condition were reached in which an increase of volume would increase $\frac{3}{2}P\overline{V}$ more than it would decrease the virial. In the case of solids, at least, P may be zero; so that the state reached would be one in which the virial increases with the volume, or the attraction between the particles does not increase so fast with a diminution of their distance as it would if the attraction were inversely as the distance.

Almost contemporaneously with Van der Waals's paper, another remarkable thesis for the doctorate was presented at Paris by Amagat. It related to the elasticity and expansion of gases, and to this subject the superb experimenter, its author, has devoted his whole subsequent life. Especially interesting are his observations of the volumes of ethylene and of carbonic acid at temperatures from 20° to 100° and at pressures ranging from an ounce to 5000 pounds to the square inch. As soon as Amagat had obtained these results, he remarked that the "coefficient of expansion at constant volume," as it is absurdly called, that is, the rate of variation of the pressure with the temperature, was very nearly constant for each volume. This accords with the equation of the virial, which gives

$$\frac{dp}{d\theta} = \frac{a}{\overline{V}} - \frac{d\Sigma \overline{Rr}}{d\theta}.$$

Now, the virial must be nearly independent of the temperature, and, therefore, the last term almost disappears. The virial would not be quite independent of the temperature, because if the temperature (i.e., the square of the velocity of the molecules) is lowered, and the pressure correspondingly lowered, so as to make the volume the same, the attractions of the molecules will have more time to produce their effects, and consequently, the pairs of molecules the closest together will be held together longer and closer; so that the virial will generally be increased by a decrease of temperature. Now, Amagat's experiments do show an excessively minute effect of this sort, at least, when the volumes are not too small. However, the observations are well enough satisfied by assuming the "coefficient of expansion at constant volume" to consist wholly of the first term, $a/\overline{V}$. Thus, Amagat's experiments enable us to determine the values of *a* and thence to calculate the virial; and this we find varies for carbonic acid gas nearly inversely to $\overline{V}^{0.9}$. There is, thus, a rough approximation to satisfying Van der Waals's equation. But the most interesting result of Amagat's experiments, for our purpose at any rate, is that the quantity *a*, though nearly constant for any one volume, differs considerably with the volume, nearly doubling when the volume is reduced fivefold. This can only indicate that the mean kinetic energy of a given mass of the gas for a given temperature is greater the more the gas is compressed. But the laws of mechanics appear to enjoin that the mean kinetic energy of a moving particle shall be constant at any given temperature. The only escape from contradiction, then, is to suppose that the mean mass of a moving particle diminishes upon the condensation of the gas. In other words, many of the molecules are dissociated, or broken up into atoms or submolecules. The idea that dissociation should be favored by diminishing the volume will be pronounced by physicists, at first blush, as contrary to all our experience. But it must be remembered that the circumstances we are speaking of, that of a gas under fifty or more atmospheres pressure, are also unusual. That the " coefficient of expansion under constant volume " when multiplied by the volumes should increase with a decrement of the volume is also quite contrary to ordinary experience; yet it undoubtedly takes place in all gases under great pressure. Again, the doctrine of Arrhenius [8] is now generally accepted, that the molecular

[8] Anticipated by Clausius as long ago as 1857; and by Williamson in 1851.

conductivity of an electrolyte is proportional to the dissociation of ions. Now the molecular conductivity of a fused electrolyte is usually superior to that of a solution. Here is a case, then, in which diminution of volume is accompanied by increased dissociation.

The truth is that several different kinds of dissociation have to be distinguished. In the first place, there is the dissociation of a chemical molecule to form chemical molecules under the regular action of chemical laws. This may be a double decomposition, as when iodhydric acid is dissociated, according to the formula

$$HI + HI = HH + II;$$

or, it may be a simple decomposition, as when pentachloride of phosphorus is dissociated according to the formula

$$PCl_5 = PCl_3 + ClCl.$$

All these dissociations require, according to the laws of thermo-chemistry, an elevated temperature. In the second place, there is the dissociation of a physically polymerous molecule, that is, of several chemical molecules joined by physical attractions. This I am inclined to suppose is a common concomitant of the heating of solids and liquids; for in these bodies there is no increase of compressibility with the temperature at all comparable with the increase of the expansibility. But, in the third place, there is the dissociation with which we are now concerned, which must be supposed to be a throwing off of unsaturated sub-molecules or atoms from the molecule. The molecule may, as I have said, be roughly likened to a solar system. As such, molecules are able to produce perturbations of one another's internal motions; and in this way a planet, i.e., a sub-molecule, will occasionally get thrown off and wander about by itself, till it finds another unsaturated sub-molecule with which it can unite. Such dissociation by perturbation will naturally be favored by the proximity of the molecules to one another.

Let us now pass to the consideration of that special substance, or rather class of substances, whose properties form the chief subject of botany and of zoölogy, as truly as those of the silicates form the chief subject of mineralogy: I mean the life-slimes, or protoplasm. Let us begin by cataloguing the general characters of these slimes. They one and all exist in two states of aggregation, a solid or nearly solid state and a liquid or nearly liquid state; but they do not pass from the former to the latter by ordinary fusion. They are readily decomposed by heat, especially in the liquid state; nor will they bear any considerable degree of cold. All their vital actions take place at temperatures very little below the point of decomposition. This extreme instability is one of numerous facts which demonstrate the chemical complexity of protoplasm. Every chemist will agree that they are far more complicated than the albumens. Now, albumen is estimated to contain in each molecule about a thousand atoms; so that it is natural to suppose that the protoplasms contain several thousands. We know that while they are chiefly composed of oxygen, hydrogen, carbon, and nitrogen, a large number of other elements enter into living bodies in small proportions; and it is likely that most of these enter into the composition of protoplasms.

Now, since the numbers of chemical varieties increase at an enormous rate with the number of atoms per molecule, so that there are certainly hundreds of thousands of substances whose molecules contain twenty atoms or fewer, we may well suppose that the number of protoplasmic substances runs into the billions or trillions. Professor Cayley has given a mathematical theory of "trees," with a view of throwing a light upon such questions; and in that light the estimate of trillions (in the English sense) seems immoderately moderate. It is true that an opinion has been emitted, and defended among biologists, that there is but one kind of protoplasm; but the observations of biologists, themselves, have almost exploded that hypothesis, which from a chemical standpoint appears utterly incredible. The anticipation of the chemist would decidedly be that enough different chemical substances having protoplasmic characters might be formed to account, not only for the differences between nerve-slime and muscle-slime, between whale-slime and lion-slime, but also for those minuter pervasive variations which characterize different breeds and single individuals.

Protoplasm, when quiescent, is, broadly speaking, solid; but when it is disturbed in an appropriate way, or sometimes even spontaneously without external disturbance, it becomes, broadly speaking, liquid. A moner in this state is seen under the microscope to have streams within its matter; a slime-mould slowly flows by force of gravity. The liquefaction starts from the point of disturbance and spreads through the mass. This spreading, however, is not uniform in all directions; on the contrary, it takes at one time one course, at another another, through the homogeneous mass, in a manner that seems a little mysterious. The cause of disturbance being removed, these motions gradually (with higher kinds of protoplasm, quickly) cease, and the slime returns to its solid condition.

The liquefaction of protoplasm is accompanied by a mechanical phenomenon. Namely, some kinds exhibit a tendency to draw themselves up into a globular form. This happens particularly with the contents of muscle-cells. The prevalent opinion, founded on some of the most exquisite experimental investigations that the history of science can show, is undoubtedly that the contraction of muscle-cells is due to osmotic pressure; and it must be allowed that that is a factor in producing the effect. But it does not seem to me that it satisfactorily accounts even for the phenomena of muscular contraction; and besides, even naked slimes often draw up in the same way. In this case, we seem to recognize an increase of the surface-tension. In some cases, too, the reverse action takes place, extraordinary pseudopodia being put forth, as if the surface-tension were diminished in spots. Indeed, such a slime always has a sort of skin, due no doubt to surface-tension, and this seems to give way at the point where a pseudopodium is put forth.

Long-continued or frequently repeated liquefaction of the protoplasm results in an obstinate retention of the solid state, which we call fatigue. On the other hand, repose in this state, if not too much prolonged, restores the liquefiability. These are both important functions.

The life-slimes have, further, the peculiar property of growing. Crystals also grow; their growth, however, consists merely in attracting matter like their own from the circumambient fluid. To suppose the growth of protoplasm of the same nature, would be to suppose this substance to be spontaneously generated in copious supplies wherever food is in solution. Certainly, it must be granted that protoplasm is but a chemical substance, and that there is no reason why it should not be formed synthetically like any other chemical substance. Indeed, Clifford has clearly shown that we have overwhelming evidence that it is so formed. But to say that such formation is as regular and frequent as the assimilation of food is quite another matter. It is more consonant with the facts of observation to suppose that assimilated protoplasm is formed at the instant of assimilation, under the influence of the protoplasm already present. For each slime in its growth preserves its distinctive characters with wonderful truth, nerve-slime growing nerve-slime and muscle-slime muscle-slime, lion-slime growing lion-slime, and all the varieties of breeds and even individual characters being preserved in the growth. Now it is too much to suppose there are billions of different kinds of protoplasm floating about wherever there is food.

The frequent liquefaction of protoplasm increases its power of assimilating food; so much so, indeed, that it is questionable whether in the solid form it possesses this power.

The life-slime wastes as well as grows; and this too takes place chiefly if not exclusively in its liquid phases.

Closely connected with growth is reproduction; and though in higher forms this is a specialized function, it is universally true that wherever there is protoplasm, there is, will be, or has been a power of reproducing that same kind of protoplasm in a separated organism. Reproduction seems to involve the union of two sexes; though it is not demonstrable that this is always requisite.

Another physical property of protoplasm is that of taking habits. The course which the spread of liquefaction has taken in the past is rendered thereby more likely to be taken in the future; although there is no absolute certainly that the same path will be followed again.

Very extraordinary, certainly, are all these properties of protoplasm; as extraordinary as indubitable. But the one which has next to be mentioned, while equally undeniable, is infinitely more wonderful. It is that protoplasm feels. We have no direct evidence that this is true of protoplasm universally, and certainly some kinds feel far more than others. But there is a fair analogical inference that all protoplasm feels. It not only feels but exercises all the functions of mind.

Such are the properties of protoplasm. The problem is to find a hypothesis of the molecular constitution of this compound which will account for these properties, one and all.

Some of them are obvious results of the excessively complicated constitution of the protoplasm molecule. All very complicated substances are unstable; and plainly a molecule of several thousand atoms may be separated in many ways into two parts in each of which the polar chemical forces are very nearly saturated. In the solid protoplasm, as in other solids, the molecules must be supposed to be moving as it were in orbits, or, at least, so as not to wander indefinitely. But this solid cannot be melted, for the same reason that starch cannot be melted; because an amount of heat insufficient to make the entire molecules wander is sufficient to break them up completely and cause them to form new and simpler molecules. But when one of the molecules is disturbed, even if it be not quite thrown out of its orbit at first, sub-molecules of perhaps several hundred atoms each are thrown off from it. These will soon acquire the same mean kinetic energy as the others, and, therefore, velocities several times as great. They will naturally begin to wander, and in wandering will perturb a great many other molecules and cause them in their turn to behave like the one originally deranged. So many molecules will thus be broken up, that even those that are intact will no longer be restrained within orbits, but will wander about freely. This is the usual condition of a liquid, as modern chemists understand it; for in all electrolytic liquids there is considerable dissociation.

But this process necessarily chills the substance, not merely on account of the heat of chemical combination, but still more because the number of separate particles being greatly increased, the mean kinetic energy must be less. The substance being a bad conductor, this heat is not at once restored. Now the particles moving more slowly, the attractions between them have time to take effect, and they approach the condition of equilibrium. But their dynamic equilibrium is found in the restoration of the solid condition, which, therefore, takes place, if the disturbance is not kept up.

When a body is in the solid condition, most of its molecules must be moving at the same rate, or, at least, at certain regular sets of rates; otherwise the orbital motion would not be preserved. The distances of neighboring molecules must always be kept between a certain maximum and a certain minimum value. But if, without absorption of heat, the body be thrown into a liquid condition, the distances of neighboring molecules will be far more unequally distributed, and an effect upon the virial will result. The chilling of protoplasm upon its liquefaction must also be taken into account. The ordinary effect will no doubt be to increase the cohesion and with that the surface-tension, so that the mass will tend to draw itself up. But in special cases, the virial will be increased so much that the surface-tension will be diminished at points where the temperature is first restored. In that case, the outer film will give way and the tension at other places will aid in causing the general fluid to be poured out at those points, forming pseudopodia.

When the protoplasm is in a liquid state, and then only, a solution of food is able to penetrate its mass by diffusion. The protoplasm is then considerably dissociated; and so is the food, like all dissolved matter. If then the separated and unsaturated sub-molecules of the food happen to be of the same chemical species as sub-molecules of the protoplasm, they may unite with other sub-molecules of the protoplasm to form new molecules, in such a fashion that when the solid state is resumed, there may be more molecules of protoplasm than there were at the beginning. It is like the jackknife whose blade and handle, after having been severally lost and replaced, were found and put together to make a new knife.

We have seen that protoplasm is chilled by liquefaction, and that this brings it back to the solid state, when the heat is recovered. This series of operations must be very rapid in the case of nerve-slime and even of muscle-slime, and may account for the unsteady or vibratory character of their action. Of course, if assimilation takes place, the heat of combination, which is probably trifling, is gained. On the other hand, if work is done, whether by nerve or by muscle, loss of energy must take place. In the case of the muscle, the mode by which the instantaneous part of the fatigue is brought about is easily traced out. If when the muscle contracts it be under stress, it will contract less than it otherwise would do, and there will be a loss of heat. It is like an engine which should work by dissolving salt in water and using the contraction during the solution to lift a weight, the salt being recovered afterwards by distillation. But the major part of fatigue has nothing to do with the correlation of forces. A man must labor hard to do in a quarter of an hour the work which draws from him enough heat to cool his body by a single degree. Meantime, he will be getting heated, he will be pouring out extra products of combustion, perspiration, etc., and he will be driving the blood at an accelerated rate through minute tubes at great expense. Yet all this will have little to do with his fatigue. He may sit quietly at his table writing, doing practically no physical work at all, and yet in a few hours be terribly fagged. This seems to be owing to the deranged sub-molecules of the nerve-slime not having had time to settle back into their proper combinations. When such sub-molecules are thrown out, as they must be from time to time, there is so much waste of material.

In order that a sub-molecule of food may be thoroughly and firmly assimilated into a broken molecule of protoplasm, it is necessary not only that it should have precisely the right chemical composition, but also that it should be at precisely the right spot at the right time and should be moving in precisely the right direction with precisely the right velocity. If all these conditions are not fulfilled, it will be more loosely retained than the other parts of the molecule; and every time it comes round into the situation in which it was drawn in, relatively to the other parts of that molecule and to such others as were near enough to be factors in the action, it will be in special danger of being thrown out again. Thus, when a partial liquefaction of the protoplasm takes place many times to about the same extent, it will, each time, be pretty nearly the same molecules that were last drawn in that are now thrown out. They will be thrown out, too, in about the same way, as to position, direction of motion, and velocity, in which they were drawn in; and this will be in about the same course that the ones last before them were thrown out. Not exactly, however; for the very cause of their being thrown off so easily is their not having fulfilled precisely the conditions of stable retention. Thus, the law of habit is accounted for, and with it its peculiar characteristic of not acting with exactitude.

It seems to me that this explanation of habit, aside from the question of its truth or falsity, has a certain value as an addition to our little store of mechanical examples of actions analogous to habit. All the others, so far as I know, are either statical or else involve forces which, taking only the sensible motions into account, violate the law of energy. It is so with the stream that wears its own bed. Here, the sand is carried to its most stable situation and left there. The law of energy forbids this; for when anything reaches a position of stable equilibrium, its momentum will be at a maximum, so that it can according to this law only be left at rest in an unstable situation. In all the statical illustrations, too, things are brought into certain states and left there. A garment receives folds and keeps them; that is, its limit of elasticity is exceeded. This failure to spring back is again an apparent violation of the law of energy; for the substance will not only not spring back of itself (which might be due to an unstable equilibrium being reached) but will not even do so when an impulse that way is applied to it. Accordingly, Professor James says, "the phenomena of habit . . . are due to the plasticity of the . . . materials." Now, plasticity of materials means the having of a low limit of elasticity. (See the *Century Dictionary,* under *solid.*) But the hypothetical constitution of protoplasm here proposed involves no forces but attractions and repulsions strictly following the law of energy. The action here, that is, the throwing of an atom out of its orbit in a molecule, and the entering of a new atom into nearly, but not quite the same orbit, is somewhat similar to the molecular actions which may be supposed to take place in a solid strained beyond its limit of elasticity. Namely, in that case certain molecules must be thrown out of their orbits, to settle down again shortly after into new orbits. In short, the plastic solid resembles protoplasm in being partially and temporarily liquefied by a slight mechanical force. But the taking of a set by a solid body has but a moderate resemblance to the taking of a habit, inasmuch as the characteristic feature of the latter, its inexactitude and want of complete determinacy, is not so marked in the former, if it can be said to be present there, at all.

The truth is that though the molecular explanation of habit is pretty vague on the mathematical side, there can be no doubt that systems of atoms having polar forces would act substantially in that manner, and the explanation is even too satisfactory to suit the convenience of an advocate of tychism. For it may fairly be urged that since the phenomena of habit may thus result from a purely mechanical arrangement, it is unnecessary to suppose that habit-taking is a primordial principle of the universe. But one fact remains unexplained mechanically, which concerns not only the facts of habit, but all cases of actions apparently violating the law of energy; it is that all these phenomena depend upon aggregations of trillions of molecules in one and the same condition and neighborhood; and it is by no means clear how they could have all been brought and left in the same place and state by any conservative forces. But let the mechanical explanation be as perfect as it may, the state of things which it supposes presents evidence of a primordial habit-taking tendency. For it shows us like things acting in like ways because they are alike. Now, those who insist on the doctrine of necessity will for the most part insist that the physical world is entirely individual. Yet law involves an element of generality. Now to say that generality is primordial, but generalization not, is like saying that diversity is primordial but diversification not. It turns logic upside down. At any rate, it is clear that nothing but a principle of habit, itself due to the growth by habit of an infinitesimal chance tendency toward habit-taking, is the only bridge that can span the chasm between the chance-medley of chaos and the cosmos of order and law.

I shall not attempt a molecular explanation of the phenomena of reproduction, because that would require a subsidiary hypothesis, and carry me away from my main object. Such phenomena, universally diffused though they be, appear to depend upon special conditions; and we do not find that all protoplasm has reproductive powers.

But what is to be said of the property of feeling? If consciousness belongs to all protoplasm, by what mechanical constitution is this to be accounted for? The slime is nothing but a chemical compound. There is no inherent impossibility in its being formed synthetically in the laboratory, out of its chemical elements; and if it were so made, it would present all the characters of natural protoplasm. No doubt, then, it would feel. To hesitate to admit this would be puerile and ultra-puerile. By what element of the molecular arrangement, then, would that feeling be caused? This question cannot be evaded or pooh-poohed. Protoplasm certainly does feel; and unless we are to accept a weak dualism, the property must be shown to arise from some peculiarity of the mechanical system. Yet the attempt to deduce it from the three laws of mechanics, applied to never so ingenious a mechanical contrivance, would obviously be futile. It can never be explained, unless we admit that physical events are but degraded or undeveloped forms of psychical events. But once grant that the phenomena of matter are but the result of the sensibly complete sway of habits upon mind, and it only remains to explain why in the protoplasm these habits are to some slight extent broken up, so that according to the law of mind, in that special clause of it sometimes called the principle of accommodation,[9] feeling becomes intensified. Now the manner in which habits generally get broken up is this. Reactions usually terminate in the removal of a stimulus; for the excitation continues as long as the stimulus is present. Accordingly, habits are general ways of behavior which are associated with the removal of stimuli. But when the expected removal of the stimulus fails to occur, the excitation continues and increases, and non-habitual reactions take place; and these tend to weaken the habit. If, then, we suppose that matter never does obey its ideal laws with absolute precision, but that there are almost insensible fortuitous departures from regularity, these will produce, in general, equally minute effects. But protoplasm is in an excessively unstable condition; and it is the characteristic of unstable equilibrium, that near that point excessively minute causes may produce startlingly large effects. Here, then, the usual departures from regularity will be followed by others that are very great; and the large fortuitous departures from law so produced, will tend still further to break up the laws, supposing that these are of

[9] "Physiologically, . . . accommodation means the breaking up of a habit. . . . Psychologically, it means reviving consciousness." Baldwin, *Psychology*, Part III, ch. i., § 5.

the nature of habits. Now, this breaking up of habit and renewed fortuitous spontaneity will, according to the law of mind, be accompanied by an intensification of feeling. The nerve-protoplasm is, without doubt, in the most unstable condition of any kind of matter; and consequently, there the resulting feeling is the most manifest.

Thus we see that the idealist has no need to dread a mechanical theory of life. On the contrary, such a theory, fully developed, is bound to call in a tychistic idealism as its indispensable adjunct. Wherever chance-spontaneity is found, there, in the same proportion, feeling exists. In fact, chance is but the outward aspect of that which within itself is feeling. I long ago showed that real existence, or thing-ness, consists in regularities. So, that primeval chaos in which there was no regularity was mere nothing, from a physical aspect. Yet it was not a blank zero; for there was an intensity of consciousness there in comparison with which all that we ever feel is but as the struggling of a molecule or two to throw off a little of the force of law to an endless and innumerable diversity of chance utterly unlimited.

But after some atoms of the protoplasm have thus become partially emancipated from law, what happens next to them? To understand this, we have to remember that no mental tendency is so easily strengthened by the action of habit as is the tendency to take habits. Now, in the higher kinds of protoplasm, especially, the atoms in question have not only long belonged to one molecule or another of the particular mass of slime of which they are parts; but before that, they were constituents of food of a protoplasmic constitution. During all this time, they have been liable to lose habits and to recover them again; so that now, when the stimulus is removed, and the foregone habits tend to reassert themselves, they do so in the case of such atoms with great promptness. Indeed, the return is so prompt that there is nothing but the feeling to show conclusively that the bonds of law have ever been relaxed.

In short, diversification is the vestige of chance-spontaneity; and wherever diversity is increasing, there chance must be operative. On the other hand, wherever uniformity is increasing, habit must be operative. But wherever actions take place under an established uniformity, there so much feeling as there may be takes the mode of a sense of reaction. That is the manner in which I am led to define the relation between the fundamental elements of consciousness and their physical equivalents.

It remains to consider the physical relations of general ideas. It may be well here to reflect that if matter has no existence except as a specialization of mind, it follows that whatever affects matter according to regular laws is itself matter. But all mind is directly or indirectly connected with all matter, and acts in a more or less regular way; so that all mind more or less partakes of the nature of matter. Hence, it would be a mistake to conceive of the psychical and the physical aspects of matter as two aspects absolutely distinct. Viewing a thing from the outside, considering its relations of action and reaction with other things, it appears as matter. Viewing it from the inside, looking at its immediate character as feeling, it appears as consciousness. These two views are combined when we remember that mechanical laws are nothing but acquired habits, like all the regularities of mind, including the tendency to take habits, itself; and that this action of habit is nothing but generalization, and generalization is nothing but the spreading of feelings. But the question is, how do general ideas appear in the molecular theory of protoplasm?

The consciousness of a habit involves a general idea. In each action of that habit certain atoms get thrown out of their orbit, and replaced by others. Upon all the different occasions it is different atoms that are thrown off, but they are analogous from a physical point of view, and there is an inward sense of their being analogous. Every time one of the associated feelings recurs, there is a more or less vague sense that there are others, that it has a general character, and of about what this general character is. We ought not, I think, to hold that in protoplasm habit never acts in any other than the particular way suggested above. On the contrary, if habit be a primary property of mind, it must be equally so of matter, as a kind of mind. We can hardly refuse to admit that wherever chance motions have general characters, there is a tendency for this generality to spread and to perfect itself. In that case, a general idea is a certain modification of consciousness which accompanies any regularity or general relation between chance actions.

The consciousness of a general idea has a certain "unity of the ego," in it, which is identical when it passes from one mind to another. It is, therefore, quite analogous to a person; and, indeed, a person is only a particular kind of general idea. Long age, in the *Journal of Speculative*

Philosophy (Vol. II, p. 156), I pointed out that a person is nothing but a symbol involving a general idea; but my views were, then, too nominalistic to enable me to see that every general idea has the unified living feeling of a person.

All that is necessary, upon this theory, to the existence of a person is that the feelings out of which he is constructed should be in close enough connection to influence one another. Here we can draw a consequence which it may be possible to submit to experimental test. Namely, if this be the case, there should be something like personal consciousness in bodies of men who are in intimate and intensely sympathetic communion. It is true that when the generalization of feeling has been carried so far as to include all within a person, a stopping-place, in a certain sense, has been attained; and further generalization will have a less lively character. But we must not think it will cease. *Esprit de corps*, national sentiment, sympathy, are no mere metaphors. None of us can fully realize what the minds of corporations are, any more than one of my brain-cells can know what the whole brain is thinking. But the law of mind clearly points to the existence of such personalities, and there are many ordinary observations which, if they were critically examined and supplemented by special experiments, might, as first appearances promise, give evidence of the influence of such greater persons upon individuals. It is often remarked that on one day half a dozen people, strangers to one another, will take it into their heads to do one and the same strange deed, whether it be a physical experiment, a crime, or an act of virtue. When the thirty thousand young people of the society for Christian

Endeavor were in New York, there seemed to me to be some mysterious diffusion of sweetness and light. If such a fact is capable of being made out anywhere, it should be in the church. The Christians have always been ready to risk their lives for the sake of having prayers in common, of getting together and praying simultaneously with great energy, and especially for their common body, for "the whole state of Christ's church militant here in earth," as one of the missals has it. This practice they have been keeping up everywhere, weekly, for many centuries. Surely, a personality ought to have developed in that church, in that "bride of Christ," as they call it, or else there is a strange break in the action of mind, and I shall have to acknowledge my views are much mistaken. Would not the societies for psychical research be more likely to break through the clouds, in seeking evidences of such corporate personality, than in seeking evidences of telepathy, which, upon the same theory, should be a far weaker phenomenon?

V. EVOLUTIONARY LOVE[1]

AT FIRST BLUSH. COUNTER-GOSPELS

PHILOSOPHY, when just escaping from its golden pupa-skin, mythology, proclaimed the great evolutionary agency of the universe to be Love. Or, since this pirate-lingo, English, is poor in such-like words, let us say Eros, the exuberance-love. Afterwards, Empedocles set up passionate-love and hate as the two co-ordinate powers of the universe. In some passages, kindness is the word. But certainly, in any sense in which it has an opposite, to be senior partner of that opposite, is the highest position that love can attain. Nevertheless, the ontological gospeller, in whose days those views were familiar topics, made the One Supreme Being, by whom all things have been made out of nothing, to be cherishing-love. What, then, can he say to hate? Never mind, at this time, what the scribe of the apocalypse, if he were John, stung at length by persecution into a rage unable to distinguish suggestions of evil from visions of heaven, and so become the Slanderer of God to men, may have dreamed. The question is rather what the sane John thought, or ought to have thought, in order to carry out his idea consistently. His statement that God is love seems aimed at that saying of Ecclesiastes that we cannot tell whether God bears us love or hatred. "Nay," says John, "we can tell, and very simply! We know and have

[1] *The Monist*, January, 1893.

trusted the love which God hath in us. God is love." There is no logic in this, unless it means that God loves all men. In the preceding paragraph, he had said, "God is light and in him is no darkness at all." We are to understand, then, that as darkness is merely the defect of light, so hatred and evil are mere imperfect stages of ἀγάπη and ἀγαθόν, love and loveliness. This concords with that utterance reported in John's Gospel: "God sent not the Son into the world to judge the world; but that the world should through him be saved. He that believeth on him is not judged: he that believeth not hath been judged already. . . . And this is the judgment, that the light is come into the world, and that men loved darkness rather than the light." That is to say, God visits no punishment on them; they punish themselves, by their natural affinity for the defective. Thus, the love that God is, is not a love of which hatred is the contrary; otherwise Satan would be a co-ordinate power; but it is a love which embraces hatred as an imperfect stage of it, an Anteros — yea, even needs hatred and hatefulness as its object. For self-love is no love; so if God's self is love, that which he loves must be defect of love; just as a luminary can light up only that which otherwise would be dark. Henry James, the Swedenborgian, says: "It is no doubt very tolerable finite or creaturely love to love one's own in another, to love another for his conformity to one's self: but nothing can be in more flagrant contrast with the creative Love, all whose tenderness *ex vi termini* must be reserved only for what intrinsically is most bitterly hostile and negative to itself." This is from *Substance and Shadow:* an *Essay on the*

Physics of Creation. It is a pity he had not filled his pages with things like this, as he was able easily to do, instead of scolding at his reader and at people generally, until the physics of creation was well-nigh forgot. I must deduct, however, from what I just wrote: obviously no genius could make his every sentence as sublime as one which discloses for the problem of evil its everlasting solution.

The movement of love is circular, at one and the same impulse projecting creations into independency and drawing them into harmony. This seems complicated when stated so; but it is fully summed up in the simple formula we call the Golden Rule. This does not, of course, say, Do everything possible to gratify the egoistic impulses of others, but it says, Sacrifice your own perfection to the perfectionment of your neighbor. Nor must it for a moment be confounded with the Benthamite, or Helvetian, or Beccarian motto, Act for the greatest good of the greatest number. Love is not directed to abstractions but to persons; not to persons we do not know, nor to numbers of people, but to our own dear ones, our family and neighbors. "Our neighbor," we remember, is one whom we live near, not locally perhaps, but in life and feeling.

Everybody can see that the statement of St. John is the formula of an evolutionary philosophy, which teaches that growth comes only from love, from — I will not say self-*sacrifice,* but from the ardent impulse to fulfil another's highest impulse. Suppose, for example, that I have an idea that interests me. It is my creation. It is my creature; for as shown in last July's *Monist,* it is a little person. I love it; and I will sink myself in perfecting it. It is not by dealing out cold justice to the circle of my ideas that I can make them grow, but by cherishing and tending them as I would the flowers in my garden. The philosophy we draw from John's gospel is that this is the way mind develops; and as for the cosmos, only so far as it yet is mind, and so has life, is it capable of further evolution. Love, recognizing germs of loveliness in the hateful, gradually warms it into life, and makes it lovely. That is the sort of evolution which every careful student of my essay *The Law of Mind*, must see that *synechism* calls for.

The nineteenth century is now fast sinking into the grave, and we all begin to review its doings and to think what character it is destined to bear as compared with other centuries in the minds of future historians. It will be called, I guess, the Economical Century; for political economy has more direct relations with all the branches of its activity than has any other science. Well, political economy has its formula of redemption, too. It is this: Intelligence in the service of greed ensures the justest prices, the fairest contracts, the most enlightened conduct of all the dealings between men, and leads to the *summum bonum*, food in plenty and perfect comfort. Food for whom? Why, for the greedy master of intelligence. I do not mean to say that this is one of the legitimate conclusions of political economy, the scientific character of which I fully acknowledge. But the study of doctrines, themselves true, will often temporarily encourage generalizations extremely false, as the study of physics has encouraged necessitarianism. What I say, then, is that the great attention paid to economical questions during our century has induced an exaggeration of the beneficial effects of greed and of the unfortunate results of sentiment, until there has resulted a philosophy which comes unwittingly to this, that greed is the great agent in the elevation of the human race and in the evolution of the universe.

I open a handbook of political economy, — the most typical and middling one I have at hand, — and there find some remarks of which I will here make a brief analysis. I omit qualifications, sops thrown to Cerberus, phrases to placate Christian prejudice, trappings which serve to hide from author and reader alike the ugly nakedness of the greed-god. But I have surveyed my position. The author enumerates "three motives to human action:

The love of self;

The love of a limited class having common interests and feelings with one's self;

The love of mankind at large."

Remark, at the outset, what obsequious title is bestowed on greed, — "the love of self." Love! The second motive *is* love. In place of "a limited class" put "certain persons," and you have a fair description. Taking "class" in the old-fashioned sense, a weak kind of love is described. In the sequel, there seems to be some haziness as to the delimitation of this motive. By the love of mankind at large, the author does not mean that deep, subconscious passion that is properly so called; but merely public-spirit, perhaps little more than a fidget about pushing ideas. The author proceeds to a comparative estimate of the worth of these motives. Greed, says he, but using, of course, another word, "is not so great an evil as is commonly supposed. . . . Every man can promote his own interests a great deal more effectively than he can promote any one else's, or than any one else can promote his." Besides, as he remarks on another page, the more miserly a man is, the more good he does. The second motive "is the most dangerous one to which society is exposed." Love is all very pretty: "no higher or purer source of human happiness exists." (Ahem!) But it is a "source of enduring injury," and, in short, should be overruled by something wiser. What is this wiser motive? We shall see.

As for public spirit, it is rendered nugatory by the "difficulties in the way of its effective operation." For example, it might suggest putting checks upon the fecundity of the poor and the vicious; and "no measure of repression would be too severe," in the case of criminals. The hint is broad. But unfortunately, you cannot induce legislatures to take such measures, owing to the pestiferous "tender sentiments of man towards man." It thus appears, that public-spirit, or Benthamism, is not strong enough to be the effective tutor of love, (I am skipping to another page), which must, therefore, be handed over to "the motives which animate men in the pursuit of wealth," in which alone we can confide, and which "are in the highest degree beneficent."[2] Yes, in the "highest degree" without exception are they beneficent to the being upon whom all their blessings are poured out, namely, the Self, whose "sole object," says the writer in accumulating wealth is his in-

[2] How can a writer have any respect for science, as such, who is capable of confounding with the scientific propositions of political economy, which have nothing to say concerning what is "beneficent," such brummagem generalisations as this?

dividual "sustenance and enjoyment." Plainly, the author holds the notion that some other motive might be in a higher degree beneficent even for the man's self to be a paradox wanting in good sense. He seeks to gloze and modify his doctrine; but he lets the perspicacious reader see what his animating principle is; and when, holding the opinions I have repeated, he at the same time acknowledges that society could not exist upon a basis of intelligent greed alone, he simply pigeon-holes himself as one of the eclectics of inharmonious opinions. He wants his mammon flavored with a *soupçon* of god.

The economists accuse those to whom the enunciation of their atrocious villainies communicates a thrill of horror of being *sentimentalists*. It may be so: I willingly confess to having some tincture of sentimentalism in me, God be thanked! Ever since the French Revolution brought this leaning of thought into ill-repute, — and not altogether undeservedly, I must admit, true, beautiful, and good as that great movement was, — it has been the tradition to picture sentimentalists as persons incapable of logical thought and unwilling to look facts in the eyes. This tradition may be classed with the French tradition that an Englishman says *godam* at every second sentence, the English tradition that an American talks about "Britishers," and the American tradition that a Frenchman carries forms of etiquette to an inconvenient extreme, in short with all those traditions which survive simply because the men who use their eyes and ears are few and far between. Doubtless some excuse there was for all those opinions in days gone by; and sentimentalism, when it was the fashionable amusement to spend one's evenings in a flood of tears over a woeful performance on a candle-litten stage, sometimes made itself a little ridiculous. But what after all is sentimentalism? It is an *ism,* a doctrine, namely, the doctrine that great respect should be paid to the natural judgments of the sensible heart. This is what sentimentalism precisely is; and I entreat the reader to consider whether to contemn it is not of all blasphemies the most degrading. Yet the nineteenth century has steadily contemned it, because it brought about the Reign of Terror. That it did so is true. Still, the whole question is one of *how much.* The Reign of Terror was very bad; but now the Gradgrind banner has been this century long flaunting in the face of heaven, with an insolence to provoke the very skies to scowl and rumble. Soon a flash and quick peal will shake economists quite out of their complacency, too late. The twentieth century, in its latter half, shall surely see the deluge-tempest burst upon the social order, — to clear upon a world as deep in ruin as that greed-philosophy has long plunged it into guilt. No post-thermidorian high jinks then!

So a miser is a beneficent power in a community, is he? With the same reason precisely, only in a much higher degree, you might pronounce the Wall Street sharp to be a good angel, who takes money from heedless persons not likely to guard it properly, who wrecks feeble enterprises better stopped, and who administers wholesome lessons to unwary scientific men, by passing worthless checks upon them, — as you did, the other day, to me, my millionaire Master in glomery, when you thought you saw your way to using my process without paying for it, and of so bequeathing to your children something to boast of their father about, — and who by a thousand wiles puts money at the service of intelligent greed, in his own person. Bernard Mandeville, in his *Fable of the Bees,* maintains that private vices of all descriptions are public benefits, and proves it, too, quite as cogently as the economist proves his point concerning the miser. He even argues, with no slight force, that but for vice civilization would never have existed. In the same spirit, it has been strongly maintained and is to-day widely believed that all acts of charity and benevolence, private and public, go seriously to degrade the human race.

The *Origin of Species* of Darwin merely extends politico-economical views of progress to the entire realm of animal and vegetable life. The vast majority of our contemporary naturalists hold the opinion that the true cause of those exquisite and marvellous adaptations of nature for which, when I was a boy, men used to extol the divine wisdom is that creatures are so crowded together that those of them that happen to have the slightest advantage force those less pushing into situations unfavorable to multiplication or even kill them before they reach the age of reproduction. Among animals, the mere mechanical individualism is vastly reënforced as a power making for good by the animal's ruthless greed. As Darwin puts it on his title-page, it is the struggle for existence; and he should have added for his motto: Every individual for himself, and the Devil take the hindmost! Jesus, in his sermon on the Mount, expressed a different opinion.

Here, then, is the issue. The gospel of Christ says that progress comes from every individual merging his individuality in sympathy with his neighbors. On the other side, the conviction of the nineteenth century is that progress takes place by virtue of every individual's striving for himself with all his might and trampling his neighbor under foot whenever he gets a chance to do so. This may accurately be called the Gospel of Greed.

Much is to be said on both sides. I have not concealed, I could not conceal, my own passionate predilection. Such a confession will probably shock my scientific brethren. Yet the strong feeling is in itself, I think, an argument of some weight in favor of the agapastic theory of evolution, — so far as it may be presumed to bespeak the normal judgment of the Sensible Heart. Certainly, if it were possible to believe in agapasm without believing it warmly, that fact would be an argument against the truth of the doctrine. At any rate, since the warmth of feeling exists, it should on every account be candidly confessed; especially since it creates a liability to onesidedness on my part against which it behooves my readers and me to be severally on our guard.

SECOND THOUGHTS. IRENICA.

Let us try to define the logical affinities of the different theories of evolution. Natural selection, as conceived by Darwin, is a mode of evolution in which the only positive agent of change in the whole passage from moner to man is fortuitous variation. To secure advance in a definite direction chance has to be seconded by some action that shall hinder the propagation of some varieties or stimulate that of others. In natural selection, strictly so called, it is the crowding out of the weak. In sexual selection, it is the attraction of beauty, mainly.

The *Origin of Species* was published toward the end of the year 1859. The preceding years since 1846 had been one of the most productive seasons, — or if extended so as to cover the great book we are considering, *the* most productive period of equal length in the entire history of science from its beginnings until now. The idea that chance begets order, which is one of the corner-stones of modern physics (although Dr. Carus considers it "the weakest point in Mr. Peirce's system,") was at that time put into its clearest light. Quetelet had opened the discussion by his *Letters on the Application of Probabilities to the Moral and Political Sciences,* a work which deeply impressed the best minds of that day, and to which Sir John Herschel had drawn general attention in Great Britain. In 1857, the first volume of Buckle's *History of Civilisation* had created a tremendous sensation, owing to the use he made of this same idea. Meantime, the "statistical method" had, under that very name, been applied with brilliant success to molecular physics. Dr. John Herapath, an English chemist, had in 1847 outlined the kinetical theory of gases in his *Mathematical Physics;* and the interest the theory excited had been refreshed in 1856 by notable memoirs by Clausius and Krönig. In the very summer preceding Darwin's publication, Maxwell had read before the British Association the first and most important of his researches on this subject. The consequence was that the idea that fortuitous events may result in a physical law, and further that this is the way in which those laws which appear to conflict with the principle of the conservation of energy are to be explained, had taken a strong hold upon the minds of all who were abreast of the leaders of thought. By such minds, it was inevitable that the *Origin of Species*, whose teaching was simply the application of the same principle to the explanation of another "non-conservative" action, that of organic development, should be hailed and welcomed. The sublime discovery of the conservation of energy by Helmholtz in 1847, and that of the mechanical theory of heat by Clausius and by Rankine, independently, in 1850, had decidedly overawed all those who might have been inclined to sneer at physical science. Thereafter a belated poet still harping upon "science peddling with the names of things" would fail of his effect. Mechanism was now known to be all, or very nearly so. All this time, utilitarianism, — that improved substitute for the Gospel, — was in its fullest feather; and was a natural ally of an individualistic theory. Dean Mansell's injudicious advocacy had led to mutiny among the bondsmen of Sir William Hamilton, and the nominalism of Mill had profited accordingly; and although the real science that Darwin was leading men to was sure some day to give a death-blow to the sham-science of Mill, yet there were several elements of the Darwinian theory which were sure to charm the followers of Mill. Another thing: anæsthetics had been in use for thirteen years. Already, people's acquaintance with suffering had dropped off very much; and as a consequence, that unlovely hardness by which our times are so contrasted with those that immediately preceded them, had already set in, and inclined people to relish a ruthless theory. The reader would quite mistake the drift of what I am saying if he were to understand me as wishing to suggest that any of those things (except perhaps Malthus) influenced Darwin himself. What I mean is that his hypothesis, while without dispute one of the most ingenious and pretty ever devised, and while argued with a wealth of knowledge, a strength of logic, a charm of rhetoric, and above all with a certain magnetic genuineness that was almost irresistible, did not appear, at first, at all near to being proved; and to a sober mind its case looks less hopeful now than it did twenty years ago; but the extraordinarily favorable reception it met with was plainly owing, in large measure, to its ideas being those toward which the age was favorably disposed, especially, because of the encouragement it gave to the greed-philosophy.

Diametrically opposed to evolution by chance, are those theories which attribute all progress to an inward necessary principle, or other form of necessity. Many naturalists have thought that if an egg is destined to go through a certain series of embryological transformations, from which it is perfectly certain not to deviate, and if in geological time almost exactly the same forms appear successively, one replacing another in the same order, the strong presumption is that this latter succession was as predeterminate and certain to take place as the former. So, Nägeli, for instance, conceives that it somehow follows from the first law of motion and the peculiar, but unknown, molecular constitution of protoplasm, that forms must complicate themselves more and more. Kölliker makes one form generate another after a certain maturation has been accomplished. Weismann, too, though he calls himself a Darwinian, holds that nothing is due to chance, but that all forms are simple mechanical resultants of the heredity from two parents.[3] It is very noticeable that all these different sectaries seek to import into their science a mechanical necessity to which the facts that come under their observation do not point. Those geologists who think that the variation of species is due to cataclysmic alterations of climate or of the chemical constitution of the air and water are also making mechanical necessity chief factor of evolution.

Evolution by sporting and evolution by mechanical necessity are conceptions warring against one another. A third method, which supersedes their strife, lies enwrapped in the theory of Lamarck. According to his view, all that distinguishes the highest organic forms from the most rudimentary has been brought about by little hypertrophies or atrophies which have affected individuals early in their lives, and have been transmitted to their offspring. Such a transmission of acquired characters is of the general nature of habit-taking, and this is the representative and derivative within the physiological domain of the law of mind. Its action is essentially dissimilar to that of a physical force; and that is the secret of the repugnance of such necessitarians as Weismann to admitting its existence. The Lamarckians further suppose that although some of the

[3] I am happy to find that Dr. Carus, too, ranks Weismann among the opponents of Darwin, notwithstanding his flying that flag.

modifications of form so transmitted were originally due to mechanical causes, yet the chief factors of their first production were the straining of endeavor and the overgrowth superinduced by exercise, together with the opposite actions. Now, endeavor, since it is directed toward an end, is essentially psychical, even though it be sometimes unconscious; and the growth due to exercise, as I argued in my last paper, follows a law of a character quite contrary to that of mechanics.

Lamarckian evolution is thus evolution by the force of habit. — That sentence slipped off my pen while one of those neighbors whose function in the social cosmos seems to be that of an Interrupter, was asking me a question. Of course, it is nonsense. Habit is mere inertia, a resting on one's oars, not a propulsion. Now it is energetic projaculation (lucky there is such a word, or this untried hand might have been put to inventing one) by which in the typical instances of Lamarckian evolution the new elements of form are first created. Habit, however, forces them to take practical shapes, compatible with the structures they affect, and in the form of heredity and otherwise, gradually replaces the spontaneous energy that sustains them. Thus, habit plays a double part; it serves to establish the new features, and also to bring them into harmony with the general morphology and function of the animals and plants to which they belong. But if the reader will now kindly give himself the trouble of turning back a page or two, he will see that this account of Lamarckian evolution coincides with the general description of the action of love, to which, I suppose, he yielded his assent.

Remembering that all matter is really mind, remembering, too, the continuity of mind, let us ask what aspect Lamarckian evolution takes on within the domain of consciousness. Direct endeavor can achieve almost nothing. It is as easy by taking thought to add a cubit to one's stature, as it is to produce an idea acceptable to any of the Muses by merely straining for it, before it is ready to come. We haunt in vain the sacred well and throne of Mnemosyne; the deeper workings of the spirit take place in their own slow way, without our connivance. Let but their bugle sound, and we may then make our effort, sure of an oblation for the altar of whatsoever divinity its savor gratifies. Besides this inward process, there is the operation of the environment, which goes to break up habits destined to be broken up and so to render the mind lively. Everybody knows that the long continuance of a routine of habit makes us lethargic, while a succession of surprises wonderfully brightens the ideas. Where there is a motion, where history is a-making, there is the focus of mental activity, and it has been said that the arts and sciences reside within the temple of Janus, waking when that is open, but slumbering when it is closed. Few psychologists have perceived how fundamental a fact this is. A portion of mind abundantly commissured to other portions works almost mechanically. It sinks to a condition of a railway junction. But a portion of mind almost isolated, a spiritual peninsula, or *cul-de-sac,* is like a railway terminus. Now mental commissures are habits. Where they abound, originality is not needed and is not found; but where they are in defect, spontaneity is set free. Thus, the first step in the Lamarckian evolution of mind is the putting of sundry thoughts into situations in which they are free to play. As to growth by exercise, I have already shown, in discussing *Man's Glassy Essence,* in last October's *Monist,* what its *modus operandi* must be conceived to be, at least, until a second equally definite hypothesis shall have been offered. Namely, it consists of the flying asunder of molecules, and the reparation of the parts by new matter. It is, thus, a sort of reproduction. It takes place only during exercise, because the activity of protoplasm consists in the molecular disturbance which is its necessary condition. Growth by exercise takes place also in the mind. Indeed, that is what it is to *learn.* But the most perfect illustration is the development of a philosophical idea by being put into practice. The conception which appeared, at first, as unitary, splits up into special cases; and into each of these new thought must enter to make a practicable idea. This new thought, however, follows pretty closely the model of the parent conception; and thus a homogeneous development takes place. The parallel between this and the course of molecular occurrences is apparent. Patient attention will be able to trace all these elements in the transaction called learning.

Three modes of evolution have thus been brought before us; evolution by fortuitous variation, evolution by mechanical necessity, and evolution by creative love. We may term them *tychastic* evolution, or *tychasm, anancastic* evolution, or *anancasm,* and *agapastic* evolution, or *agapasm.* The doctrines which represent these as severally of principal importance, we may term *tychasticism, anancas-*

ticism, and *agapasticism.* On the other hand the mere propositions that absolute chance, mechanical necessity, and the law of love, are severally operative in the cosmos, may receive the names of *tychism, anancism,* and *agapism.*

All three modes of evolution are composed of the same general elements. Agapasm exhibits them the most clearly. The good result is here brought to pass, first, by the bestowal of spontaneous energy by the parent upon the offspring, and, second, by the disposition of the latter to catch the general idea of those about it and thus to subserve the general purpose. In order to express the relation that tychasm and anancasm bear to agapasm, let me borrow a word from geometry. An ellipse crossed by a straight line is a sort of cubic curve; for a cubic is a curve which is cut thrice by a straight line; now a straight line might cut the ellipse twice and its associated straight line a third time. Still the ellipse with the straight line across it would not have the characteristics of a cubic. It would have, for instance, no contrary flexure, which no true cubic wants; and it would have two nodes, which no true cubic has. The geometers say that it is a *degenerate* cubic. Just so, tychasm and anancasm are degenerate forms of agapasm.

Men who seek to reconcile the Darwinian idea with Christianity will remark that tychastic evolution, like the agapastic, depends upon a reproductive creation, the forms preserved being those that use the spontaneity conferred upon them in such wise as to be drawn into harmony with their original, quite after the Christian scheme. Very good! This only shows that just as love cannot have a contrary, but must embrace what is most opposed to it, as a degenerate case of it, so tychasm is a kind of agapasm. Only, in the tychastic evolution progress is solely owing to the distribution of the napkin-hidden talent of the rejected servant among those not rejected, just as ruined gamesters leave their money on the table to make those not yet ruined so much the richer. It makes the felicity of the lambs just the damnation of the goats, transposed to the other side of the equation. In genuine agapasm, on the other hand, advance takes place by virtue of a positive sympathy among the created springing from continuity of mind. This is the idea which tychasticism knows not how to manage.

The anancasticist might here interpose, claiming that the mode of evolution for which he contends agrees with agapasm at the point at which tychasm departs from it. For it makes development go through certain phases, having its inevitable ebbs and flows, yet tending on the whole to a foreordained perfection. Bare existence by this its destiny betrays an intrinsic affinity for the good. Herein, it must be admitted, anancasm shows itself to be in a broad acception a species of agapasm. Some forms of it might easily be mistaken for the genuine agapasm. The Hegelian philosophy is such an anancasticism. With its revelatory religion, with its synechism (however imperfectly set forth), with its "reflection," the whole idea of the theory is superb, almost sublime. Yet, after all, living freedom is practically omitted from its method. The whole movement is that of a vast engine, impelled by a *vis a tergo*, with a blind and mysterious fate of arriving at a lofty goal. I mean that such an engine it *would* be, if it really worked; but in point of fact, it is a Keely motor. Grant that it really acts as it professes to act, and there is nothing to do but accept the philosophy. But never was there seen such an example of a long chain of reasoning, — shall I say with a flaw in every link? — no, with every link a handful of sand, squeezed into shape in a dream. Or say, it is a pasteboard model of a philosophy that in reality does not exist. If we use the one precious thing it contains, the idea of it, introducing the tychism which the arbitrariness of its every step suggests, and make that the support of a vital freedom which is the breath of the spirit of love, we may be able to produce that genuine agapasticism, at which Hegel was aiming.

A THIRD ASPECT. DISCRIMINATION

In the very nature of things, the line of demarcation between the three modes of evolution is not perfectly sharp. That does not prevent its being quite real; perhaps it is rather a mark of its reality. There is in the nature of things no sharp line of demarcation between the three fundamental colors, red, green, and violet. But for all that they are really different. The main question is whether three radically different evolutionary elements have been operative; and the second question is what are the most striking characteristics of whatever elements have been operative.

I propose to devote a few pages to a very slight examination of these questions in their relation to the historical development of human thought. I first formulate for the reader's convenience the briefest possible definitions of the three conceivable modes of development of thought, distinguishing also two varieties of anancasm and three of agapasm. The tychastic development of thought, then, will consist in slight departures from habitual ideas in different directions indifferently, quite purposeless and quite unconstrained whether by outward circumstances or by force of logic, these new departures being followed by unforeseen results which tend to fix some of them as habits more than others. The anancastic development of thought will consist of new ideas adopted without foreseeing whither they tend, but having a character determined by causes either external to the mind, such as changed circumstances of life, or internal to the mind as logical developments of ideas already accepted, such as generalizations. The agapastic development of thought is the adoption of certain mental tendencies, not altogether heedlessly, as in tychasm, nor quite blindly by the mere force of circumstances or of logic, as in anancasm, but by an immediate attraction for the idea itself, whose nature is divined before the mind possesses it, by the power of sympathy, that is, by virtue of the continuity of mind; and this mental tendency may be of three varieties, as follows: First, it may affect a whole people or community in its collective personality, and be thence communicated to such individuals as are in powerfully sympathetic connection with the collective people, although they may be intellectually incapable of attaining the idea by their private understandings or even perhaps of consciously apprehending it. Second, it may affect a private person directly, yet so that he is only enabled to apprehend the idea, or to appreciate its attractiveness, by virtue of his sympathy with his neighbors, under the influence of a striking experience or development of thought. The conversion of St. Paul may be taken as an example of what is meant. Third, it may affect an individual, independently of his human affections, by virtue of an attraction it exercises upon his mind, even before he has comprehended it. This is the phenomenon which has been well called the *divination* of genius; for it is due to the continuity between the man's mind and the Most High.

Let us next consider by means of what tests we can discriminate between these different categories of evolution. No absolute criterion is possible in the nature of things, since in the nature of things there is no sharp line of demarcation between the different classes. Nevertheless, quantitative symptoms may be found by which a sagacious and sympathetic judge of human nature may be able to estimate the approximate proportions in which the different kinds of influence are commingled.

So far as the historical evolution of human thought has been tychastic, it should have proceeded by insensible or minute steps; for such is the nature of chances when so multiplied as to show phenomena of regularity. For example, assume that of the native-born white adult males of the United States in 1880, one-fourth part were below 5 feet 4 inches in stature and one-fourth part above 5 feet 8 inches. Then by the principles of probability, among the whole population, we should expect

	216	under	4	feet	6	inches,		216	above	6	feet	6	inches
	48	"	4	"	5	"		48	"	6	"	7	"
	9	"	4	"	4	"		9	"	6	"	8	"
less than	2	"	4	"	3	"	less than	2	"	6	"	9	"

I set down these figures to show how insignificantly few are the cases in which anything very far out of the common run presents itself by chance. Though the stature of only every second man is included within the four inches between 5 feet 4 inches and 5 feet 8 inches, yet if this interval be extended by thrice four inches above and below, it will embrace all our 8 millions odd of native-born adult white males (of 1880), except only 9 taller and 9 shorter.

The test of minute variation, if *not* satisfied, absolutely negatives tychasm. If it *is* satisfied, we shall find that it negatives anancasm but not agapasm. We want a positive test, satisfied by tychasm, only. Now wherever we find men's thought taking by imperceptible degrees a turn contrary to the purposes which animate them, in spite of their highest impulses, there, we may safely conclude, there has been a tychastic action.

Students of the history of mind there be of an erudition to fill an imperfect scholar like me with envy edulcorated by joyous admiration, who maintain that ideas when just started are and can be little more than freaks, since they cannot yet have been critically examined, and further that everywhere and at all times progress has been so gradual that it is difficult to make out distinctly what original step any given man has taken. It would follow that tychasm has been the sole method of intellectual development. I have to confess I cannot read history so; I cannot help thinking that while tychasm has sometimes been operative, at others great steps covering nearly the same ground and made by different men independently, have been mistaken for a succcssion of small steps, and further that students have been reluctant to admit a real entitative "spirit" of an age or of a people, under the mistaken and unscrutinized impression that they should thus be opening the door to wild and unnatural hypotheses. I find, on the contrary, that, however it may be with the education of individual minds, the historical development of thought has seldom been of a tychastic nature, and exclusively in backward and barbarizing movements. I desire to speak with the extreme modesty which befits a student of logic who is required to survey so very wide a field of human thought that he can cover it only by a reconnaissance, to which only the greatest skill and most adroit methods can impart any value at all; but, after all, I can only express my own opinions and not those of anybody else; and in my humble judgment, the largest example of tychasm is afforded by the history of Christianity, from about its establishment by Constantine, to, say, the time of the Irish monasteries, an era or eon of about 500 years. Undoubtedly the external circumstance which more than all others at first inclined men to accept Christianity in its loveliness and tenderness, was the fearful extent to which society was broken up into units by the unmitigated greed and hard-heartedness into which the Romans had seduced the world. And yet it was that very same fact, more than any other external circumstance, that fostered that bitterness against the wicked world of which the primitive gospel of Mark contains not a single trace. At least, I do not detect it in the remark about the blasphemy against the Holy Ghost, where nothing is said about vengeance, nor even in that speech where the closing lines of Isaiah are quoted, about the worm and the fire that feed upon the "carcasses of the men that have transgressed against me." But little by little the bitterness increases until in the last book of the New Testament, its poor distracted author represents that all the time Christ was talking about having come to save the world, the secret design was to catch the entire human race, with the exception of a paltry 144,000, and souse them all in a brimstone lake, and as the smoke of their torment went up forever and ever, to turn and remark, "There is no curse any more." Would it be an insensible smirk or a fiendish grin that should accompany such an utterance? I wish I could believe St. John did not write it; but it is his gospel which tells about the "resurrection unto condemnation," — that is of men's being resuscitated just for the sake of torturing them; — and, at any rate, the Revelation is a very ancient composition. One can understand that the early Christians were like men trying with all their might to climb a steep declivity of smooth wet clay; the deepest and truest element of their life, animating both heart and head, was universal love; but they were continually, and against their wills, slipping into a party spirit, every slip serving as a precedent, in a fashion but too familiar to every man. This party feeling insensibily grew until by about A.D. 330 the luster of the pristine integrity that in St. Mark reflects the white spirit of light was so far tarnished that Eusebius, (the Jared Sparks of that day), in the preface to his History, could announce his intention of exaggerating everything that tended to the glory of the church and of suppressing whatever might disgrace it. His Latin contemporary Lactantius is worse, still; and so the darkling went on increasing until before the end of the century the great library of Alexandria was destroyed by Theophilus, [4] until Gregory the Great, two centuries later, burnt the great library of Rome, proclaiming that "Ignorance is the mother of devotion," (which is true, just as oppression and injustice is the mother of spirituality), until a sober description of the state of the church would be a thing our not too nice newspapers would treat as "unfit for publication." All this movement is shown by the application of the test given above to have been tychastic. Another very much like it on a small scale, only a hundred times swifter, for the study of which there are documents by the library-full, is to be found in the history of the French Revolution.

Anancastic evolution advances by successive strides with pauses between. The reason is that in this process a habit of thought having been overthrown is supplanted by the next strongest. Now this next strongest is sure to be widely disparate from the first, and as often as not is its direct contrary. It reminds one of our old rule of making the second candidate vice-president. This character, therefore, clearly distinguishes anancasm from tychasm. The character which distinguishes it from agapasm is its purposelessness. But external and internal anancasm have to be examined separately. Development under the pressure of external circumstances, or cataclysmine evolution, is in most cases unmistakable enough. It has numberless degrees of intensity, from the brute force, the plain war, which has more than once turned the current of the world's thought, down to the hard fact of evidence, or what has been

[4] See *Draper's History of Intellectual Development*, chap. x.

taken for it, which has been known to convince men by hordes. The only hesitation than can subsist in the presence of such a history is a quantitative one. Never are external influences the only ones which affect the mind, and therefore it must be a matter of judgment for which it would scarcely be worth while to attempt to set rules, whether a given movement is to be regarded as principally governed from without or not. In the rise of medieval thought, I mean scholasticism and the synchronistic art developments, undoubtedly the crusades and the discovery of the writings of Aristotle were powerful influences. The development of scholasticism from Roscellin to Albertus Magnus closely follows the successive steps in the knowledge of Aristotle. Prantl thinks that that is the whole story, and few men have thumbed more books than Carl Prantl. He has done good solid work, notwithstanding his slap-dash judgments. But we shall never make so much as a good beginning of comprehending scholasticism until the whole has been systematically explored and digested by a company of students regularly organized and held under rule for that purpose. But as for the period we are now specially considering, that which synchronised the Romanesque architecture, the literature is easily mastered. It does not quite justify Prantl's dicta as to the slavish dependence of these authors upon their authorities. Moreover, they kept a definite purpose steadily before their minds, throughout all their studies. I am, therefore, unable to offer this period of scholasticism as an example of pure external anancasm, which seems to be the fluorine of the intellectual elements. Perhaps the recent Japanese reception of western ideas is the purest instance of it in history. Yet in combination with other elements, nothing is commoner. If the development of ideas under the influence of the study of external facts be considered as external anancasm, — it is on the border between the external and the internal forms, — it is, of course, the principal thing in modern learning. But Whewell, whose masterly comprehension of the history of science critics have been too ignorant properly to appreciate, clearly shows that it is far from being the overwhelmingly preponderant influence, even there.

Internal anancasm, or logical groping, which advances upon a predestined line without being able to foresee whither it is to be carried nor to steer its course, this is the rule of development of philosophy. Hegel first made the world understand this; and he seeks to make logic not merely the subjective guide and monitor of thought, which was all it had been ambitioning before, but to be the very mainspring of thinking, and not merely of individual thinking but of discussion, of the history of the development of thought, of all history, of all development. This involves a positive, clearly demonstrable error. Let the logic in question be of whatever kind it may, a logic of necessary inference or a logic of probable inference (the theory might perhaps be shaped to fit either), in any case it supposes that logic is sufficient of itself to determine what conclusion follows from given premises; for unless it will do so much, it will not suffice to explain why an individual train of reasoning should take just the course it does take, to say nothing of other kinds of development. It thus supposes that from given premises, only one conclusion can logically be drawn, and that there is no scope at all for free choice. That from given premises only one conclusion can logically be drawn, is one of the false notions which have come from logicians' confining their attention to that Nantucket of thought, the logic of non-relative terms. In the logic of relatives, it does not hold good.

One remark occurs to me. If the evolution of history is in considerable part of the nature of internal anancasm, it resembles the development of individual men; and just as 33 years is a rough but natural unit of time for individuals, being the average age at which man has issue, so there should be an approximate period at the end of which one great historical movement ought to be likely to be supplanted by another. Let us see if we can make out anything of the kind. Take the governmental development of Rome as being sufficiently long and set down the principal dates.

B.C. 753, Foundation of Rome.
B.C. 510, Expulsion of the Tarquins.
B.C. 27, Octavius assumes title Augustus.
A.D. 476, End of Western Empire.
A.D. 962, Holy Roman Empire.
A.D. 1453, Fall of Constantinople.

The last event was one of the most significant in history, especially for Italy. The intervals are 243, 483, 502, 486, 491 years. All are rather curiously near equal, except the first which is half the others. Successive reigns of kings would not commonly be so near equal. Let us set down a few dates in the history of thought.

B.C. 585, Eclipse of Thales. Beginning of Greek philosophy.
A.D. 30, The crucifixion.
A.D. 529, Closing of Athenian schools. End of Greek philosophy.
A.D. 1125, (Approximate) Rise of the Universities of Bologna and Paris.
A.D. 1543, Publication of the "De Revolutionibus" of Copernicus. Beginning of Modern Science.

The intervals are 615, 499, 596, 418, years. In the history of metaphysics, we may take the following:

B.C. 322, Death of Aristotle.
A.D. 1274, Death of Aquinas.
A.D. 1804, Death of Kant.

The intervals are 1595 and 530 years. The former is about thrice the latter.

From these figures, no conclusion can fairly be drawn. At the same time, they suggest that perhaps there may be a rough natural era of about 500 years. Should there be any independent evidence of this, the intervals noticed may gain some significance.

The agapastic development of thought should, if it exists, be distinguished by its purposive character, this purpose being the development of an idea. We should have a direct agapic or sympathetic comprehension and recognition of it, by virtue of the continuity of thought. I here take it for granted that such continuity of thought has been sufficiently proved by the arguments used in my paper on the "Law of Mind" in *The Monist* of last July. Even if those arguments are not quite convincing in themselves, yet if they are reënforced by an apparent agapasm in the history of thought, the two propositions will lend one another mutual aid. The reader will, I trust, be too well grounded in logic to mistake such mutual support for a vicious circle in reasoning. If it could be shown directly that there is such an entity as the "spirit of an age" or of a people, and that mere individual intelligence will not account for all the phenomena, this would be proof enough at once of agapasticism and of synechism. I must acknowledge that I am unable to produce a cogent demonstration of this; but I am, I believe, able to adduce such arguments as will serve to confirm those which have been drawn from other facts. I believe that all the greatest achievements of mind have been beyond the powers of unaided individuals; and I find, apart from the support this opinion receives from synechistic considerations, and from the purposive character of many great movements, direct reason for so thinking in the sublimity of the ideas and in their occurring simultaneously and independently to a number of individuals of no extraordinary general powers. The pointed Gothic architecture in several of its developments appears to me to be of such a character. All attempts to imitate it by modern architects of the greatest learning and genius appear flat and tame, and are felt by their authors to be so. Yet at the time the style was living, there was quite an abundance of men capable of producing works of this kind of gigantic sublimity and power. In more than one case, extant documents show that the cathedral chapters, in the selection of architects, treated high artistic genius as a secondary consideration, as if there were no lack of persons able to supply that; and the results justify their confidence. Were individuals in general, then, in those ages possessed of such lofty natures and high intellect? Such an opinion would break down under the first examination.

How many times have men now in middle life seen great discoveries made independently and almost simultaneously! The first instance I remember was the prediction of a planet exterior to Uranus by Leverrier and Adams. One hardly knows to whom the principle of the conservation of energy ought to be attributed, although it may reasonably be considered as the greatest discovery science has ever made. The mechanical theory of heat was set forth by Rankine and by Clausius during the same month of February, 1850; and there are eminent men who attribute this great step to Thomson.[5] The kinetical theory of gases, after being started by John Bernoulli and long buried in oblivion, was reinvented and applied to the explanation not merely of the laws of Boyle, Charles, and Avogadro, but also of diffusion and viscosity, by at least three modern physicists separately. It is well known that the doctrine of natural selection was presented by Wallace and by Darwin at the same meeting of the British Association; and Darwin in his "Historical Sketch" prefixed to the later editions of his book shows that both were anticipated by obscure forerunners. The method of spectrum analysis was claimed for Swan as well as for Kirchhoff, and there were others who perhaps had still better claims. The authorship of the Periodical Law of the Chemical Elements is disputed between a Russian,

[5] Thomson, himself, in his article *Heat* in the *Encyclopedia Britannica*, never once mentions the name of Clausius.

a German, and an Englishman; although there is no room for doubt that the principal merit belongs to the first. These are nearly all the greatest discoveries of our times. It is the same with the inventions. It may not be surprising that the telegraph should have been independently made by several inventors, because it was an easy corollary from scientific facts well made out before. But it was not so with the telephone and other inventions. Ether, the first anæsthetic, was introduced independently by three different New England physicians. Now ether had been a common article for a century. It had been in one of the pharmacopœias three centuries before. It is quite incredible that its anæsthetic property should not have been known; it was known. It had probably passed from mouth to ear as a secret from the days of Basil Valentine; but for long it had been a secret of the Punchinello kind. In New England, for many years, boys had used it for amusement. Why then had it not been put to its serious use? No reason can be given, except that the motive to do so was not strong enough. The motives to doing so could only have been desire for gain and philanthropy. About 1846, the date of the introduction, philanthropy was undoubtedly in an unusually active condition. That sensibility, or sentimentalism, which had been introduced in the previous century, had undergone a ripening process, in consequence of which, though now less intense than it had previously been, it was more likely to influence unreflecting people than it had ever been. All three of the ether-claimants had probably been influenced by the desire for gain; but nevertheless they were certainly not insensible to the agapic influences.

I doubt if any of the great discoveries ought, properly, to be considered as altogether individual achievements; and I think many will share this doubt. Yet, if not, what an argument for the continuity of mind, and for agapasticism is here! I do not wish to be very strenuous. If thinkers will only be persuaded to lay aside their prejudices and apply themselves to studying the evidences of this doctrine, I shall be fully content to await the final decision.

Supplementary Essay

THE PRAGMATISM OF PEIRCE

BY

JOHN DEWEY

THE term pragmatism was introduced into literature in the opening sentences of Professor James's California Union address in 1898. The sentences run as follows: "The principle of pragmatism, as we may call it, may be expressed in a variety of ways, all of them very simple. In the *Popular Science Monthly* for January, 1878, Mr. Charles S. Peirce introduces it as follows:" etc. The readers who have turned to the volume referred to have not, however, found the word there. From other sources we know that the name as well as the idea was furnished by Mr. Peirce. The latter has told us that both the word and the idea were suggested to him by a reading of Kant, the idea by the *Critique of Pure Reason,* the term by the "Critique of Practical Reason."[1] The article in the *Monist* gives such a good statement of both the idea and the reason for selecting the term that it may be quoted *in extenso.* Peirce sets out by saying that with men who work in laboratories, the habit of mind is molded by experimental work much more than they are themselves aware. "Whatever statement you may make to him, he [the experimentalist] will either understand as meaning that if a given prescription for an experiment ever can be and ever is carried out in act, an experience of a given description will result, or else he will see no sense at all in what you say." Having himself the experimental mind and being interested in methods of thinking, "he framed the theory that a *conception,* that is, the rational purport of a word or other expression, lies

[1] See article on "Pragmatism," in *Baldwin's Dictionary,* Vol. 2., p. 322, and the *Monist,* Vol. 15, p. 162.

exclusively in its bearing upon the conduct of life; so that, since obviously nothing that might not result from experiment can have any direct bearing upon conduct, if one can define accurately all the conceivable experimental phenomena which the affirmation or denial of a concept could imply, one will have therein a complete definition of the concept, and *there is absolutely nothing more in it.* For this doctrine, he invented the name *pragmatism.*"

After saying that some of his friends wished him to call the doctrine practicism or practicalism, he says that he had learned philosophy from Kant, and that to one "who still thought in Kantian terms most readily, *praktisch* and *pragmatisch* were as far apart as the two poles, the former belonging to a region of thought where no mind of the experimentalist type can ever make sure of solid ground under his feet, the latter expressing relation to some definite human purpose. Now quite the most striking feature of the new theory was its recognition of an inseparable connection between rational cognition and human purpose." [2]

From this brief statement, it will be noted that Peirce confined the significance of the term to the determination of the meaning of terms, or better, propositions; the theory was not, of itself, a theory of the test, or the truth, of propositions. Hence the title of his original article: *How to Make Ideas Clear.* In his later writing, after the term had been used as a theory of truth, — he proposed the more limited "pragmaticism" to designate his original specific meaning.[3] But even with respect to the meaning of propositions, there is a marked difference between his pragmaticism and the pragmatism of, say, James. Some of the critics (especially continental) of the latter would have saved themselves some futile beating of the air, if they had reacted to James's statements instead of to their own as-

[2] Kant discriminates the laws of morality, which are *a priori,* from rules of skill, having to do with technique or art, and counsels of prudence, having to do with welfare. The latter he calls pragmatic; the *a priori* laws practical. See *Metaphysics of Morals,* Abbott's trans., pp. 33 and 34.

[3] See the article in the *Monist* already mentioned, and another one in the same volume, p. 481, "The Issues of Pragmaticism."

sociations with the word "pragmatic." Thus James says in his California address: "The effective meaning of any philosophic proposition can always be brought down to some particular consequence, in our future practical experience, whether active or passive; the point lying rather in the fact that the experience must be *particular,* than in the fact that it must be *active.*" (Italics mine.)

Now the curious fact is that Peirce puts more emphasis upon practise (or conduct) and less upon the particular; in fact, he transfers the emphasis to the general. The following passage is worth quotation because of the definiteness with which it identifies meaning with both the future and with the general. "The rational meaning of every proposition lies in the future. How so? The meaning of a proposition is itself a proposition. Indeed, it is no other than the very proposition of which it is the meaning: it is a translation of it. But of the myriads of forms into which a proposition may be translated, which is that one which is to be called its very meaning? It is, according to the pragmaticist, that form in which the proposition becomes applicable to human conduct, not in these or those special circumstances nor when one entertains this or that special design, but that form which is most applicable to self-control under every situation and to every purpose." Hence, "it must be simply the general description of all the experimental phenomena which the assertion of the proposition virtually predicts." Or, paraphrasing, pragmatism identifies meaning with formation of a habit, or way of acting having the greatest generality possible, or the widest range of application to particulars. Since habits or ways of acting are just as real as particulars, it is committed to a belief in the reality of "universals." Hence it is not a doctrine of phenomenalism, for while the richness of phenomena lies in their sensuous quality, pragmatism does not intend to define these (leaving them, as it were, to speak for themselves), but "eliminates their sential element, and endeavors to define the rational purport, and this it finds in the purposive bearing of the word or proposition in question." Moreover, not only are generals real, but they are physically efficient. The meanings "the air is stuffy" and "stuffy air is unwholesome" may determine, for example, the opening of the window. Accordingly on the ethical side, "the pragmaticist does not make the *summum bonum* to consist in action, but makes it to consist in that process of evolution whereby the existent comes more and more to embody those generals . . . ; in other words, becomes, through action an embodiment of rational purports or habits generalized as widely as possible."[4]

The passages quoted should be compared with what Peirce has to say in the Baldwin Dictionary article. There he says that James's doctrine seems to commit us to the belief "that the end of man is action — a stoical maxim which does not commend itself as forcibly to the present writer at the age of sixty as it did at thirty. If it be admitted, on the contrary, that action wants an end, and that the end must be something of a general description, then the spirit of the maxim itself . . . would direct us toward something different from practical facts, namely, to general ideas. . . . The only ultimate good which the practical facts to which the maxim directs attention can subserve is to further the development of concrete reasonableness. . . . Almost everybody will now agree that the ultimate good lies in the evolutionary process in some way. If so, it is not in individual reactions in their segregation, but in something general or continuous. Synechism is founded on the notion that the coalescence, the becoming continuous, the becoming governed by laws, the becoming instinct with general ideas, are but phases of one and the same process of the growth of reasonableness. This is first shown to be true with mathematical exactitude in the field of logic, and is thence inferred to hold good metaphysically. It is not opposed to pragmaticism . . . but includes that procedure as a step."

Here again we have the doctrine of pragmaticism as a doctrine that meaning or rational purport resides in the setting up of habits or generalized methods, a doctrine passing over into

[4] It is probably fair to see here an empirical rendering of the Kantian generality of moral action, while the distinction and connection of "rational purport" and "sensible particular" have also obvious Kantian associations.

the metaphysics of synechism. It will be well now to recur explicitly to Peirce's earlier doctrine which he seems to qualify — although, as he notes, he upheld the doctrine of the reality of generals even at the earlier period. Peirce sets out, in his article on the "Fixation of Belief," with the empirical difference of doubt and belief expressed in the facts that belief determines a habit while doubt does not, and that belief is calm and satisfactory while doubt is an uneasy and dissatisfied state from which we struggle to emerge; to attain, that is, a state of belief, a struggle which may be called inquiry. The sole object of inquiry is the fixation of belief. The scientific method of fixation has, however, certain rivals: one is that of "tenacity" — constant reiteration, dwelling upon everything conducive to the belief, avoidance of everything which might unsettle it — the will to believe. The method breaks down in practice because of man's social nature; we have to take account of contrary beliefs in others, so that the real problem is to fix the belief of the community; for otherwise our own belief is precariously exposed to attack and doubt. Hence the resort to the method of authority. This method breaks down in time by the fact that authority can not fix all beliefs in all their details, and because of the conflict which arises between organized traditions. There may then be recourse to what is "agreeable to reason" — a method potent in formation of taste and in esthetic productions and in the history of philosophy, — but a method which again fails to secure permanent agreements in society, and so leaves individual belief at the mercy of attack. Hence, finally, recourse to science, whose fundamental hypothesis is this: "There are real things, whose characters are entirely independent of our opinions about them; those realities affect our senses according to regular laws, and . . . by taking advantage of the laws of perception, we can ascertain *by reasoning* how things really are, and any man if he have sufficient experience and reason enough about it, will be led to the one true conclusion."[5]

It will be noted that the quotation employs the terms "reality" and "truth," while it makes them a part of the state-

[5] P. 26.

ment of the *hypothesis* entertained in scientific procedure. Upon such a basis, what meanings attach to the terms "reality" and "truth"? Since they are general terms, their meanings must be determined on the basis of the effects, having practical bearings, which the object of our conception has. Now the effect which real things have is to cause beliefs; beliefs are then the consequences which give the general term reality a "rational purport." And on the assumption of the scientific method, the *distinguishing* character of the *real* object must be that it tends to produce a single universally accepted belief. "All the followers of science are fully persuaded that the processes of investigation, if only pushed far enough, will give one certain solution to every question to which they can be applied." "This activity of thought by which we are carried, not where we wish, but to a foreordained goal, is like the operation of destiny. . . . This great law is embodied in the conception of truth and reality. The opinion which is fated to be ultimately agreed to by all *who investigate,* is what we mean by the truth, and the object represented in this opinion is the real."[6] In a subsequent essay (on the "Probability of Induction") Peirce expressly draws the conclusion which follows from this statement; viz., that this conception of truth and reality makes everything depend upon the character of the methods of inquiry and inference by which conclusions are reached. "In the case of synthetic inferences we know only the degree of trustworthiness of our proceeding. As all knowledge comes from synthetic inference, we must also infer that all human certainty consists merely in our knowing that the processes by which our knowledge has been derived are such as must generally have led to true conclusions"[7] — true conclusions, once more, being those which command the agreement of competent inquiries.

Summing up, we may say that Peirce's pragmaticism is a doctrine concerning the meaning, conception, or rational purport of objects, namely, that these consist in the "effects, which might conceivably have practical bearings, we conceive the ob-

[6] P. 56–57. [7] P. 105.

ject of our conception to have. Then, our conception of these effects is the whole of our conception of the object."[8] "Our idea of anything is our idea of its sensible effects," and if we have any doubt as to whether we really believe the effects to be sensible or no, we have only to ask ourselves whether or no we should act any differently in their presence. In short, our own responses to sensory stimuli are the ultimate, or testing, ingredients in our conception of an object. In the literal sense of the word pragmatist, therefore, Peirce is more of a pragmatist than James.

He is also less of a nominalist. That is to say, he emphasizes much less the *particular* sensible consequence, and much more the habit, the generic attitude of response, set up in consequence of experiences with a thing. In the passage in the Dictionary already quoted he speaks as if in his later life he attached less impcrtance to action, and more to "concrete reasonableness" than in his earlier writing. It may well be that the relative emphasis had shifted. But there is at most but a difference of emphasis. For in his later doctrine, concrete rationality means a change in existence brought about *through* action, and through action which embodies conceptions whose own specific existence consists in habitual attitudes of response. In his earlier writing, the emphasis upon habits, as something generic, is explicit. "What a thing means is simply what habits it involves."[9] More elaborately, "Induction infers a rule. Now the belief of a rule is a habit. That a habit is a rule, active in us, is evident. That every belief is of the nature of a habit, in so far as it is of a general character, has been shown in the earlier papers of this series."[10]

The difference between Peirce and James which next strikes us is the greater emphasis placed by the former upon the method of procedure. As the quotations already made show, everything ultimately turned, for Peirce, upon the trustworthiness of the procedures of inquiry. Hence his high estimate of logic, as compared with James — at least James in his later days. Hence also

[8] P. 45. [9] P. 43. [10] P. 151.

his definite rejection of the appeal to the Will to Believe — under the form of what he calls the method of tenacity. Closely associated with this is the fact that Peirce has a more explicit dependence upon the social factor than has James. The appeal in Peirce is essentially to the consensus of those who have investigated, using methods which are capable of employment by all. It is the need for social agreement, and the fact that in its absence "the method of tenacity" will be exposed to disintegration from without, which finally forces upon mankind the wider and wider utilization of the scientific method.

Finally, both Peirce and James are realists. The reasonings of both depend upon the assumption of real things which really have effects or consequences. Of the two, Peirce makes clearer the fact that in philosophy at least we are dealing with the *conception* of reality, with reality as a term having rational purport, and hence with something whose meaning is itself to be determined in terms of consequences. That "reality" means the object of those beliefs which have, after prolonged and coöperative inquiry, becomes stable, and "truth" the quality of these beliefs is a logical consequence of this position. Thus while "we may define the real as that whose characters are independent of what anybody may think them to be . . . it would be a great mistake to suppose that this definition makes the idea of reality perfectly clear."[11] For it is only the outcome of persistent and conjoint inquiry which enables us to give intelligible meaning in the concrete to the expression "characters independent of what anybody may think them to be." (This is the pragmatic way out of the egocentric predicament.) And while my purpose is wholly expository I can not close without inquiring whether recourse to Peirce would not have a most beneficial influence in contemporary discussion. Do not a large part of our epistemological difficulties arise from an attempt to define the "real" as something given prior to reflective inquiry instead of as that which reflective inquiry is forced to reach and to which when it is reached belief can stably cling?

[11] P. 53.

BIBLIOGRAPHY OF PEIRCE'S PUBLISHED WRITINGS

I. Writings of General Interest.[1]

A. Three papers in the *Journal of Speculative Philosophy*, Vol. 2 (1868).

1. "Questions Concerning Certain Faculties Claimed for Man," pp. 103–114.
2. "Some Consequences of Four Incapacities," pp. 140–157.
3. "Ground of Validity of the Laws of Logic," pp. 193–208.

These three papers, somewhat loosely connected, deal mainly with the philosophy of discursive thought. The first deals with our power of intuition, and holds that "every thought is a sign." The second, one of the most remarkable of Peirce's writings, contains an acute criticism of the Cartesian tradition and a noteworthy argument against the traditional emphasis on "images" in thinking. The third contains, *inter alia*, a refutation of Mill's indictment of the syllogism. The same volume of the *Journal* contains two unsigned communications on Nominalism and on the Meaning of Determined.

B. Review of Fraser's "Berkeley," in the *North American Review*, Vol. 113 (1871), pp. 449–472.

This paper contains an important analysis on medieval realism, and of Berkeley's nominalism. (A Scotist realism continues to distinguish Peirce's work after this.)

C. "Illustrations of the Logic of Science," in *Popular Science Monthly*, Vols. 12–13 (1877–1878). Reprinted in Pt. I of this volume. The first and second papers were also published in the *Revue Philosophique*, Vols. 6–7 (1879).

D. Ten papers in the *Monist*, Vols. 1–3 (1891–1893), and 15–16 (1905–1906). The first five are reprinted in Pt. II of this volume.

The sixth paper, "Reply to the Necessitarians," Vol. 3, pp. 526–570, is an answer to the criticism of the foregoing by the editor of the *Monist*, Vol. 2, pp. 560ff.; cf. Vol. 3, pp. 68ff. and 571ff., and McCrie, "The Issues of Synechism," Vol. 3, pp. 380ff.

[1] The following classification is arbitrary, as some of Peirce's most significant reflections occur in papers under headings II. and III. It may, however, be useful.

7. "What Pragmatism Is?" Vol. 15, pp. 161–181.

8. "The Issues of Pragmaticism," Vol. 15, pp. 481–499.

9. "Mr. Peterson's Proposed Discussion," Vol. 16, pp. 147ff.

10. "Prolegomena to an Apology for Pragmaticism," Vol. 16, pp. 492–546.

The last four papers develop Peirce's thought by showing its agreement and disagreement with the pragmatism of James and Schiller. The last paper contains his Method of Existential Graphs.

E. "The Reality of God," in the *Hibbert Journal*, Vol. 7 (1908), pp. 96–112. (This article contains brief indications of many of Peirce's leading ideas.)

F. Six Papers in the *Open Court*, Vols. 6–7 (1893).

1. "Pythagorics" (on the Pythagorean brotherhood), pp. 3375–3377.
2. "Dmesis" (on charity towards criminals), pp. 3399–3402.
3. "The Critic of Arguments (I.), Exact Thinking," pp. 3391–3394.
4. "The Critic of Arguments (II.), The Reader is Introduced to Relatives," pp. 3415-3419. (The last two contain a very clear succinct account of the general character of Peirce's logic.)
5. "What is Christian Faith?" pp. 3743–3745.
6. "The Marriage of Religion and Science," pp. 3559–3560.

G. Articles in Baldwin's "Dictionary of Philosophy": Individual, kind, matter and form, possibility, pragmatism, priority, reasoning, sign, scientific method, sufficient reason, synechism, and uniformity.

H. "Pearson's Grammar of Science," in *Popular Science Monthly*, Vol. 58 (1901), pp. 296–306. (A critique of Pearson's conceptualism and of his utilitarian view as to the aim of science.)

II. Writings of Predominantly Logical Interest.

A. Five Papers on Logic, read before the American Academy of Arts and Sciences. Published in the *Proceedings of the Academy*, Vol. 7 (1867).

1. "On an Improvement in Boole's Calculus of Logic," pp. 250–261. (Suggests improvements in Boole's logic, especially in the representation of particular propositions. The association of probability with the notion of relative frequency became a leading idea of Peirce's thought.)
2. "On the Natural Classification of Arguments," pp. 261–287. (A suggestive distinction between the leading principle and the premise of an argument. Contains also an interesting note (pp. 283–284) denying the posi-

tivistic maxim that, "no hypothesis is admissible which is not capable of verification by direct observation.")

3. "On a New List of Categories," pp. 287–298. The categories are: Being, Quality (Reference to a Ground), Relation (Reference to a Correlate), Representation (Reference to an Interpretant), Substance. "Logic has for its subject-genus all symbols and not merely concepts." Symbols include terms, propositions, and arguments.

4. "Upon the Logic of Mathematics," pp. 402–412. "There are certain general propositions from which the truths of mathematics follow syllogistically."

5. "Upon Logical Comprehension and Extension," pp. 416–432. (Interesting historical references to the use of these terms and an attack on the supposed rule as to their inverse proportionality.)

B. "Description of a Notation for the Logic of Relations," in *Memoires of the American Academy*, Vol. 9 (1870), pp. 317–378. (Shows the relation of inclusion between classes to be more fundamental than Boole's use of equality. Extends the Booleian calculus to DeMorgan's logic of relative terms.)

C. "On the Algebra of Logic," *American Journal of Mathematics*, Vol. 3 (1880), pp. 15–57. (Referred to by Schroeder as Peirce's *Hauptwerk* in "Vorlesungen über die Algebra der Logik," Vol. 1., p. 107.)

D. "On the Logic of Number," *American Journal of Mathematics*, Vol. 4 (1881), pp. 85–95.

E. "Brief Description of the Algebra of Relatives," Reprinted from ??, pp. 1–6.

F. "On the Algebra of Logic: A Contribution to the Philosophy of Notation," *American Journal of Mathematics*, Vol 7 (1884), pp. 180–202.

G. "A Theory of Probable Inference" and notes "On a Limited Universe of Marks" and on the "Logic of Relatives" in "Studies in Logic by members of the Johns Hopkins University," Boston, 1883, pp. 126–203.

H. "The Regenerated Logic," *Monist*, Vol. 7, pp. 19–40.

"The Logic of Relatives," *Monist*, Vol. 7, pp. 161–217. (An elaborate development of his own logic of relatives, by way of review of Schroeder's book.)

I. Miscellaneous Notes, etc.

1. Review of Venn's "Logic of Chance," *North American Review*, July, 1867.

2. "On the Application of Logical Analysis to Multiple Al-

gebra," *Proceedings of the American Academy,* Vol. 10 (1875), pp. 392–394.

3. "Note on Grassman's 'Calculus of Extension,'" *Proceedings of the American Academy,* Vol. 13 (1878), pp. 115–116.
4. "Note on Conversion," *Mind,* Vol. 1, p. 424.
5. Notes and Additions to Benjamin Peirce's "Linear Associative Algebra," *American Journal of Mathematics,* Vol. 4 (1881), pp. 92ff., especially pp. 221–229.
6. "Logical Machines," *American Journal of Psychology,* Vol. 1 (1888).
7. "Infinitesimals," *Science,* Vol. 11 (1900), p. 430.
8. "Some Amazing Mazes," *Monist,* Vol. 18 (April and July, 1908), and Vol. 19 (Jan., 1909).
9. "On Non-Aristotelian Logic" (Letter), *Monist,* Vol. 20.

J. A Syllabus of Certain Topics of Logic. 1903. Boston. Alfred Mudge & Son (a four page brochure).

K. Articles in Baldwin's "Dictionary of Philosophy" on: laws of thought, leading principle, logic (exact and symbolic), modality, negation, predicate and predication, probable inference, quality, quantity, relatives, significant, simple, subject, syllogism, theory, truth and falsity universal, universe, validity, verification, whole and parts.

III. Researches in the Theory and Methods of Measurement.

A. General and Astronomic.

1. "On the Theory of Errors of Observation," *Report of the Superintendent of the U. S. Coast Survey* for 1870, pp. 220–224.
2. "Note on the Theory of Economy of Research," *Report of the U. S. Coast Survey* for 1876, pp. 197–201. (This paper deals with the relation between the utility and the cost of diminishing the probable error.)
3. "Apparatus for Recording a Mean of Observed Times," *U. S. Coast Survey,* 1877. Appendix No. 15 to *Report* of 1875.
4. "Ferrero's Metodo dei Minimi Quadrati," *American Journal of Mathematics,* Vol. 1 (1878), pp. 55–63.
5. "Photometric Researches," *Annals of the Astronomical Observatory of Harvard College,* Vol. 9 (1878), pp. 1–181.
6. "Methods and Results. Measurement of Gravity. Washington. 1879.
7. "Methods and Results. A Catalogue of Stars for Observations of Latitude. Washington. 1879.

8. "On the Ghosts in Rutherford's 'Diffraction Spectra,'" *American Journal of Mathematics*, Vol. 2 (1879), pp. 330–347.

9. "Note on a Comparison of a Wave-Length with a Meter," *American Journal of Science*, Vol. 18 (1879), p. 51.

10. "A Quincuncial Projection of the Sphere," *American Journal of Mathematics*, Vol. 2 (1879), pp. 394, 396.

11. "Numerical Measure of Success of Predictions," *Science*, Vol. 4 (1884), p. 453.

12. "Proceedings Assay Commission" Washington, 1888. (Joint Reports on Weighing.)

B. Geodetic Researches. The Pendulum.

1. "Measurement of Gravity at Initial Stations in America and Europe," *Report of the U. S. Coast Survey*, 1876, pp. 202–237 and 410–416.

2. "De l'influence de la flexibilité du trépied sur l'oscillation du pendule a réversion," Conférence Geodesique Internationale (1877) Comptes Rendus, Berlin, 1878, pp. 171–187. (This paper was introduced by Plantamour and was followed by the notes of Appolzer.)

3. "On the Influence of Internal Friction upon the Correction of the Length of the Second's Pendulum," *Proceedings of the American Academy*, Vol. 13 (1878), pp. 396–401.

4. "On a Method of Swinging Pendulums for the Determination of Gravity proposed by M. Faye," *American Journal of Science*, Vol. 18 (1879), pp. 112–119.

5. "Results of Pendulum Experiments," *American Journal of Science*, Vol. 20 (1880).

6. "Flexure of Pendulum Supports," *Report of the U. S. Coast Survey*, 1881, pp. 359–441.

7. "On the Deduction of the Ellipticity of the Earth from the Pendulum Experiment," *Report of the U. S. Coast Survey*, 1881, pp. 442–456.

8. "Determinations of Gravity at Stations in Pennsylvania," *Report of U. S. Coast Survey*, 1883, Appendix 19 and pp. 473–486.

9. "On the Use of the Noddy," *Report of the U. S. Coast Survey*, 1884, pp. 475–482.

10. "Effect of the Flexure of a Pendulum upon the Period of Oscillation," *Report of the U. S. Coast Survey*, 1884, pp. 483–485.

11. "On the Influence of a Noddy, and of Unequal Temperature upon the Periods of a Pendulum," *Report of the U. S. Coast and Geodetic Survey* for 1885, pp. 509–512.

C. Psychologic. "On Small Differences in Sensation" (in co-operation with J. Jastrow), *National Academy of Sciences*, Vol. 3 (1884), pp. 1–11.

IV. Philologic.

"Shakespearian Pronunciation" (in coöperation with J. B. Noyes), *North American Review*, Vol. 98 (April, 1864), pp. 342–369.

V. Contributions to the *Nation*.

Lazelle, Capt. H. M., One Law in Nature. *Nation*, Vol. 17, No. 419.

Newcomb, S., Popular Astronomy. Vol. 27, No. 683.

Read, C., Theory of Logic, 1878. Vol. 28, No. 718.

Rood, O. N., Modern Chromatics, 1879. Vol. 29, No. 746.

Note on the *American Journal of Mathematics*. Vol. 29, No. 756.

Jevons, W. S., Studies in Deductive Logic, 1880. Vol. 32, No. 822.

Ribot, Th., The Psychology of Attention, 1890. Vol. 50, No. 1303.

James, W., The Principles of Psychology, 1890. Vol. 53, Nos. 1357 and 1358.

Comte, A. (F. Harrison, editor), The New Calendar of Great Men, 1892. Vol. 54, No. 1386.

Lobatchewsky, N. (Translator: G. B. Halsted), Geometrical Researches on the Theory of Parallels, 1891. Vol. 54, No. 1389.

Lombroso, C., The Man of Genius, 1891. Vol. 54, No. 1391.

Note on William James' abridgment of his Psychology, 1892. Vol. 54, No. 1394.

McClelland, W. J., A Treatise on the Geometry of the Circle, 1891. Vol. 54, No. 1395.

Buckley, Arabella B., Moral Teachings of Science, 1892. Vol. 54, No. 1405.

Hale, E. E., A New England Boyhood, 1893. Vol. 57, No. 1468.

Mach, E. (Translator: T. J. McCormack), The Science of Mechanics, 1893. Vol. 57, No. 1475.

Ritchie, D. G., Darwin and Hegel, 1893. Vol. 57, No. 1482.

Huxley, T. H., Method and Results, 1893. Vol. 58, No. 1489.

Scott, Sir Walter, Familiar Letters of Sir Walter Scott. Vol. 58, No. 1493.

Gilbert, W. (Translator: P. F. Mottelay), Magnetic Bodies. Vol. 58, No. 1494 and No. 1495.

Forsyth, A. R., Theory of Functions of a Complex Variable, 1893; and Harkness, J., A Treatise on the Theory of Functions, 1893; and Picard, E., Traité d'analyse, 1893. Vol. 58, No. 1498.

A Short Sketch of Helmholtz, Sept. 13, 1894. Vol. 59, No. 1524.

Windelband, W. (Translator: J. H. Tufts), A History of Philosophy; and Falkenberg, R. (Translator: A. C. Armstrong), History of Modern Philosophy; and Bascom, J., An Historical Interpretation of Philosophy; and Burt, B. C., A History of Modern Philosophy. Vol. 59, Nos. 1526 and 1527.

Spinoza (Translators: W. H. White and Amelia H. Stirling), Ethics, 1894. Vol. 59, No. 1532.

Watson, J., Comte, Mill, and Spencer, 1895. Vol. 60, No. 1554.

Jones, H., A Critical Account of the Philosophy of Lotze, 1895; and Eberhard, V., Die Grundbegriffe der ebenen Geometrie, 1895; and Klein, F. (Translator: A. Ziwet), Riemann and his Significance for the Development of Modern Mathematics, 1895; and Davis, N. K., Elements of Inductive Logic, 1895. Vol. 61, No. 1566.

Benjamin, P., The Intellectual Rise in Electricity, 1895. Vol. 62, No. 1592.

Baldwin, J. M., The Story of the Mind, 1898. Vol. 67, No. 1737.

Darwin, G. H., The Tides and Kindred Phenomena in the Solar System, 1898. Vol. 67, No. 1747.

Marshall, H. R., Instinct and Reason, 1898. Vol. 68, No. 1774.

Britten, F. J., Old Clocks and Watches and their Makers, 1899. Vol. 69, No. 1778.

Renouvier, Ch., et Prat, L. La Nouvelle Monadologie, 1899. Vol. 69, No. 1779.

Mackintosh, R., From Comte to Benjamin Kidd, 1899; and Moore, J. H., Better-World Philosophy, 1899. Vol. 69, No. 1784.

Ford, P. L., The Many-sided Franklin, 1899. Vol. 69, No. 1793.

Avenel, G. d', Le Mécanisme de la vie moderne, 1900. Vol. 70, No. 1805.

Reid, W., Memoirs and Correspondence of Lyon Playfair, 1899. Vol. 70, No. 1806.

Stevenson, F. S., Robert Grosseteste, 1899. Vol. 70, No. 1816.

Thilly, F., Introduction to Ethics, 1900. Vol. 70, No. 1825.

Wallace, A. R., Studies, Scientific and Social, 1900. Vol. 72, No. 1854.

Sime, J., William Herschel and His Work, 1900. Vol. 72, No. 1856.

Rand, B. (Editor), The Life, Unpublished Letters, and Philosophical Regimen of Anthony, Earl of Shaftesbury, 1900; and Robertson, J. M. (Editor), Characteristics of Men, *etc.*, by Shaftesbury, 1900. Vol. 72, No. 1857.

Bacon, Rev. J. M., By Land and Sea, 1901. Vol. 72, No. 1865.

Jordan, W. L., Essays in Illustration of the Action of Astral Gravitation in Natural Phenomena, 1900. Vol. 72, No. 1876.

Goblot, E., Le Vocabulaire Philosophique, 1901. Vol. 72, No. 1877.

Fraser, A. C. (Editor), The Works of George Berkeley, 1901. Vol. 73, No. 1883.

Frazer, P., Bibliotics, 1901. Vol. 73, No. 1883.

Caldecott, A., The Philosophy of Religion in England and America, 1901. Vol. 73, No. 1885.

Review of four physical books. Vol. 73, No. 1887.

Maher, M., Psychology: Empirical and Rational, 1901. Vol. 73, No. 1892.

Mezes, S. E., Ethics, 1901. Vol. 73, No. 1895.

Report of the Meeting of the National Academy of Sciences, Philadelphia, 1901. Vol. 73, No. 1899.

Crozier, J. B., History of Intellectual Developments on the Lines of Modern Evolution. Vol. III., 1901, Vol. 74, No. 1908.

Richardson, E. C., Classification, Theoretical and Practical, 1901. Vol. 74, No. 1913.

Vallery-Radot, R. (Translator: Mrs. R. L. Devonshire), The Life of Pasteur. Vol. 74, No. 1914.

Giddings, F. H., Inductive Sociology, 1902. Vol. 74, No. 1918.

Report on the Meeting of the National Academy of Sciences, Washington, D. C., 1902. Vol. 74, No. 1921.

Emerson, E. R., The Story of the Vine, 1902. Vol. 74, No. 1926.

Joachim, H. H., A Study of the Ethics of Spinoza, 1901. Vol. 75, No. 1932.

Review of four chemistry text-books, 1902. Vol. 75, No. 1934.

Royce, J., The World and the Individual, Vol. II., 1901. Vol. 75, No. 1935. (For a review of Vol. I., probably by Peirce, see 1900, Vol. 70, No. 1814.)

Thorpe, T. E., Essays in Historical Chemistry, 1902. Vol. 75, No. 1938.

Paulsen, F., Immanuel Kant: His Life and Doctrine, 1902. Vol. 75, No. 1941.

Aikens, H. A., The Principles of Logic, 1902. Vol. 75, No. 1942.

Drude, P., The Theory of Optics, 1902. Vol. 75, No. 1944.

Valentine, E. S., Travels in Space, 1902; and Walker, F., Aerial Navigation, 1902. Vol. 75, No. 1947.

Baillie, J. B., The Origin and Significance of Hegel's Logic, 1901. Vol. 75, No. 1950.

Forsyth, A. R., Theory of Differential Equations, Vol. IV., 1902. Vol. 75, No. 1952.

Ellwanger, G. W., The Pleasures of the Table, 1902. Vol. 75, No. 1955.

Earle, Alice M., Sundials and Roses of Yesterday, 1902. Vol. 75, No. 1956.

Smith, Rev. T., Euclid: His Life and System, 1902. Vol. 76, No. 1961.

Report on the Meeting of the National Academy of Sciences, Washington, D. C., 1903. Vol. 76, No. 1974.

Hibben, J. G., Hegel's Logic, 1902. Vol. 76, No. 1977.

Mellor, J. W., Higher Mathematics for Students of Chemistry and Physics, 1903. Vol. 76, No. 1977.

Sturt, H. C. (Editor), Personal Idealism, 1902. Vol. 76, No. 1979.

Baldwin, J. M., Dictionary of Philosophy and Psychology, Vol. II., 1902. Vol. 76, No. 1980.

Note on Kant's Prolegomene edited in English by Dr. P. Carus, 1903. Vol. 76, No. 1981.

Smith, N., Studies in the Cartesian Philosophy, 1902. Vol. 77, No. 1985.

Hinds, J. I. D., Inorganic Chemistry, 1902. Vol. 77, No. 1986.

Clerke, Agnes M., Problems in Astrophysics, 1903. Vol. 77, No. 1987.

Michelson, A. A., Light Waves and their Uses, 1903; and Fleming, J. A., Waves and Ripples in Water, 1902. Vol. 77, No. 1989.

Note on Sir Norman Lockyer. Vol. 77, No. 1794.
Note on British and American Science, 1903. Vol. 77, No. 1996.
Welby, Lady Victoria, What is Meaning? 1903; and Russell B, The Principles of Mathematics, 1903. Vol. 77, No. 1998.
Note on the Practical Application of the Theory of Functions, 1903. Vol. 77, No. 1999.
Fahie, J. J., Galileo. Vol. 78, No. 2015.
Halsey, F. A., The Metric Fallacy, and Dale, S. S., The Metric Failure in the Textile Industry. Vol. 78, No. 2020.
Newcomb, S., The Reminiscences of an Astronomer, 1903. Vol. 78, No. 2021.
Boole, Mrs. M. E., Lectures on the Logic of Arithmetic, 1903; and Bowden, J., Elements of the Theory of Integers, 1903. Vol. 78, No. 2024.
Report on the Meeting of the National Academy of Sciences, Washington, D. C., 1904. Vol. 78, No. 2026.
Lévy-Bruhl, L. (Translator: Kathleen de Beaumont-Klein), The Philosophy of Auguste Comte, 1903. Vol. 78, No. 2026.
Turner, W., History of Philosophy, 1903. Vol. 79, No. 2036.
Duff, R. A., Spinoza's Political and Ethical Philosophy. Vol. 79, No. 2038.
Allbutt, T. C., Notes on the Composition of Scientific Papers, 1904. Vol. 79, No. 2039.
Sylvester, J. J., The Collected Mathematical Papers of, Vol. I. Vol. 79, No. 2045.
Renouvier, Ch., Les Derniers Entretiens, 1904, and Dewey, J., Studies in Logical Theory, 1903. Vol. 79, No. 2046.
Royce, J., Outlines of Psychology. Vol. 79, No. 2048.
Straton, G. M., Experimental Psychology and its Bearing upon Culture. Vol. 79, No. 2055.
Report on the Meeting of the National Academy of Sciences, New York, 1904. Vol. 79, No. 2057.
Boole, Mrs. M. E., The Preparation of the Child for Science, 1904. Vol. 80, No. 2062.
Royce, J., Herbert Spencer, 1904. Vol. 80, No. 2065.
Strutt, R. J., The Becquerel Rays and the Properties of Radium, 1904. Vol. 80, No. 2066.
Schuster, A., An Introduction to the Theory of Optics, 1904. Vol. 80, No. 2071.
Findlay, A., The Phase Rule and its Application, 1904. Vol. 80, No. 2074.
Report on the Meeting of the National Academy of Sciences, Washington, D. C., 1905. Vol. 80, No. 2078.
Flint, R., Philosophy as Scientia Scientiarum, 1904; and Peirce, C. S., A Syllabus of Certain Topics of Logic, 1903. Vol. 80, No. 2079.
Arnold, R. B., Scientific Fact and Metaphysical Reality, 1904, also a Note on Mendeleeff's Principles of Chemistry. Vol. 80, No. 2083.

Note on Ida Freund's The Study of Chemical Composition. Vol. 80, No. 2086.

Carnegie, A., James Watt, 1905. Vol. 80, No. 2087.

Ross, E. A., Foundations of Sociology, 1905, and Sociological Papers, 1905, published by the Sociological Society. Vol. 81, No. 2089.

Wundt, W. (Translator: E. B. Titchener), Principles of Physiological Psychology, 1904. Vol. 81, No. 2090.

Roscoe, H. E., A Treatise on Chemistry, Vol. I., 1905, and de Fleury, M., Nos Enfants au Collége, 1905. Vol. 81, No. 2097.

Varigny, H. de, La Nature et la Vie, 1905. Vol. 81, No. 2101.

Note on Mr. G. W. Hill's Moon Theory. Vol. 81, 2103.

Report on the Meeting of the National Academy of Sciences, New Haven, 1905. Vol. 81, No. 2108.

Gosse, E., Sir Thomas Browne, 1905. Vol. 81, No. 2111.

Rutherford, E., Radio-Activity, 1905. Vol. 82, No. 2116.

Wallace, A. R., My Life, 1905. Vol. 82, No. 2121.

Haldane, Elizabeth S., Descartes. Vol. 82, No. 2125.

Report on the Meeting of the National Academy of Sciences, Washington, D. C., 1906. Vol. 82, No. 2130.

Rogers, H. J. (Editor), Congress of Arts and Sciences, Universal Exposition, St. Louis, 1904. Vol. 82, No. 2136.

Loeb, J., The Dynamics of Living Matter; and Mann, G., Chemistry of the Proteids. Vol. 83, No. 2140.

Roscoe, H. E., The Life and Experiences of Sir Henry Enfield Roscoe. Vol. 83, No. 2141.

Marshall, T., Aristotle's Theory of Conduct. Vol. 83, No. 2150.

Joseph, H. W. B., An Introduction to Logic. Vol. 83, No. 2156.

Other Articles and Reviews

Old Stone Mill at Newport, *Science,* 4, 1884, 512.

Criticism on "Phantasms of the Living," *Proc. Am Soc. Psychical Research,* Vol. 1, No. 3 (1887).

Napoleon Intime, *The Independent,* December 21 and December 28, 1893.

Decennial Celebration of Clark University, *Science,* 11 (1900), p. 620.

Century's Great Men of Science, *Smithsonian Institute Reports,* 1900.

Campanus *Science,* 13 (1901), p. 809.

French Academy of Science, N. Y. Evening *Post,* March 5, 1904.